The Path to Nirodha

The Path to Nirodha

Why and How of Meditation

Irv Jacob

authorHOUSE®

AuthorHouse™
1663 Liberty Drive
Bloomington, IN 47403
www.authorhouse.com
Phone: 1-800-839-8640

Published by AuthorHouse   11/20/2012

ISBN: 978-1-4772-9085-9 (sc)
ISBN: 978-1-4772-9084-2 (e)

Library of Congress Control Number: 2012921804

THE TURNING OF THE WHEEL: THE MIDDLE WAY

CHAPTER CONTENTS

Introduction

I have the sense of real, present time when I think, look out of my eyes, touch a loved-one, or smell my breakfast, etc., and of course so does everyone else, I trust. I know that others have this same sense of real time in the way I do, first because they tell me they do, and secondly it just makes sense that we are all the same in this aspect of our humanity. I accept this as an ordinary fact of life; even my cat has his own personality and is quite self-willed because he is always in the right place at the right time. But how is it that I have this sense consciousness? And we each do; is this completely random? Or arbitrary? It is an example of what in Buddhism is referred to as "thusness or suchness," as we will learn. This is a sense of being present "In the moment", and this is the way of our natures, or it can be said—the nature of our species.

The next inkling we might have about being human is to see meaning, precedence and purpose about our lives, because that is how we analyze other phenomena of nature and culture (i.e. buildings and relics). At some point we have all heard the expressions: "That . . . must have happened for a reason." or, "It will all work out for the best." These are often comforting thoughts in the face of tragedy or temporary misfortune, or we might come from the opposite direction, and be on a Search for Meaning, which we will discuss in chapter eight. For example, losing our job today could put us in the position of finding a really good job tomorrow, or finding success along a different path to financial recovery. These conjectures are natural enough but are no more than our tendency as humans to rely on superstitions; and our tendency to create all sorts of preliminary theories, rules and taboos is well documented in human social history (anthropology). So our inclination to create explanations (beliefs) for sequential facts is part of human nature, but this temptation isn't necessary to our survival. What is necessary is to accept our role as a functioning member of some society and to develop our relationships and shared purposes as we go. This is why the Buddha taught that one-third part of Buddhism is to Take Refuge in the Sangha, to associate, console, encourage, learn from and share with like-minded people. As we embrace Buddhism (and the Dharma) we accept our part of being interdependent, interconnected members of humanity, rather than a law unto ourselves.

This interconnectedness is what keeps us alive, whether we realize this consciously or not. We learn as we mature, perhaps gradually we develop a kind of humility, a sense of shared mission in life as we develop our Buddhist religious practice. We do this because we learn to relieve suffering, to be happier, to help others, to be compassionate and to prevent future suffering, (this is how we'll Take Refuge in the Buddha) and to benefit from surrendering our thoughts of uniqueness as an acknowledgment of our gift of life. We don't dwell on the reality of our individuality so often, which is probably good because to obsess about this self-consciousness can be debilitating, instead every day we accept our shared lives and the causes of our existence for what they are, simple facts, and this enables our personalities and our intellect to take over, and to be and live at our highest potential.

This book is dedicated to showing how to tap into and develop, observe and utilize the " . . . very subtle or extraordinary level of the mind."

During the time I initially prepared this introduction, I wrote this poem:

> I see Wind blowing
> dancing, singing in the tree
> and know about life.
>   I.J. Hall, Feb. 17, 2012

This is a simple confession of being present in the moment, no particular moment, but in each moment when I am reminded by my perceptions that my consciousness is alive and well.

This is not an explanation of the characteristics of the wind, it is not a story about a tree as much as a reflection back to the reader as s/he senses what is so basic about life that it too often goes without saying. There is a subtle acknowledgment here about safety, about accepting the beauty of nature, peacefulness, deductions and introspection. Gratefully I live where I can look out the window past the trees and see my little corner of the world as a safe place, and this is not trivial, and when I meditate I share this merit with everyone and know how special this simple, quiet contemplation is. I don't need any theories or philosophizing to do this profound act of sharing and mindfulness.

It is curious that the most useful moments in meditation are when there is no connection to any ego centeredness, but rather it is during the time when we surrender to following an age old path to peace and tranquility; this comes from a sense of connectedness to the whole of humanity. Rather than thinking this is my issue, this is my mind, this is my solution, which seems such a natural reaction; we can relax in the same way that Buddhists have been doing for 2500 years. We can watch our breath the

---

In this book we learn why meditation is important, and that it is a journey of looking deeply, to touch our true nature and reach into our Hearts.

---

same way the Buddha did, we can experience Piti-jhana to identify emotional issues in our lives the same way our neighbor does (we study this beginning in Chapter Five), and we can solve our problems, aversions and inhibitions that we identify in the same way monks have been doing all along in history. The solutions, not surprisingly, are basically of the same sort for each of us. That is the message of the clever expression—that we are all part of the *same nose hole society*. I don't know who said that first, but when understood, it unites us all with compassion and humility, rather than expanding our egos, which would tend to separate us from a very wholesome connection to society.

Also beginning in chapter five is a discussion or layering of the "Dhammacakkappavattana Sutta: Setting the Wheel of Dhamma in Motion" which in Buddhist teachings is not only presumed to be the very first teaching of the Buddha just after his enlightenment given to the five monks with whom he previously associated, but refers us to the twelve frames of reference resulting from a simple format. In order to reach Purification, which is something of a technical term, it is necessary to follow the twelve permutations of Dharma. There are many translations and the text is so arcane that it is a little difficult to parse out of it the precise intention. I accept that it explains three stages of progress in our practice: first, we recognize "what is" suffering or stress etc., and obtain direct knowledge of each of the Four Noble Truths. Then second: we are encouraged to develop an understanding of "what is to be" by self-awakening until we have full awakening in relation to each of the Four Noble Truths. Then third: we come to realize what "has come to be" and arise to an unbinding from attachment, craving etc., relating to each of the Four Noble Truths of our lives and in the process overcoming many of the 108 (corresponding to the number of beads on the mala, prayer necklace) defilements. (That is three topics X four truths, thus twelve permutations.) Each subsequent chapter incorporates one of the resulting twelve permutations, i.e. Chapter Eight deals with "recognizing" the significance of the elements of the Eight-fold Path. Hopefully this format is not intrusive to the sequence of the discussion and explanations relating to the step-by-step meditation scheme of Anapanasati which is also developed one in each of the sixteen chapters. The development of Purification begins after chapter four, after the careful explanation of the purpose of following our breaths, we learn how to have a calm mind, and presumably the reader has a good grasp and proficiency with vipassana, mindfulness meditation by that juncture.

The teaching of mindfulness that is preliminary and central to Buddhist meditation brings us back to our real sense of present time-space in a healthy way, and we rest in this energetic, clean self-consciousness as a mental state of peacefulness and aesthetic pleasure. Indeed this sense of present, momentary reality is a tool of purification that we utilize to relieve stress and torments, we utilize our sense of Direct Awareness to neutralize the emotional loads associated with unpleasant thoughts and negative social relationships. It was part of Buddha's wisdom that he developed the techniques to co-opt and use our personal identities not only for enjoying a tranquil peace, but also for the purpose of gaining enlightenment and for arriving at the peace of nirvana. It is a positive trade-off to develop our Hearts to essentially surrender our "I-ness" to gain a more complete and intimate association with humanity, and a more functional and beneficial way of life. As we surrender our greed, cravings, attachments, and our need for selfishness, we become part of an enlightened culture. As we accept our role in society we gain a breadth of soul, as it were; we are greater than the singularity of the moment of our births.

As we grow and learn we develop our abilities, and hopefully receive the aid we need to fulfill our talents. Not everyone does of course, but those who can develop and expand their natural spirituality, be introspective, be skillful in pursuit of a better society, ought to fulfill their talents for the sake of all others and for their own peace of mind. These objectives are facilitated when we understand and utilize

the concise explanation that comes from a Tibetan tradition[1]
of how our minds are organized into 1) coarse, or ordinary
content; 2) the subtle level of mindfulness—the "awareness
on the mind's moment-by-moment fleeting movements", and
3) the very-subtle awareness of "karmic propensities", thus
we think before we act. In this third stage we can unpack our
cravings and natural urges and change our lives. The chapters
in this book are grouped according to these three categories of
mind as a way of giving a context to the flow of the discussion
about Purification. Each subject spills into the next to provide
continuity. This is a kind of collecting or schema, to help focus
and advance the discussion.

We often hear about the benefits of meditation from many
practical perspectives, but I believe the most important benefit
occurs as we learn how to develop our Hearts.[2] As we practice
the principles of "Concentration" we develop our ability to
reach the subtle level of our minds. As we utilize "Insight"
meditation we exercise and reach into our Hearts and the
very-subtle level of our minds. The Tibetan tradition teaches
us about "advance pliancy", and we learn about shifting gears

---

[1]   "According to Buddhist psychology, there are three levels to the
mind. 1. The coarse level pertains to ordinary content in the stream
of consciousness, for example, thoughts, percepts, bodily sensations,
and emotions. [Calm Mind] 2. On the subtle level there is no
content. [Citta—The Heart: The Pure Mind] The skilled meditator
learns to hold awareness on the mind's moment-by-moment fleeting
movements prior to these movements being constructed into coarse
content [thinking before we act.] 3. At the very subtle level of mind
the skilled meditator learns to hold [buddhahood: the enlightened
mind] awareness on karmic propensities [i.e. inclinations, motivating
factors] prior to their manifestation in the time-space matrix of the
ordinary mental continuum [urges, instincts and cravings.]" (Brown)

[2]   "Mastery of the concentration stages of meditation opens up the subtle
level of the mind. Mastery of the special-insight stages opens up the
very subtle or extraordinary level of the mind. Advanced pliancy
entails shifting through these levels of mind with considerable skill,
much like shifting gears in a car." (Brown, pp. 155-156)

and steering through our minds. This becomes an automatic mental activity, just as we may have developed competence and learned as a teenager how to drive a car. When we operate consciously inside our developed Hearts, we can satisfy and fulfill the challenges and teachings of Buddhism, i.e. which is when our egos can disappear and become irrelevant.

When we develop our minds in meditation we seek to reach past the mindfulness level, to a conceptual level that pervades our personalities with a nobility of purpose and action that reflects well, not only on ourselves, but on our teachers, parents and ancestors. "The one whose victory cannot be undone,\ Whose victory does not go anywhere in the world—\ By what path will you lead him,\ The trackless Buddha of infinite range?" (Dhammapada, vs. 179) This book is dedicated to showing how to tap into and develop the Buddha inside each of us, observe and utilize the capacities of the ". . . very subtle or extraordinary level of the mind."

When I reread the content of each chapter, I found a way to utilize and model this skill of observation. I noticed that there were features and benefits of meditation that were identified, surprisingly more than I expected to find. I collected these for each chapter into a preview list which might help emphasize these, might motivate the reader to continue, and help the reader understand the scope of each chapter better. This was an exercise for me also, like calisthenics for my Heart. Likewise I collected the key words, usually the first time each appeared. This should help the reader do a "find" search of the electronic file of this book for topics that are of immediate interest. This is not intended to be pedantic, or a burden to the reader, but a useful collection of ideas as a quick summary.

Throughout the day we can evaluate our mental status as a simple kind of meditation, and when we move beyond casual-perfunctory thinking we move into the realm of Pure Mind. Each tradition of Buddhism deals with these relationships, sometimes the words are different as with the Theravada (Thailand) teaching about the organization of our minds, as a fundamental aspect of Dharma. There is the 1) calm mind (coarse or ordinary content), 2) the pure mind (subtle), and

3) the enlightened mind (very-subtle), the second and third are for sure works in progress based on our efforts of "mind development".[3] This is a slightly different explanation than the previous Tibetan taxonomy, but both are useful for purposes of discussion. After only a very brief introduction and orientation, a Practitioner should be able to achieve a calm mind, or know how to go there at any time, even during stressful periods.

Each Practitioner should also have a good idea what it takes to have a pure mind, although that is a more sophisticated concept, in the sense that it involves accepting a particular set of assumptions (The Precepts) and teachings (intended by this author, Wee, to refer to the twelve permutations of Purification) about how to live ethically. Developing that capacity is a continuous task; it involves applying the lessons we learn from Dharma into our actual experience of life. The Stream Enterer gets a glimpse of what it means to obtain enlightenment as each level of mind development emerges, not an occult state, but a natural, confident, very possible and capable achievement; not unlike developing the competence of an accomplished musician. That is the promise of this book, to explain and guide each Practitioner to the ultimate achievement of their optimum potential (and hey, I expect to get to that point too).

The presumption that we can obtain purification seems in a way pompous and arrogant: but Purification of our

---

3 "Mind (citta)—is **heart**, thing that perceives something, thinks and feels. It is a state of consciousness with these basic mental relationships. It is the natural state that is aware of sense-objects or always perceives sense-objects. Mind can be named 'perceiver' only . . . In respect of practice to develop mind, there are three kinds of mind we should notice to know and understand. They are *1) calm mind, 2) pure mind and 3) enlightened mind.* Noticing [the status of our] mind will enable us to understand how to practice [to develop further the] mind, [we can see] how much we make progress in practicing [developing] it, whether we make any progress." (Wee, pg. 78)

Hearts is very private. We will learn and develop this as one of the fruits of meditation.

One of the most fundamental lessons repeated by the Buddha was a description of the world based on its essential qualities or characteristics. He said that all of life, nature and material is 1) impermanent, *aniccam*, subject to change more or less continuously; 2) unsatisfying, *dukkham*, or a condition that counts for the suffering we might experience; and 3) not possessed of or influenced by an eternal soul, instead subject to numerous and unique causes, *anatta*. This is one of the teachings found in every tradition of Buddhism with which I have become acquainted. When we learn about reality in these terms we are able to understand how and why so many of the vagaries of our lives occur. Stating this taxonomy is easy, since it is taught in each Buddhist tradition perhaps using different words, but explaining all the implications takes a good deal of care, practice, encouragement and elaboration; the most important implications are to be unfolded in this book, some as original insights.

Even if the language of Buddhism is sometimes curious or abstract, it can convey powerful and useful meanings. The poetry of the Lotus Sutra is often inspiring and promises rewards as the teachings of an epic poem.[4] These poetic illusions and devices are inspiring and hopeful, as they describe the possibility of success. Nirvana is functionally a grace from

---

[4] "The Buddha said to the monks: 'In future ages if there are good men or good women who, on hearing the Devadatta chapter of the Lotus Sutra of the Wonderful Law, believe and revere it with pure hearts and harbor no doubts or perplexities, they will never fall into hell or the realm of hungry spirits or of beasts, but will be born in the presence of the Buddhas of the ten directions, and in the place where they are born they will constantly hear this sutra. If they are born among human or heavenly beings, they will enjoy exceedingly wonderful delights, and if they are born in the presence of a Buddha, they will be born by transformation from lotus flowers.' Devadatta." (Watson, pg. 185)

the natural force of our Buddha nature that pervades our own innate buddhahood, it gives worth and value to even the most unschooled and corrupt among us; it simply remains for each of us to open the flower of this virtue one pedal at a time.

Gradually we learn about and develop 1) benevolence 2) compassion 3) giving happiness and 4) impartiality—the *four infinite virtues*. These can become well developed mental capabilities and personality traits beyond the simple real-time consciousness we feel as a beginning point of being human. In order to achieve these Purifications, absent entering a monastery or wat, we need to develop a sincere and active practice of meditation such as that described in this book and referred to in the introduction of Satipatthana Sutta (which is also included in its entirety as Appendix I.) This ancient guided meditation follows and develops the four foundations of meditation, *the body, feelings, mind and contents (or qualities) of the mind.*[5] This reads as if it were easy enough to do, but it is a full-fledged admonition directing our effort to study these four foundations of meditation also found in Anapanasati, which underlie the organization of this book.

We begin with the basics in our ordinary lives (call this Dharma): the simple natural structure of our humanity, the six senses, "the six sense organs and their objects" as these are described in the classic Buddhist tradition.[6] These teachings

---

[5]   "There is the case where a monk remains focused on the ***body*** in & of itself—ardent, alert, & mindful—putting aside greed & distress with reference to the world. [S/he] remains focused on *feelings* ardent, alert, & mindful—putting aside greed & distress with reference to the world. [S/he remains focused on] ***Mind***, ardent, alert, & mindful—putting aside greed & distress with reference to the world. [S/he remains focused on] ***Mental qualities*** in & of themselves—ardent, alert, & mindful—putting aside greed & distress with reference to the world." (Satipatthana)

[6]   "Learn in your daily life from the. . . functions of 1) seeing, 2) listening, 3) smelling, 4) tasting, 5) touching and 6) thinking. There is the body, and organs of the body which have contact with the things around the body. . . If you want to study Buddha-dharma and know

moved from the oral tradition to the written Dharma, and come to us in numerous books and sutras. When the beginning Practitioner has given as much effort to each of the subsequent three foundations of meditation as to the first—body and senses—then they should expect to achieve some worthwhile results, but obviously we have to go the whole distance more than once to get the results we can expect to achieve—relief from suffering. "Don't start from a book or a sermon or a preaching."(Buddhadasa)

The general guide for all our effort is the teaching of the "middle way". "There are these two extremes that are not to be indulged in by one who has gone forth. Which two? That which is devoted to sensual pleasure with reference to sensual objects: base, vulgar, common, ignoble, unprofitable; and that which is devoted to self-affliction: painful, ignoble, unprofitable. Avoiding both of these extremes, *the middle way realized by the Tathagata*—producing vision, producing knowledge—leads to calm, to direct knowledge, to self-awakening, to Unbinding." (Appendix II) We are to start with meditation, the practice of watching and following our breathing, and developing our minds based on our increasing capacity for mindfulness (notwithstanding that this advice comes from a book.) Even this book will come up wanting and only points the way that we have to travel (practice) on our own. Along the way we can take notes, write in a journal and write poems as a way to track our progress, and perhaps we can have some fun too; that is not too much to ask.

Buddha-dharma, you must begin your study upon these things. . . starting your practice with these six pairs of ayatana: the six sense organs and their objects when they are functioning in your daily life. Don't start from a book or a sermon or a preaching. That's useless if you want to get at the heart of Dharma." (Buddhadasa, 1982, pp. 10-11)

PART I
Calm mind

Chapter One

Long Breaths

Key Words:

agitation, skillful, determinant, productive mind, internal motivation, grasping, bliss, sati, Anapanasati, mindfulness, Foundations of Meditation, following, Bud-dho

Why Should I Meditate?

A productive mind is capable of meditation and developing useful insights. A calm mind is one that is fit to do this work. Single pointed clarity gives the energy to proceed with insight and contemplation of the Dharma. Using our breath in meditation is an intimate and personal activity that no one else can manipulate or influence. Accumulate experiences in meditation (and apply these) until these become a source of wisdom. Meditation develops the frame of reference to understand how each piece of the mental puzzle fits into an idiosyncratic whole. We can hope and expect to eliminate one problem at a time, developing a life free of defilements. Meditation is a journey of looking deeply, to touch our true nature [and reach into our Hearts.] We can train [our] mind to attain perfect and efficient mindfulness—ready to know the truth (Dharma). We watch the breath get refined . . . there's

3

just awareness . . . called meeting the Buddha . . . this is what *bud—dho* means. When we sense that mental calm and relaxation is the case—we have arrived—we're living with the Buddha. Purification of our Hearts? We learn this as a fruit of meditation. We learn in a deeper way, through personal experience rather than through thinking, that the breath is intimately associated with the body (it is the body conditioner). We use a focus on breath as object lesson to develop a calm mind. Emotions and feelings underlay our thinking; we discover and unravel this subtle and beautiful capacity during meditation.

It might seem at first thought that a calm mind is a rather trivial state for most people of normal faculties. How hard can it be? But in point of fact, for first time meditators, having a distracted and uncomfortably active mind, full of random and wandering thoughts, is the most commonly reported result. When we stop and sit, our minds keep going as if these had a life of their own, which is precisely the case. When we ride on a bus or train and the vehicle stops, the background out the window seems to keep moving for a short time, and our minds cause this, and do the same when we begin to meditate. This stopping and sitting is an unnatural state, perhaps this relates to a primitive need to be defensive, alert and paranoid in a hostile world; a survival mechanism. Buddhists have stories about the Monkey Mind, and the difficulty of trying to train an elephant—to describe the normal state of our overactive mental functioning. The Tibetan monk Rinpoche Mingyur is one of the best meditation teachers, he suggests that our typical experience is characterized as "The ordinary conditions of dullness, distraction, or agitation that confront the mind." (Mingyur) Settling into a pattern of relaxed and comfortable meditation is not counter-intuitive; on the surface it seems like a perfectly reasonable way to relax, rather, it is just counter-cerebral. It goes against the grain of our normally active, agitated mind. In the next few paragraphs we look at and expand several important lessons he gives in a very concise and succinct instruction.

The first, best strategy is to accept the thoughts we perceive even though these threaten to flood us like a swollen river, one at a time. Look at your thoughts that arise as if they were objects of interest. Mingyur says that "You gain greater strength [and determination] and progress through working with these conditions . . ." whatever they are. Most thoughts are trivial renditions, restatements of actual events, etc., or just nuisance ideas, but the odd thought might be useful and deliver some insight worth pausing for. It is neither helpful nor skillful to try to create a blank mind, and there is no shame, at least initially, in having concepts and ideas jumping around. That is an essential part of inspiration and creativity, after all. On an organized basis this is called "brainstorming" and can be sublimated into a problem solving technique. The best strategy is to expect to benefit from your thoughts; in fact it is skillful to use your thinking for good purposes, to examine a specific event of suffering for example. Eventually it will be possible to identify the causes and determinants of that suffering and proceed to choose a path in order to eliminate and/or prevent that suffering. Thus a calm mind is one that is fit for work, not dead but capable of contemplation and progressing toward a worthwhile goal; not a blank, silent box.

So we don't initially have a calm mind, we begin to learn how to achieve a productive mind, capable of meditation and developing useful insights, and this is a goal worth achieving. Do we want to be more productive? And productive of what? In any or each case, developing the skill to meditate will accelerate our ability to accomplish the goals we choose or accept (as with an assigned task from our employer). Many of the verses of The Dhammapada, one of the most popular sources of inspiring poetry in the Buddhist literary heritage, are directed at encouraging the development of the mind and mental control. "The mind is hard to restrain, light\ Flying where it will.\ Control of it is good.\ Mind controlled brings happiness." (Dhammapada, vs. 35) Each time we meditate our experience is going to be slightly or entirely different, and that is the good news. The devil is in the details, however, and that is what we need to accumulate, knowledge of the ten thousand teachings of Buddhism as is suggested in the Zen tradition.

Gaining this knowledge is not the same as experiencing some kind of "bliss, clarity, or some other wonderful experience". In an important way we have to take our pick, because our mind can't really accomplish anything and rest in a state of bliss at the same time. Rinpoche Mingyur suggests that we will have more motivation to meditate if we cut short our experience of bliss, etc.[7] This may seem counter-intuitive, but coming from such an authority it is worth heeding this admonition. When I read that for the first time I was surprised and more than a little perplexed. But I learned that there is the need to meditate for the sake of meditation (that is: training our minds) and meditation to achieve a predetermined objective. Both these kinds of meditation are possible and useful for Buddhist practitioners, along with the occasional need to just be at peace and enjoy the passing of time. Even though it would seem that we would want to extend the time when we have "bliss, clarity . . . etc." rather than stopping, there are several good reasons for doing so. Thus these peaceful experiences are not the most skillful, nor even the best results of meditation, as we will soon learn. However, this single pointed clarity can give us the energy to proceed with insight and contemplation of the Dharma, which are more valuable achievements.

---

[7] "The most important lesson I learned was to avoid becoming attached to my positive experience if it was peaceful. As with every mental experience, bliss, clarity, and non-conceptuality spontaneously come and go. You didn't create them, you didn't cause them, and you can't control [or force] them. They are simply natural qualities of your mind. I was taught that when such very positive experiences occur to stop right there, before the sensations dissipate. Contrary to my expectations, when I stopped practicing as soon as bliss, clarity, or some other wonderful experience occurred, the effects actually lasted much longer than when I tried to hang on to them. I also found that I was much more eager to meditate the next time I was supposed to practice." (Mingyur)

The main message is to relax and not try to force too much to happen or result from the very beginning. Axiom: If we find ourselves bored, or lacking stimulation, that is when we can remind ourselves that we are most likely achieving a good mental state, ready for work. Boredom is an involuntary acknowledgment by an inexperienced meditator that our minds are running at a slower pace. In our ordinary lives, some people find that they are entertained and stimulated so much, and they have become accustomed to so much activity and depend so much on external stimulation from music, television or social chatting with friends (more on this later) that the very thought of meditation is abhorrent. I know of people who think they have to have a radio playing and talking at them in order to sleep because they have become accustomed to having external stimulation, and having peace and quiet irritates them. More on this later.

This brings up the question: How much of our thinking can we actually control? How much of what comes to mind is a result of our own biology, nurturing, DNA, IQ, or based on the environment or books we have chosen to read? Listening to music, for example, is a way to distract our minds into any number of states of calm or excitement, but listening to music is not meditation. Most people in our society are addicted to this and other kinds of distraction. Does it seem strange to call what is otherwise considered so normal and ordinary an addiction? Having a calm mind is an achievement, and a very useful one as every student knows who is trying to read or focus to prepare for an examination. This kind of focus is not strictly speaking meditation because it is still based on external input, but there are some useful analogues. Meditation is something internal we will for ourselves, a continuing process that we learn and practice to control; while studying is often based on outside pressures and assignments from teachers, etc. There is guided meditation, and this is a half-way point that can inspire Insight and can be beneficial especially for beginners. Meditation is an assignment we give ourselves—even when guided vocally by another person—and we are willing participants. The more we can internalize our motivation when we set out to meditate, the better and easier it will be to succeed. The best students are also the ones who have this kind of self-directed motivation. Listening to peaceful music can be a very useful prelude to meditation, like a period of transition from the daily grind. Sounding a gong and lighting candles serves something of the same purpose, although there is more involved in those rituals.

What is more important as a goal for meditation, to recognize suffering or to recognize and amplify joy and happiness? Or is this in an important way of saying the same thing with different words? If life means suffering, does that mean we are doomed, or is that just a marketing gimmick to get us to follow the Buddhist path? If to live means to suffer, because our human nature is not perfect and neither is the world we live in, So!? Why does that have to impinge on us? We are as special as we work to make ourselves, yet we can never take ourselves away from the natural hazards of life, growing old, or perhaps suffering from some disease or disability. During our lifetime, we inevitably have to endure physical suffering such as pain, sickness, injury, tiredness, isolation, the difficulties of old age, and eventually death; and all of these compounded when they occur to our loved ones. We recognize that we inevitably have to endure serious psychological suffering like sadness, fear, ennui, frustration, empathy, anger, disappointment, and depression (and the list goes on) at one time or another. Although there are different degrees of suffering and there are also positive experiences in life that we perceive as the opposite of suffering, such as ease, comfort, achievement and happiness. So? Unraveling these questions in specific detail is what we can hope to gain during meditation and we can achieve this kind of profound enlightenment after sustained practice.

Life in its totality is imperfect and incomplete, complex and exciting, because our world is subject to impermanence, according to the standard Buddhist diatribe. Yet when we recognize these defects and limitations of nature in advance, we anticipate impermanence as is taught by Anapanasati;

this impermanence does not need to make us suffer! We can make an end to it, and that is the promise of Buddhism. I like to repeat the idea that suffering is what we add to pain; likewise it is *how we experience* the many emotions and events just mentioned, and many more. This means we are never able to keep permanently what we strive for, and just as happy moments pass by like an enjoyable movie that comes to an end, we and our loved ones will pass away one day too. So when we understand this, we can be prepared for the negatives, and amplify the positive happiness—thus we learn to take all the negatives in stride. To understand that, is to begin to understand what it means to not cling to or crave certain outcomes or relationships. This talk is all so theoretical, however, in meditation we take the theory and apply it to the here and now that is in part why we practice and develop the skill to be mindful.

We use our minds and thoughts in Buddhism because, as with breathing, it is the most intimate and personal activity of our lives that presumably no one else can manipulate or influence. If we live in a busy household with an active job (i.e. teaching), we have constant interaction with many different kinds of people, the time we set aside for meditation is like a reprieve from the nuisance of all that hustle and bustle. Using the breath as a tool to enhance meditation is literally like a breath of fresh air, and for this reason alone it would have stood the test of time as the most productive way of pursuing meditation. (There are other reasons for using the breath that we will discuss later.) Furthermore, our breath and thoughts are features and aspects of our lives that travel with us, available each minute of the day, and we can accumulate experiences in meditation until these become a source of wisdom without these being detracted by—or distracted by other people. If we accept the goal of eliminating suffering, we set out to recognize the non-productive habits that confront our lives, such as craving, clinging and attaching our egos to outcomes. "Grasping or clinging too tightly to a wonderful

9

experience is the one real danger of meditation . . ."[8] because we might think that is our goal rather than developing our skill using our breath to change our lives. Since one tendency we have to overcome in our ordinary day is the *grasping and clinging* of other aspects of our lives (we discuss this again in chapter fourteen), it is skillful to start with not holding on to this kind of meditation experience. That by itself does not lead to elimination of suffering, we will instead gradually own our achievements and build on these, but "wonderful experiences" once analyzed, are just a collection of humble, temporary mental states that may or may not be repeated. We should know in advance that these are the same experiences that have occurred for so many monks and meditators throughout history, and more importantly, we are self-selected to be part of that honorable and prestigious tradition. Being an active Buddhist is in one way like being a leader or politician for most Western practitioners, it is something we choose to do for our own psychic satisfaction, or out of a sense of some positive need.

We all have ambitions, i.e. for financial success or a long-term, committed partner in life—that come in every conceivable color and size, most of which we acquire from our parents, siblings or peers at school. We have these because of our cultural training, such as a desire to possess and acquire not only materials but useful and enlightening experiences. We don't leave our ambitions outside the door of the sala with our sandals, but we do from the very beginning need to exercise some discernment, to learn some humility at a very beginning stage. Our ambitions can be counterproductive if they make us impatient for results or quick knowledge. We

---

[8]   "Even more important, I discovered that ending my meditation practice at the point at which I experienced something of bliss, clarity or nonconceptuality [a quiet Heart] was a great exercise in learning to let go of the habit of dzinpa (Tibetan), or grasping. Grasping or clinging too tightly to a wonderful experience is the one real danger of meditation, because it's so easy to think that this wonderful experience is a sign of realization. . ." (Mingyur)

need to learn to take instructions and have patience even though we may not understand the subtle "whys" of what we are being told to do. Our minds carry all this baggage, and in the beginning we don't know the answers let alone all the questions (and here I am speaking from self-critical personal experience). Using our breath appropriately is what helps us put all that in order and helps us make sense out of our circumstances—or make changes. Remember, "*Realization*" is a technical Buddhist term, the last stage of purification so we will need some patience to get to chapter thirteen when we begin to discuss that level of achievement. If a beginning meditator objects to or doesn't understand the importance of using breath as an object of meditation now, the best advice is to be patient and do it anyway, eventually it will make a lot of sense.

We can only gradually develop the frame of reference to understand how each piece of the puzzle of our minds fits into an idiosyncratic whole. We can expect too much, be too over confident, be too ambitious for results, and cling or grasp for the bliss and clarity we might momentarily achieve. Even having "*recognition*" about our lives, personalities, talents and limitations is an advanced but essential step, one we will hopefully achieve (beginning with chapter five), even if gradually. Before that, the best we can hope for is to see, look at and know the truth about our lives and eliminate one problem at a time, then move on to the next. That is the message of the preliminary Buddhist training—to use the body as the first object or foundation of meditation—the breath is presumed to be connected inextricably to the body (as the body-conditioner). That is just the beginning of developing a life unencumbered by defilements.

Mingyur is generous and gentle enough not to be discouraging in his coaching when he delivers his strict teaching. When we experience peace and tranquility, and perhaps this comes very soon after we begin, it is just a starting off point. It is more productive to work with the "ordinary conditions of dullness, distraction, or agitation"[9] in our practice. When we greet this normal thinking with a welcoming and sympathetic Heart, we shower ourselves with love and compassion. We show a willingness to accept our human natures as reasonable and highly functional, albeit initially naive. The goal, to end suffering, is a fabulous achievement, but our initial experience is likely to be anything but regular or consistent.

The best strategy for developing the skill of purposeful meditation is to simply learn how to focus on breathing, in and out. When we are mindful of our breaths, we tend to relax, settle our minds and more efficiently eliminate the rush of thoughts and distractions. This is traditionally most closely associated with Buddhist meditation, and although this technique is taught by many other traditions and religions, it remains useful after more than 2500 years of discussion. While being conscious of our breaths, we can follow this next guided meditation as a brief practice and set of instructions. Throughout this book, as stated in the introduction, we will be moving gradually through the sixteen steps of Anapanasati meditation together, dwelling on and considering each of the four Foundations of Meditation, discussing each step of Purification, and using the breath which is probably the most skillful single aspect of this whole process.

—Breathe normally. Begin with the eyes open.[10] Watch the breath and even try counting to ten in-and-out breaths, which is a staple of Zen meditation. We each perhaps mediate for

---

[9]   "But in most cases it's just a passing phase, a glimpse of the true nature of the mind, as easily obscured as when clouds obscure Sun. Once that brief moment of pure awareness has passed, you have to deal with the ordinary conditions of dullness, distraction, or agitation that confront the mind. And you gain greater strength [of Heart] and progress through working with these conditions rather than by trying to cling to experiences of bliss, clarity, or non-conceptuality." (Mingyur, pg. 219)

[10]   "Meditating with the eyes open will help us to stay awake and will keep the eyes cool and comfortable . . .Gaze at the tip of the nose without crossing your eyes which causes fatigue." (Buddhadasa)

our own reasons, but when we wish to touch our true nature, this is the most skillful way of doing it.[11] When we watch our breaths we are beginning to experience mindfulness, we are conscious of the activity of our minds in that very moment of awareness.[12]—Notice the strength, sound and speed of your breath.—Mindfulness is nothing more than this focus on or awareness of our breaths (or another thought or image we might choose as an object.) There is no mystery, just insight, literally looking in; it is the underlying animation and activity of the reflexive pronoun "myself or mine". There is no doctrine that contradicts any religion that I know about as we begin simply to develop the skill to control our minds and make our thinking process be a tool for purifying our lives. Yet there is the promise "In the village, a sage should go about/ Like a bee, which, not harming/ Flower, color or scent/ Flies off with the nectar." (Dhammapada, vs. 49) As each of us gains in our ability to control our minds and thinking, then we will find ways to add to our communities (like pollinating flowers and making honey).

Begin with normal breathing and to the extent that you can do this, you can create a calm mind. Just watch the breath traveling from the nose to the abdomen.[13] Place your hands on your lap in normal meditation Lotus posture, right hand resting on left palm, then roll this slightly or shift it so that you can feel

---

[11] "To meditate means to be invited on a journey of looking deeply in order to touch our true nature [reach into our Hearts] and to recognize that nothing is lost." (Hanh, pg. 225)

[12] "First we talk about Sati. Our intention should be to develop *sati (mindfulness or reflective awareness)* by being actively mindful of each in-breath and out-breath. We train in sati by noting that we are about to breathe in or breathe out . . . How are we breathing in? Breathe in a relaxed way." (Buddhadasa, 1988)

[13] "Sati means mindfulness. The importance of the Dhamma practice is that we can train [our] mind to attain perfect and efficient mindfulness to know the truth [the three characteristics] of the body: it is impermanent, suffering and subject to decay at last." (Wee, pg. 184)

the movement of your diaphragm and stomach[14] to help focus your attention. "Keep the mind constantly focused on the breathing in and out smoothly . . . This is the . . . foundation for all the rest . . ." (Buddhadasa) If there is incense in the room you will notice the pleasant odor of this as you breathe, but when following the breath this will be only a passing distraction, although perhaps it will make the session more peaceful and complex, incorporating this sense of smell as well as what is for Buddhists the sixth sense.

When I want to go to sleep or do stretching for my joints and muscles I find it beneficial to meditate using this same breathing technique but adding the mental chant "bud—dho" with normal in and—out breathing respectively. "This is called meeting with the Buddha . . ."[15] This is widely used in Thailand and practiced by the "forest tradition" of Buddhism. This is something we need to do each day on our own cushion, lying

---

[14]   "What is the out-breath like? Use sati to note the ordinary breath . . . and train sati by using a technique called '**following**,' or 'chasing.' We imagine the in-breath starting from the tip of the nose and ending at the navel . . . contemplate the breath as if chasing it, without ever losing it. Do not allow empty spaces where the mind might wander but keep the mind constantly focused on the breathing in and out smoothly . . . This is the first lesson to learn, the foundation for all the rest . . . " (Buddhadasa)

[15]   "When you feel tired, stop all your thoughts. Don't think of anything at all. Focus the mind in at the mind, and keep the mind with the breath: buddho, buddho. Let go of everything outside. . . Focus on the breath. Gather the mind at the breath. . . We get acquainted with coarse breathing. We get acquainted with refined breathing. . . We keep watching the breath get more and more refined until there's no more breath. There's just awareness, wide awake. . . This is called meeting with the Buddha. . .This is what buddho means: what's aware, awake, serene. When that's the case we're living with the Buddha. We've met with awareness. We've met with brightness. . . The real Buddha is awareness that's serene and bright. When you meet with this, that's all you have to know. Let everything gather right here." (Ajahn Chah, pp. 6-7)

in bed, walking, standing or sitting in a chair, because it is foundational to the practice of Buddhist meditation. So come back to this—but now we move on.

Next we want to change the natural breath into first of all long, extended breathing. We will make a study of this altered breathing, and see how it affects our body and feelings.[16] Fill the lungs slowly and completely taking as much time as necessary, it is an unnatural way to breathe. This is just a study, it is not routine in Buddhism to change the breath. How does this help with the purification of our Hearts? The answer to this question will become self-evident, but we will have to learn this for ourselves as one of the fruits of meditation.

First we examine long breaths. Breathe with long, slow breaths [counting to yourself to ten slowly] without holding, fill the lungs completely. Continue. (Do this for one minute.) Follow this guided meditation coming from the Suan Mokkh, Thailand, teachings.

"The **first lesson** is the contemplation [and chasing] of the long breath [in more detail.] . . . its properties, qualities, influence, and flavor.

When a breath is long, how pleasant is it?

Is it natural and ordinary?

What kinds of calmness and happiness arise?

In what ways is it different from a short breath?

Observe how the body works in relation to long breaths. Place a hand on your abdomen.

How does the body move when there is a long inhalation?

In what places does the body expand?

Where does it contract?

---

[16] "Now we are about to contemplate the different kinds of breath [as well], long and short, coarse and fine, easy and uneasy. Begin to observe the various kinds by experiencing them with sati. . . The goal is to know [our own individual] reactions to these various properties of the breath. . . we must learn to know when these qualities influence our awareness, our sensitivity, our mind . . ." (Buddhadasa, pp. 30-31)

With the deepest possible long breath, does the chest expand or contract?

Does the abdomen expand or contract? [continue slow, deep breathing]

(The chest expands with long breaths.) In order to know the nature of the long breath, we study all the secrets and attributes of the long breath. We are able to contemplate its long duration, learning to protect and maintain it. In fact, we become experts in all matters concerned with the long breath. Practicing with the **long breath is lesson one** . . . We learn in a deeper way, through personal experience rather than through thinking, that the breath is intimately associated with the body." (Buddhadasa)

(Return to normal relaxed breathing.) It is possible to change the body chemistry to the point of hallucination or emotional distortion, but this is not the goal, so keep the duration of long breathing to about one minute during each sitting. Evaluate what the effects are of this long breath for yourself.[17] —Our academic minds are like vanilla ice cream, certainly it is a flavor but it seems neutral—like a can of base-tint paint ready for additional colors—and ready for other flavors; often with our academic minds we are ignorant of emotions and feelings that underlie our thinking.

We can discover this subtle and beautiful capacity we have for spontaneity and emotions during meditation, just as we learn to recognize the flavors of our breaths. Again, changing or manipulating the breath is not an important part of meditation for Buddhists (as it is for Yoga), except to the extent that we learn about the character and effect of the different breaths. Once we have learned, and occasionally perhaps we practice this lesson again, we almost always meditate with normal breathing, focusing on observing the breath as it comes naturally in and out. We use this focus, also

---

[17] "It is also important for us to note the effect or flavor of each kind of breath. The flavors that arise as different kinds of feeling are: happiness, dukkha (suffering), annoyance, and contentment . . ." (Buddhadasa, 1988, pp. 35-39)

16

as an object lesson to help us develop a calm mind, breathing bud—dho, and just as importantly, for developing our skill at being mindful.

Gradually we learn to enjoy meditation more than stimulating our minds through other external, sensual entertainment such as bungee jumping, para-sailing, watching sit-coms on TV, or other less complicated pleasures. Using our breath to begin our meditation practice can be thought of as a ritual, as we will see, connecting with a sacred determinant of life. In ancient times the observation of the breath was equivalent to seeing or being in contact with the spiritual nature or soul of a person. This leads us to the accomplishment of Nirodha, even if initially we don't see it, we will be changing the way we enjoy spending our time. We become like a flower—"The scent of flowers is not blown against the wind/ Not sandalwood or tagara or jasmine./ But the scent of the good is blown against the wind: A good [wo/]man perfumes all directions." (Dammapada, vs. 54) As our meditation training progresses and our virtues compound, we develop influence beyond simply being blown by the wind, we develop the control of our own lives.

Chapter Two

Short Breaths

Key Words:

mystical breath, ritual, insight, natural truth, temple, breath-body, health, wisdom, body conditioner, flesh-body, occultism

Why Should I Meditate?

In meditation we learn about the characteristics of our breath and how this affects our bodies, emotions and how this is a very serious religious activity. Eventually we observe ourselves and the breath, less for information and more as an important ritual. Meditation is natural, occultism or mysticism is **not** typically pursued by Buddhist traditions. In Meditation we act in a certain way toward the *breath-body* and have an effect on the *flesh-body, and* we can exploit this fact. Once we get the good habit started—this relaxed, normal, clear breathing will dominate our lives. We seek to reinforce qualities of our natural mind—peace, clarity, openness, relaxation—present in our Heart just as it is. Meditation can be an end in itself at times, a peaceful retreat, and a place to feel at home. We use meditation to actively improve our lives (to reduce suffering) and learn how to breathe properly to improve our health. In meditation we focus on one subject at a time, as "object" for insight, and this is skillful and effective in reducing suffering. The music we create is our purpose when we sing and play a horn; and we use our breath in meditation to a productive end.

When does it happen that our breath pattern changes involuntarily? When we exercise we very quickly begin to breathe more frequently and perhaps more deeply. If we exercise extensively, we can reach the limit of how fast our breath can refresh and feed our bodies the oxygen and other elements we need from the air we exchange. This capability is a measure of the endurance and capacity of athletes. In a very different context our breath can change if we suddenly encounter a circumstance of danger or threat. I notice if I am walking along a strange street in an unknown town at night, I am looking deep into every shadow and my breath reflects this anxiety. I breathe faster, more shallow, and feel other physical reactions associated with fear and suspicion. So, I seldom do this! Curiously, this is more or less the same reaction I feel before I make a presentation in front of a group, or even when walking in front of an audience at a public gathering. Perhaps that is why I don't do that very often either. Thus we can study our own lives and learn a lot about the foundation principles of meditation.

There was no science as such during the time of the Buddha, no scientific method but there were of course keen observations and logical thinking. So knowing about the practical effects of breath and connecting this to life and emotional states was well developed 2,500 years ago based on the same kind of experience we can have every day. Beyond that, the breath was given a mystical status, numinous, as both a signal of life and a cause of life, so the mystical breath figures prominently in many Buddhist teachings. We know that the breath doesn't cause life, just as kissing doesn't create babies. But it is a determinant, a necessary adjunct to life; they both exist simultaneously and necessarily. The Precept against killing—*taking away the breath*—was very significant for the

Buddha, more so than for the other religions of the day which practiced animal and even human sacrifices. The Precepts of not using the breath to generate loud, rude speech or for false speech is as much to do with violating the sacred status of the breath, as it is about being polite and honest, respectively. This connection has been lost in historical texts as far as I know, but it came to me as one of those spontaneous insights. So when we begin to learn about the characteristics of our breath and how this affects our bodies and emotions, this is a very serious religious activity. When we do this meditation using the breath year after year, eventually we observe the breath less for information and more as an important ritual. Observing and using the breath is central to developing a calm mind fit for Insight and Concentration, it is the beginning of our practice each sitting and remains important as a meditation tool. Once we know what there is to know about any particular object, we just keep using our normal breath as part of our meditation practice.

Remember what we studied in the last chapter about long breaths. Now follow this directed meditation step by step and test the technique of breathing **short breaths**—Begin by softly counting in your mind one (in)-two (out), gradually quicken the pace. "Find out [for yourself] why short breaths have different flavors than long breaths . . . Finally, we can discover the various causes that render our breathing either long or short. We gradually learn this by [observing] ourselves . . . This **second lesson is the contemplation of short breath** [in more detail.] . . . its properties, qualities, influence, and flavor.

When a breath is short, how pleasant is it? (Continue following quick breaths.)

Is it natural and ordinary?

What kinds of calmness or nervousness arise?

In what ways is it different from a long breath?

Observe how the body works in relation to short breaths. Place a hand on your abdomen.

How does the body move when there is a short inhalation?

In what places does the body expand?

Where does it contract? How much effort does it take?

With these short breaths, how does the chest expand or contract?

Does the abdomen expand or contract?

Looking from the other direction, what kind of mood makes the breath short?

There is a compression of time-space and you are active and busy while chasing short breaths. Study this more on your own. Keep these questions in mind for future reference . . ." (Buddhadasa)

(Breathe normally.) It is better to study the long and short breath briefly in each sitting. Prolonged artificial breathing can lead to changes in the body's chemistry and even affect the mind's ability to concentrate. Again, achieving these altered states of consciousness is not a goal or tool of Buddhism in general, in the same way that occultism or mysticism is **not** taught or pursued by almost all Buddhist traditions. That's easy to say but there has always been an element of superstition or mysticism (at least a special Dharma language) in most Buddhism, at least as it is practiced in various Asian countries. Consider the Buddha's words as he explains his original teaching "turning the wheel." "But as soon as this—my three-round, twelve-permutation knowledge & vision concerning these four noble truths as they have come to be—was truly pure, then I did claim to have directly awakened to the right self-awakening unexcelled in the cosmos with its deities, Maras & Brahmas, with its contemplatives & brahmans, its royalty & commonfolk. Knowledge & vision arose in me: 'Unprovoked is my release. This is the last birth. There is now no further becoming'." (Appendix II) What should we make of this? Should we use our breaths to create these special altered states of consciousness to advance our full-awakening? Or do these "deities" just act as metaphors to explain the special personality traits of humans, most of which are to be avoided? How can one person achieve non-returning ("the last birth . . . no further becoming.") if the rest of us have a different fate? Or do we?

21

Now when we learn about the ordinary breath as it is extensively used in Buddhist meditation, we learn that it consists of a group of elements and life giving energy and it is believed that the breath is sacred and conditions the flesh body to be healthy, calm and pure. Does the breath have any effect on our wisdom? Because of the connections between our breath, our lungs and blood, then to all the body; the breath as air, even though just a natural element of Earth like soil, heat or water (and now we know that air contains all four of these elements), it has a special place in Buddhist traditions.[18] Some effects are subtle, calming; some are more noticeable and easier to describe. Identify as many as possible during each of your next few meditation sessions. Consider that scientists have determined (now after 2,500 years) that breathing patterns during sleep, i.e. sleep apnea, have consequences for our health and possibly for longevity. So eventually we will realize that having a healthy, normal pattern of breathing 24 hours a day, will help us prevent suffering in our lives. That is just one of the physical, practical benefits; there are many others that are less measurable. Can regular, calm breath affect our wisdom?

What is this wisdom we hear so much about? Historically "'Wisdom meant a lot of different things. But it was always associated with knowledge, frequently applied to human social situations, involved judgment and reflection, and was almost always embedded in a component of compassion.'

---

[18] ". . .we can master [the flesh-body] by using the breath. If we act in a certain way toward the breath-body, there will also be a specific effect upon the flesh-body. This is why we take the breath as the object of our training. Supervising the breath, to whatever degree, is equivalent to regulating the flesh-body to the same degree. This point will be more clearly understood when we have trained up to that particular stage of *anapanasati* . . . Every kind of breath is noted and analyzed. Long breaths, short breaths, calm breaths, violent breaths, fast breaths, slow breaths—we learn to know them all [by following and observing them.] We examine the nature, characteristics, and functions of each kind of breath that arises." (Buddhadasa, 1988, pp.7-8)

(Vivian Clayton) The Hebrew term for wisdom, chokhmah, suggested that the concept resided in both the mind and the heart. Indeed, the melding of these two ancient concepts in a single word anticipates one of the burning issues in modern neuroscience: the degree to which mind and body, cognition and emotion, are similarly melded. Not distinct parts, mind you, but marbled together." (Hall, pg. 45) When we evaluate wisdom we think of the elements of cognitive (or knowledge), affective (emotional concerns) and being reflective. This is like many other personal characteristics that often defy explanation, "we all know it when we see it, we just don't see it very often." (Hall, pg. 51)

Now having studied so much about breathing during meditation, I try to think about breathing normally whenever I happen to notice, of course this can't be every moment of the day, and in fact it is very seldom. But once we get good habits started, this relaxed, normal, clear breathing will dominate our lives. I want to emphasize a few points about meditation in general: our breathing can influence our health, "peace, openness, relaxation, and clarity" are available in our minds when we release them naturally, and when we reduce effort and expectations we gain more.[19] This technique of being mindful of and using our breaths is easy enough to adopt,

---

[19] "Actually, the essence of meditation practice is to let go of all your expectations about meditation. All the qualities of your natural mind—peace, openness, relaxation, and clarity—are present in your mind and Heart just as it is. You don't have to do anything different. You don't have to shift or change your awareness. All you have to do while observing your mind [and breath] is to recognize the qualities these already have. This is one of the most basic teachings of Buddhism. Breath alone is well worth knowing, even if only in terms of health. If we know how to breathe properly [naturally,] we may improve our health. Thus, the body and everything associated with the body—the breath, the emotions, our minds, [our Hearts,] our health—is considered to be a very important subject. [Thus] we may get very immediate benefits from this very first stage of anapanasati." (Buddhadasa, 2005, pg. 96)

and later we learn about reciting or chanting mantras and special sounds, and using our normal breaths in meditation is of course a functional aspect of this religious practice. Breathing is natural, but using this breath skillfully does take some training and coaching, it doesn't just come naturally; we noticed this same truth from the experience of our agitated, distracted mind when we first began meditation.

Once we are trained well to understand and "read" our breath we prepare ourselves for success in meditation. This kind of being in the present, comfortable with our breathing, is different than our most common condition of having thoughts about our past full of pain or emotions, or the future full of hopes and ambitions. ". . . The 'sacred now.' This is a state of being fully present . . ."[20] I like this idea that what we are doing, even in the beginning of our meditation practice, might be in some way sacred. This idea and belief ought to help motivate people to progress and move to step five, when our emotions begin to be examined in detail.

In our culture we have traditions about our breath, "take a few deep breaths" to calm down and change our emotional state, we breathe rapidly into a bag to reduce our anxiety; we relax by taking a deep breath and a sigh. What results are most common? The long breath slows down our minds and brings ease and comfort. Short breaths are caused by anxiety, and in turn can create "uneasiness, agitation and discomfort."[21] These natural truths are now accepted and

---

[20]   "Another major benefit of mindfulness meditation practice is that it brings you into what is sometimes called the 'sacred now.' This is a state of being fully present such that you are both 'in time' and 'not in time.' Mystics in most contemplative traditions throughout the ages have extolled this as an exalted state but have seldom given instructions for how to achieve it. . . When you are stuck in either past or future thinking, you create suffering for yourself and miss much of the actual experience of the gift of having embodied consciousness. " (McLeod, pg. 49)

[21]   " . . .that the long breath brings ease and comfort? While the short breath leads to abnormality, that is, uneasiness, agitation, and discomfort.

repeated in psychology training and therapy throughout the Western culture, a truth long accepted by the Eastern or Asiatic cultures. Count ten breaths to reduce your response to anger, is a common teaching. In my experience of historical and practical Christianity, Islam or Judaism, I don't remember this issue of learning about or using the breath to have been in any way significant. (I could be mistaken.) Musicians and singers especially learn to control their breathing, and learn to generate breath and air-force from deep in their diaphragms. I played the cornet initially (later I learned to play the euphonium) when I was eleven years old, and was taught about how to breathe and expel air to make my instrument create the desired sounds (which did not always happen). I learned about the length of notes, and how to read music, all associated with the more trivial aspect of using my breath productively. Even for meditation, the breath is essentially indirectly consequential for the intended purpose, which is to reduce suffering, etc.; it is a vehicle or tool, in the background of our mindfulness as we develop our skill in contemplating objects and developing insights. The music that we create is our purpose when we sing and play a horn, once we practice and develop competence we don't spend any time thinking about the breath, we just use it. It is a means, a determinant, to an end.

Based on what we have studied, how should we use our breath to calm our minds? The best advice is to make it as natural as possible, unaffected by emotions or irregular practices. There is more to consider beyond our breathing, and we come to that in the next chapter. Breathers (and we all are) try to be natural: "Irrigators lead the water;/ Fletchers shape the arrow;/ Carpenters shape the wood;/ The wise control themselves." (Dhammapada, vs. 80) Which means, we can control our breaths when we need to.

Thus through our ability to regulate the breath, we know how to make the body either comfortable or uncomfortable." (Buddhadasa, 1988, pg. 39)

I was taught in my youth in a Christian religion that the body, my ordinary human body, is a temple. Their idea is that our spirit and soul reside in the body so therefore we have to keep our bodies pure to respect and give reverence to our spirits. This is one of the teachings that is worthwhile from this tradition, a concept that can be carried over to any religious practice. We know that we can control the appearance of our bodies in a general way, fitness, weight control, recuperation from injury, plastic surgery, etc. In Buddhism we tend to take our bodies for granted, especially ascetics and vegetarians; we watch them and try not to attach too much importance to our appearance, but I like the temple idea. This has some useful repercussions for health, self-respect, and alertness. When we think of our bodies as a reflection of our minds, then we recognize that keeping our bodies in perfect tune is a good idea. Thus we can use our breath to bless and sanctify our body/temple.

The benefit derived from learning to control our breathing extends well beyond our physical health, although that is considerable. We can learn to control and level out our emotions and the reactions we have to our own feelings in many circumstances. After using long breaths and short breaths we notice that we can have a significant control on the causes of our suffering, by controlling our emotions.[22] We will discuss this effect on our emotions in more detail in chapters five and six. This focus on breath seemed so rudimentary and even trivial to me when I was first introduced to it. Why not focus on a Buddha icon or a photo? Gradually I learned that in order to be inside my mind without distractions, to extract from my memories the causes of suffering as it were, it was more skillful to focus on something more neutral and internal, as the breath is. In that way I have been able to focus on one

---

[22] ". . . that it is possible to regulate, control, limit, and manage the emotions by using the breath. We can make the emotions correct, balanced, useful, and beneficial through the breath . . . our practice is not complete until we can see this clearly." (Buddhadasa, 1988, pg. 40)

subject at a time (to be used as an object for insight), and this has been more skillful and effective in reducing suffering. I can do this anywhere I am; I don't need to go to a temple where I see a certain image or icon. I do go to the temple for special occasions, or when it is convenient, but in between those times, my sacred breath connects me to this world of Buddhism just fine. Meditation can be an end in itself at times, a peaceful retreat, but most of the time we use our meditation to actively improve our lives, and that is when having a single object, and using the normal breath to bring that about—thus one pointed meditation—is appropriate and beneficial.

Chapter Three

Breath-body

Key Words:

Satipatthana, anatta, contemplation, causes, Buddhadasa Bikkhu, religion, sixth sense, Zen/jhana, visualization, Taking Refuge

Why Should I Meditate?

In meditation we learn fundamental truths that set Buddhism apart such as training to breathe in/out calming bodily fabrication. Meditation is valuable for seeing truth and for realizing anatta. We come face to face with the myriad causes of creation, humanity and the foundational causes of life (breath). In Buddhist meditation we gain confidence in our beliefs or change. We condition and calm the flesh-body by regulating [and following or chasing] the breath-body then return to our Hearts to exam our thoughts and our lives. Meditation is not a luxury of the well educated and affluent since it is free and accessed by everyone even in Western societies. We can practice compassion and refuge by following our breath and thus develop empathy. In meditation we learn about and understand the cycle of life through the generations of which we are an essential part. When we breathe in unison during group meditation we join with 2,500 years of monks and devotees who did the same.

In the process of explaining each kind of breath, and observing our breath's characteristics, I have given the clues and preliminary description of both the physical body which is obvious as we can see in a mirror, and the breath-body (this is known as kaya-sankhara—body-conditioner), which is not so obvious. What is our breath made of? Our modern science can teach us this, but the ancient religion of Buddhism depends on this simple practice of first learning about the breath, then using it as the centerpiece of meditation.[23] The particles absorbed from our breath are suffused throughout our body (for good and for bad) in both our blood and our bones and sinews. Yet knowing that the breath has a kind of numinous importance, also for the development of our minds, we are learning a fundamental truth that perhaps sets Buddhism apart. This is a teaching and practice that is found in most Buddhist traditions and in Yoga, however the why of it is not always explained so explicitly as here in these chapters.

Once we recognize the significance of using the breath, or even if we don't, and we are comfortable being mindful of breathing in and out without other serious distractions, then we can begin to follow our breath from its entrance through our noses, to the bottom of our lungs, with the rise and fall of our diaphragms and stomachs. Obviously this is a visualization exercise, and it is a seeing that occurs in our mind's eye, or sixth sense, our imagination. I have found that it is helpful, when sitting in meditation postures with my right hand lying on my left, to move the hands slightly so they make contact

---

[23] "Breathing in long, he discerns that he is breathing in long; or breathing out long, he discerns that he is breathing out long. Or breathing in short, he discerns that he is breathing in short; or breathing out short, he discerns that he is breathing out short. He trains himself to breathe in sensitive to the entire body and to breathe out sensitive to the entire body. He trains himself to breathe in calming bodily fabrication and to breathe out calming bodily fabrication." (Satipatthana)

with my abdomen, thus I sense the movement in and out, and this helps me follow and visualize the cycle of breathing. This leads to the next or third step, which is to recognize the breath as a "body" in a metaphorical and religious way.[24] After I learned these details I became curious with an unanswered question: What else is at stake here, what was the original ancient significance of the "breath-body"? Does this derive from the mysticism of yoga and the teachings of chakra? The Buddha was a yogi so he learned all there was to know about contemporary traditions. If we study yoga breathing, we have the responsibility to test those techniques for efficacy beyond these first three steps of Anapanasati.

It is easy to recognize the importance of the breath when we have a cold or allergy symptoms and our noses and sinuses are all plugged up. When we don't have uninterrupted and clear passing of our breaths, we notice right away and feel uncomfortable, it can even cause a sense of panic. It is possible to meditate successfully by following the air through the mouth with the tongue pressing against the roof of the mouth behind the teeth and holding the lips only slightly open, then the passing of the breath will be felt at that point just as well.

People who are prone to stress can experience hyperventilation, too much of a good thing, and that is the opposite extreme. So balancing our breathing with our level of activity is normally an unconscious task, done very well by our bodies autonomous brain functioning; seldom are we ever mindful of these operations—in the same way that we

---

[24] "In step three, the aim is to experience all kaya, all bodies [in addition to the breath-body.] . . .While practicing the [long and short breaths] . . . we investigated this fact [that the breath conditions our flesh-and-blood body.] . . .Now we contemplate in a deeper way that there are two kaya (bodies). We should continuously observe this while breathing in and breathing out in a relaxed way . . . We should analyze this experience to see clearly that there are two groups and that they condition each other. Contemplate this thoroughly until it becomes obvious . . ." (Buddhadasa)

are unaware of the continuing functioning of our hearts. But in Buddhism we use this natural, otherwise ordinary breathing as a mechanism to not only enhance our mindfulness—watching our breath in real time with the focus of our consciousness—but it is a determinant of our very life—thus of the character of our life—and it has a sacred significance and "we contemplate in a deeper way that there are two kaya (bodies)." Thus our breath serves well to initiate our calm and functional meditative state, and we need to take a second step and recognize the nature of this second "body". This is a threshold point, and the important work of meditation is just beginning.

What does it mean that our breath is a determinant of our lives? Just as soil, water, nitrogen, etc., are determinants of the growth of plants, our breath is a necessary ingredient and activity to sustain our lives. It is an obvious sign of life, but not a cause of life by way of having an origin function. Yet as a determinant it has influence over our flesh-bodies, emotions and even the health of our minds, delivering the oxygen and feeding the brain one essential ingredient. Now these relationships are well understood by medical science, but in the time of The Buddha, it was only understood circumstantially and in the most general terms. So the breath is a cause of the continuation of our life once it has been set in motion by so many other preceding causes, nevertheless a sacred cause.

Our breath, if contaminated with cigarette smoke, coal mining dust or polluted air, can be a determining factor in diseases such as cancer and emphysema. I have never heard of any ill effects associated with incense, but it stands to reason that we ought not overdo even this kind of pleasant experience either by intensity or by frequency. Some people are allergic to incense and perfumes and we need to respect those medical conditions in our Sangha. It is easy to imagine that with poor sanitation and unclean living conditions, incense would have served a useful function as an air-freshener 2,500 years ago, and was considered a luxury. It is used now to remind practitioners of the pleasant nature of the Dharma in modern religious contexts. There is no intoxicating effect, but I find most scents relaxing, calming and pleasant. Using incense is a way of engaging our sense of smell in the meditative function (just as I suggested that we can move our hands to feel our breaths, or use our mouths) and the smell of incense is helpful to remind us of this second "body" associated with our breathing. Our sense of smell which obviously depends on our breath as well is otherwise not involved to any great extent in meditative activities. Thus the smell of incense can remind us of our interconnected relationships with other people, our similarities and connection to all of humanity, because breathing is one thing that we obviously have in common. Beyond that, it is skillful to inventory our six senses occasionally to see how we use each, and how they are contributing to our meditation practice. If we are distracted or irritated in any way by incense, we can simply do without using it, or remove ourselves to a place with fresh, clean air.

The causes of our life are mostly obscure to us, and this is just as well, because it is not necessary for any purpose I know to dwell on this history other than just to be thankful and appreciative to our parents and uphold the expectations and love of our families. But it is easy for someone like me born into the democratic, more or less egalitarian society of the USA to dismiss the significance of the details of birth and status. The status of one's birth, race, gender and physical condition are still hugely influential in determining suffering in life for most of the world's population. So many people will never know the kind of comfort, albeit modest by most Western standards, that I have experienced during my life, and it continues today. I don't feel guilty, because I see so many people around me that live in so much more luxury, but I do recycle and try to minimize my "carbon footprint". But as we practice and develop our compassion for others, we must find ways to share beyond the stipulated way of paying honest taxes that are used to serve the general public and the world in so many ways. That kind of institutional giving existed during the time of Buddha but the landlords and kings (i.e. Asoka) used their extracted revenue to build monuments and luxurious palaces, and that seems to also be an aspect of human nature, i.e. Angkor Wat that developed 1500 years after Buddha. Our physical condition, heritage and sustenance are likewise determinants of our lives, however elaborate or simple these might be.

Of course our families do have claims on our reciprocal love and our resources, and the best way to fulfill this obligation is to be successful and operate with our talents at the highest and most effective level of our intelligence. The operation of the breath-body is analogous to how we operate in the world, we serve and protect it, and it nourishes us. Thus our breath is a determinant of suffering or the relief of suffering.[25] There is likewise the consideration of protecting our flesh-body by having adequate, healthy and comfortable shelter, otherwise we can't protect and benefit from the sacred nature of our breaths. This sensitive understanding and the broader perspective of our breath-body can be thought of as an allegory for the way we live our lives and how we share and exploit our talents, interconnected with others in and outside of our Sangha, using our talents to help other people as well as our own families. Just as our birth status is a determinant and conditioning factor of who we are, what we make of ourselves through our education and vocational effort, and even how we comport ourselves in our religious pursuits, it puts us in a position to do good for our neighbors and perhaps for humanity.

Anatta is the concept in Buddhism that brings us face to face with the myriad causes of our creation and includes an understanding of how essential the determinant of our breath-body is and how it fits into the greater picture. Recall that breath is, in ancient Buddhism, associated with life and

---

[25] "The specific aim of this third step is to come to understand (1) that there are two groups and (2) that one group conditions, nourishes, and supports the other group. The breath-body group nourishes the flesh-body group . . . See them arise together, fall together, coarsen together, become fine together, grow comfortable together, and become uncomfortable together . . . This is valuable for seeing truth more extensively, even for realizing anatta . . . [this] is the natural process of conditioning." (Buddhadasa, 1988, pg. 47)

the source of life. Our breath is diffused throughout our bodies continuously, in both a real way and in a metaphorical way as an ephemeral mist or vapor. As we follow our breath we are following the very spark of life in our bodies both in a religious way and in a simple physiological way. As we use our talents we contribute to the functioning of the world in a significant way, we give metaphorical breath to the world in a poetic sense. So this is not a trivial activity with or without the modern science that explains all we know about life science. This is in part how watching our breaths becomes a ritual in its own right, not unlike lighting candles or incense, it is a functional part of our religious life that unites us with the welfare of every being in a very positive and complex way. Just in writing and explaining what I perceived by intuition about the second body, the breath-body, it has increased my understanding of the relevance of this ritual of following our breaths during meditation.

Once we come to believe that there is no eternal element in our body that lives on after life, which is explained by most Buddhist traditions, then meditating by using the breath is more significant because it becomes a ritual that replaces the supplication and devotion we might otherwise have directed to a god or first cause, or to a non-existent eternal substance. Buddhists usually don't teach (at least not modern Buddhism) a creation story about a first cause, so we are left to the direct observation of our breaths in order to be intimate with the causes of our lives.[26] Recall that this was one of the questions the Buddha refused to answer or conjecture about. But one step at a time; so we will return to a discussion of anatta and

---

[26] "There is no atta (anatta), no self, (not a spirit) no soul involved (no ghost in the body.) For ancient Buddhists the breath was as important as the Soul or Higher Self for yogi or as these are for most religions today. Although it is beyond the specific objective of this step, such an understanding can have the highest benefit. For now, however, our purpose in understanding this conditioning is to be able to calm the flesh-body by regulating [and following] the breath-body." (Buddhadasa, 1988, pp. 43-44)

other causes of our lives in later chapters. Learning to track and follow the breath well, is not a trivial process, this is the way we calm the breath, our minds and the entire body. As the mind is following the breath we are deliberately mindful of the path of the breath from the origin outside our nose to the depths of our lungs and the muscles that propel it.[27] The calming process of gentle breathing will be important in the subsequent stage of meditation and I find that this prepares me to be receptive to intuition, creativity as well as jhana. This is very much a part of Dharma, and indeed is fundamental to all the wisdom that grows and the good that comes about and is beneficial based on Buddhism.[28]

We need to practice this process of following our breaths once we learn about the different characteristics of our breathing. That's why in Zen and other Buddhist traditions, learning to count to ten breaths is a preliminary exercise; the teachings build on that basic skill. If we can succeed with understanding and following our breath, we can succeed

---

[27]   "Run after it, so to speak. Set mindfulness to following the breath as it comes in and as it goes out between two points—one inside and one outside. These points are purely imaginary [in the sixth sense.] Suppose. . . The incoming breath starts at the tip of the nose and ends at the navel. The out-going breath starts at the navel and ends at the tip of the nose. Don't be concerned with the breath anywhere else but at these two points and the path that the breath follows between them. . . Sit and contemplate breathing in this way for a while. . . imagine that there is a channel or a tube going from the tip of the nose to the navel. As the breath flows in and out along this path, the mind follows it along the same path. This method is also a good way to counter sleepiness. If the breath becomes too still or too quiet, you may breathe in with more force, even if need be, with enough force to make an audible sound." (Buddhadasa, 1982, pp. 32-33)

[28]   "Just like a deep lake,\ Clear and undisturbed,\ The wise grow peaceful\ On hearing Dhamma teachings. \\ Good people go everywhere;\ The good don't boast, from desire for sensual things;\ Touched by happiness or sorrow,\ The wise do not display excitement or depression." (Dhammapada, vs. 82-83)

with meditation,[29] it is the entry point for Insight as well as Concentration. This is the process of developing mindfulness, the idea that our minds are calm and conscious of our breath—in the same way when we began meditation, of being conscious and reflective about the various thoughts that entered our minds. We initially watched these thoughts with the objective of making our minds quieter and calmer, now we watch the breath deliberately to achieve more or less the same purpose. Once we have mastered this, we will return over and over to an examination of our thoughts and our lives.

I often wonder why I have been so blessed with health and a strong, immune physical constitution. Did I do something right to deserve this, do I breathe correctly and thus keep my health stable? As I age I notice the changing elements of my body, deterioration of muscle tone, and more sensitivity to repetitive motions and reduced capability for work. This is all to be expected, so I don't suffer from these phenomena, I accept them and compensate for them. I have always accepted the advice of experts to keep my immunizations and inoculations up to date, and generally take (ibuprofen) pain relievers (over the counter) whenever I begin to work hard or incur some kind of pain. I get regular physical exams, brush, floss and get my teeth cleaned and checked regularly, and now take low levels of medication to reduce my blood pressure and keep my cholesterol under safe levels (and a small aspirin each day). I take a vitamin pill each day even though it is probably not necessary, and try to eat whole foods, low salt and a good variety of proteins and nutrients; but no fetishes, no focus on "organic" or vegetarian; just a conservative diet which I have practiced for 60 years more or less. I could exercise more of course, and eat less and perhaps benefit from and enjoy a more rigorous fitness program, but I don't. I regularly work around the house and garden actively and enjoy that

---

[29] "Once we have understood this clearly [about the conditioner] and are convinced by our experience of this process with each in-breath and out-breath, then we have realized success in our practice of step three [Anapanasati.]" (Buddhadasa, 1988, pg. 47)

productive exercise. Maybe the key is to be honest and kind in general, and to be considerate generally. In ancient times speaking the truth was considered a metaphysical ritual around the time of The Buddha. (Armstrong) Listening to others in the tradition of Kwan Yin (Chinese Bodhisattva), is a worthwhile activity. Perhaps living a compassionate life is just as important for longevity as a conscientious approach to nutrition and a moderate life style.

In order to follow (or chase) the breath we simply relax (and repeat) and visualize the breath all the way back and forth along the path of our nose, wind-pipes and lungs.[30] Wrinkle the nose if needed to focus attention. Elsewhere it is taught that this is to be thought of as meeting and hosting the Buddha in our being (Bud—dho), as part of devotion and Taking Refuge. I have the luxury of leisure time to enjoy and benefit from this meditation practice. Taking my sustenance away from myself and giving everything to others won't help very many people and only momentarily, these trivialities are not determinants of our lives in the same way as the essential, pure, gentle breath because we can certainly live without them. It is probably too late for me to become a hunter/gatherer, or even a mendicant monk, I believe. Using my resources to develop my talents and sharing these with others may help somebody in a meaningful way, including members of my family, Sangha members and grandchildren when they come of age. Understanding this cycle of life is no less useful than learning to follow our breath from origin to destination.

When sitting in a group, follow this instruction called **chasing** (following), whispering "Bud—dho" with each

---

[30] "When we realize and dwell on [normal, relaxed] inhalation, we feel the air touching the upper part of the nose tip. We have to watch it [to] know the touch of the air. When breathing in, the belly rises. This is a bodily feeling of inhalation. Realizing inhalation, [air coming in] we chant 'Bud' [silently.] Likewise, when breathing out, we feel the air touching the lower part of the nose tip and the upper lip. When breathing out, the belly falls. This is exhalation. Realizing exhalation, we chant 'Dho' [silently.]" (Wee)

breath—repeating in a soft voice until the group is breathing and chanting in unison, the room will begin to vibrate noticeably with spiritual energy. This can be a powerful sharing and bonding experience. Sharing this sacred breath through hearing multiplies this significance, in a similar way as feeling the abdomen expand and contract with your hands gives you another possible study aid. This is an object lesson in releasing the sense of I and aloneness, and gaining a sense of we and unity with other humans. Imagine that you are together with all the monks and practitioners who have meditated over the 2,500 years since the Buddha, and they are all there making the same whispering sounds, chanting. When we touch a sensitive center of connectedness in our conscious, mindful sixth sense, this is a place in our Hearts.

I believe I have made a good start to answering the initial question: "What else is at stake here, what was the original ancient significance of the 'breath-body'?" There may be more to know, and I will keep looking and invite the reader to do the same. At the meditation retreat in Thailand, when I went to Suan Mokkh, I was told that learning to chase the breath well was significantly more important than learning to guard the breath at a point, which comes next. I'm still not sure why, perhaps it is simply a more complex challenge, and perhaps the other ideas in this chapter give some suggestions as to why that is.

In summary, our modern science can explain that our bodies are made of both solid elements or molecules, and gaseous elements. Most of these gaseous elements come from our breath, one of many transient determinants and causes of life (thus the need for clean air is sacred), so the ancient idea of a breath-body can be understood in this more or less esoteric way. If there are mystical forces that help us and give us strength, i.e. connected to our mitochondrial DNA, chakras or whatever—whether we understand these or not—so much the better. And for Buddhism, this mythical breath actually takes on the significant role of the Spirit or Soul as it has become explained by many religions including Christianity. And likewise in Buddhism, as we sit to meditate, we are touching on one of the very foundational causes of the continuation of life in an intimate and spiritual way (a spirituality that is not occult but part of our reality). If we think of Buddhism as a nature religion, that idea is justified because our first and most intimate connection to nature is through our breath as we are awakened and cry out immediately after birth, and we use that same, innocent breath as a tool in mediation.

Chapter Four

Guarding

Key Words:

Heart, enlightenment, spiritual practice, guarding point, ekaggata, directing/ manipulating, apologizing, kammaniya (fit for work), delusion, walking meditation, direct awareness, Concentration/samadhi, meaningfulness.

Why Should I Meditate?

This mindfulness (awareness) helps make the mind function well. Meditation creates connections with our Hearts as we learn to develop this as a resource. We may notice that we no longer need to apologize or regret our actions as often as in the past. We develop the self-control to behave with no harmful, unproductive addictions, and we may notice there are no obstacles to showing and receiving love with our families and friends. In meditation our ability to feel and show compassion expands. Because of meditation the flesh body will become very gentle, relaxed and tranquil (your heart beat may slow down). You can calm the mind to the point where your bodily functions will be as chimes from your Heart. We create the guarding point, a place to locate thoughts and watch them carefully as objects. In meditation, useful concepts might flicker bye that we can gradually flesh-out and utilize. Holding objects with direct awareness can diffuse the emotional load of our thoughts and unfold the truths in our Hearts. We practice this guarding process, because it can help us achieve a reduction of suffering in our lives. In meditation we are eliminating suffering, and preventing suffering by guiding the changes and determinants of our lives. I use this guarding point for contemplating physical health and enhancing immune responses. In Pali this state called *ekaggata,* which means 'to have a single peak, focus, or apex', and this is where thoughts gather to be used for our personal, skillful work of meditating.

The first training that most people encounter when they begin their acquaintance with Buddhism is Mindfulness training. My memories of traveling to Suan Mokkh on the peninsula of Southern Thailand, (near Surat Thani) are vivid; riding the noisy train from Bangkok for an all day trip to Chaiya, (the night sleepers had sold out) passing quickly the rice fields, then the graceful coconut, palm trees and banana plantations, watching the rugged mountains that border Myanmar to the west pass slowly, taking in all the sights and cacophony of noise like a foreign observer, which I was of course, assiduously avoiding all the local food (which was probably very safe). The physical aspects of the trip, getting there, are secondary to the intention of the training after arriving, however, these details make up part of the atmosphere and recollection, where in other circumstances the actual pilgrimage, the tiredness and discomfort, the bouncing and vibrating, the hard seats, the swollen feet, are the point; on this trip these seemed like trivial irritations, part of the ascetic preparation (and a stark contrast) for the release of sitting hour after hour in meditation for ten days. Being mindful as one travels is reasonably easy as the circumstances of the travel force themselves indelibly into your consciousness.

This mindfulness can be taught by various techniques—walking meditation, by observing the body, as well as by observing the breath. This mindfulness seems like such a simple concept, but the trick is to sustain a peaceful watching of the mind, the thoughts, uninterrupted for a period of twenty minutes or more, as a preliminary goal, without being taken away into some kind of day dreaming, elaboration of a thought or a rewinding of a personal drama. Training to achieve this skill, and then practicing, helps make the mind function well and creates connections with our Hearts as we learn to develop this as a resource. "The mind is gentle and tranquil and is most suitable for carrying out its function when it is overwhelmingly under the influence of our Hearts."[31] This is mindfulness at its best and the author, Buddhadasa Bikkhu, was the founding leader of Suan Mokkh, a stripped down almost secular Wat. Nonetheless, this training is ambitious, and from this skillful fourth step of Anapanasati, all of our spiritual practice flourishes. We will know that we have achieved success with our mindfulness training when we no longer need to apologize for or regret our actions as often as in the past—the beginning of Nirodha. We will have developed the self-control to behave the way we see is best, there are no unproductive addictions and no obstacles to showing and receiving love with our families and friends in a normal and productive way. That is, our ability to feel and show compassion has expanded. What a blessing this is! And we need to keep practicing mindfulness training until we reach this stage of competence and beyond.

The same foundations of meditation that we are pursuing here from the Theravada tradition are also found and used in the Tibetan traditions as the "mental continuum", presumably all kinds of cognitive activity relating to 1) the body, 2) feeling tone, 3) our state of consciousness, 4) and the contents of consciousness. Each can sustain mindfulness, and it is

---

[31] "It enhances the tranquility of the mind, thus enabling it to think well, remember well and also perform other duties well. The mind is gentle and tranquil and is most suitable for carrying out its function when it is overwhelmingly under the influence of our Hearts. It is thus called '*Kammaniya*' meaning 'fit for work'. Hence the mind is fit enough to think, memorize, decide or whatever function it sets about to do." (Buddhadasa, 2003, pp. 28-29)

interesting to see how the same teachings that flourish in Thailand, also can be found in Tibet.[32] The entire practice of Anapanasati is not exotic or esoteric; it is based on successful *mindfulness*, (direct awareness of our breath) which as we need to remember is one step along the Eight-fold Path, think of it as one/one-hundredth part of the Dharma.

Even before we have accomplished this skillful goal of deliberately turning on mindfulness, however, we can utilize the breathing techniques we have developed. We can use our meditation skills for "calming the body-conditioner." This means that as we inhale and exhale we relax to the point where our bodily functions will be as chimes from our Hearts. This fourth step of our meditation moves in five segments, and the last one is—once we have identified an image or object at guarding point we have developed—then we consider and contemplate that object in order to gain insight from it.[33] This is where the best work of meditation is achieved.

---

[32] "The object of mindfulness is referred to as the support of mindfulness . . . there are four types of supports: 1. the body [which we have just studied,] 2. feeling tone [which comes next,] 3. our state of consciousness [our citta or heart/minds,] 4. and the contents of consciousness [i.e. knowledge, memories, dharma, wisdom.] Each of these four is a distinct class of internal events within the mental continuum. Each can serve as a vehicle for mindfulness, and we study four parts of each support in a tetrad. Practicing mindfulness of the body [as with walking meditation] is considered to be easier than the others, so it is often practiced first in the series. Any posture will do to fully master mindfulness, using all four supports as recommended." (Brown, pg. 140)

[33] ". . .we are still following the breath, and we make the body-conditioner (the breath) calmer and calmer . . . The flesh body will become very gentle, relaxed and tranquil . . . (your heart beat may slow down). Then there will also arise a calming of the mind . . .To summarize, here are five techniques, 'skillful means' for calming the body, tools we have already used.

1. following the breath;—chasing then monitoring and
2. guarding the breath at a certain point;—this may

For many people, the second step of "guarding the breath at a certain point" is the primary objective, and it becomes second nature, the competency of Buddhist meditation. This is the basis for Insight meditation where we can begin the real work of changing our characters and our lives toward a goal of Purification. Yet as we have seen in the first three chapters, there are several other preliminary achievements that we can benefit from when we develop those skills; these are also attributes of mindfulness.

Practice this guarding process especially well, for one thing because it is handy to help us achieve the reduction of suffering in our lives, then it becomes the pivotal point for the next three steps.[34] I recall hearing and reading a derogatory phrase "contemplating your navel", used by someone to suggest that another person is wasting their time, just sitting around doing nothing. Now I see that this phrase perhaps derives from this same meditation technique; some traditions (Burmese) use the lower end of the breath cycle as the guarding point rather than the nostrils. The location of the focus of guarding is not

---

3. give rise to an image at that guarding point; -then we can

4. manipulate these images or "objects" in such a way as to gain power over them [directing]; and in a skillful way we can

5. select one image and contemplate it in a more concentrated way until the body becomes truly calm and peaceful. (Buddhadasa)

[34] "The technique of calming the breath is 'Watching' or being on guard. There is no longer a running after the breath, there is just a careful scrutiny. The best place to watch is at the nostrils. When the in-coming breath or the out-going breath makes contact with the nostrils, don't follow it. Just be mindful of that at that point. If you are carefully on guard and watching for the in-coming and out-going breaths, the mind will have no opportunity to wander to some other plaice. . . You will notice that there will be short gaps after the in-coming breath is completed and before the in-coming breath begins. . . mindfulness must be carefully established at its post lest it wander off seeking some other attraction. . . each step of the practice must be done fully and carefully so that it will be possible to practice the later steps." (Buddhadasa, 1982, pp. 33-34)

as important as our ability to hold that single point and return to it effortlessly at the beginning of each meditation sitting.

When I was in college I noticed that I would tire easily when studying and get sleepy. When I had an eye exam the optometrist noticed that my eyes, when relaxed, tracked out of parallel, my muscles naturally pulled my eyes out of focus to the outside, so I was making unconsciously extra effort to bring my eyes back to focus when I read, which I was doing a great deal of every day. He suggested that I do some simple exercises to develop my focus ability inward in a cross-eyed way. I was never good as a child doing the cross-eyed facial expression, and apparently that was why. So my exercise was to practice several times a day with a pencil having my eyes follow the pencil from the end of my arm to my nose and back. I developed this visual following of my pencil, so to speak. Or I would put the pencil at the tip of my nose and bring my eyes to it and hold that focus, then look out at a distance, back and forth. In only a few weeks I noticed that my ability to cross my eyes had improved, and I have maintained that muscular talent to this day. I didn't notice any dramatic reduction in my drowsiness, however. When I studied I still had to make a serious effort to stay focused (mindful) of the material I was trying to incorporate into my brain. I remember having to stand in the late evening when I had to complete some particularly difficult section of reading. But then, my major in college was Economics, "the dismal science", so perhaps this fatigue was also a symptom of the nature of the academic subject. When I read Buddhist commentaries now I sometimes experience fatigue, but usually I am very interested in the material, and have made it part of my practice to read a good deal of teachings and historical commentaries. My eyes are serving me well in all this, and I have no particular handicap or challenge in this respect, even as the rest of my body ages. Because I am naturally a little near-sighted, I read easily (and can cross my eyes at will) and for long periods without any correction. I suggest this history as an example of what training to follow the breath, then developing a guarding position might involve, and why it is not necessarily a natural habit before we develop it into our practice.

Arguably, developing this guarding point may be the most skillful competency, because this is where it is best to locate thoughts and watch them carefully as objects, and useful concepts might flicker bye—that we can gradually flesh-out and utilize. I have found that this holding and observation activity can diffuse the emotional load on many thoughts, thus eliminating suffering and preventing suffering by guiding me to change the determinants of my life. (I always wear comfortable and practical shoes or sandals now, rather than any that might be of a more fashionable style. This is a simple example of a "determinant of suffering" that I have changed in my life.) We can manipulate the image or thought (at the guarding point) that we collect to focus on, until we become calm with it.[35] The amount of time required for holding the object will vary with each effort, there is no rule about this, whatever seems to get "skillful" results. In yoga teaching, using the navel as the guarding point is associated with the location of chakra points and follows an ancient tradition of teachings associated with the general idea of the breath-body. Recall that Buddha was a yogi before he reached enlightenment, and he never denied, repudiated or argued against studying chakras, he suggested what he thought was a more skillful method of relieving suffering, plain and simple. He did warn against conceptualizing, philosophizing and creating theories based on mystical practices, in that sense he was a teacher who advocated very practical, even prosaic methods.

---

[35] "[. . .Choose] one image to be the specific object of samadhi (concentration, collectedness) until there is complete calmness . . . This citta [focused thought,] this sati [insight,] is not allowed to go anywhere; it must stay at the chosen point [along the path of the breath.] It guards the breath passing in and passing out; hence, the results are equivalent to "following," except that guarding is more subtle . . .(stable). Generally, we use the furthest point on the nose where the breath makes contact." (Buddhadasa, 1988, pp. 47-49)

I find that it is more natural to locate my guarding point in my sinus area where my breath is filtered, moisturized and even my softest breath makes sure contact with the inside of my nasal cavity. When air is hot I can feel drying and heat, when air is cold I can feel that directly. For me this is easier to locate than outside the tip of the nose, where I seldom feel anything especially when my breath is calm and slight. It is distracting for me when I have to try to find and notice my breath where it is not obvious. That is the main point, don't get distracted, find a place where breath becomes natural, where the mind can be calm.[36] This is not the same as putting random marks on a blank page, because we are learning what the marks, letters and words are because of the compassionate effort of so many teachers who have preceded us.

Another location which I have discovered as being useful is the end of my breath cycle in the diaphragm area that I can feel easily with my hands. (This is also taught by meditation teachers from Myanmar, I understand.) I naturally place my hands on my lap during meditation, and by moving them only slightly to be against my stomach, I can sense the expansion and contraction of breathing, thus create a guarding point. I like to use this guarding point for contemplating physical health issues, and enhancing immune responses. Perhaps it's just a superstition on my part. Of course when we spend our time "contemplating our navel" we run the risk of being accused of wasting our time, but at least we can laugh about that, knowing what it is all about.

Return to this fourth step of the sixteen stage meditation practice (Anapanasati) of Theravada (guarding) as often as desired, because studying the breath, as in the first two steps, is not necessary each time we meditate. Continue the process of guarding using the five skillful techniques just listed, until it becomes second nature. Once we have done the preliminary three steps in meditation and we have created an image to

---

[36] "The monk who with calm mind\ Has entered an empty house,\ Who has right insight into dhammas,\ Has joy beyond the human." (Dhammapada, vs. 373)

47

guard we are well on our way: This is the practical explanation of vipassana meditation, which is skillful Insight meditation, to which we must return during every meditation sitting. "We can change from one image to another . . . manipulate them, to play with them . . ."[37] We have been essentially preparing the mechanics, now we are ready to achieve some useful results. Don't get stuck in the place of meditating just for the sake of meditating, because what we want is results for our lives, not just pleasant, blissful and jhana kinds of experience although these will naturally occur, if not in every sitting perhaps often. But then we move our mindfulness back to the guarding point and contemplate a pertinent object for the benefit of our lives since we are on the track of Nirodha.

The breath is simply something for the mind to hold to so that you can reach the real thing, just as when you follow the tracks of an ox: *You're not after the tracks of the ox.* **You follow its tracks because you want to reach the ox. Here you're keeping track of the breath so as to reach the real thing: awareness. (Boowa)**

---

[37] "Choose an image that is most fitting and proper, and then contemplate it with full attention in order to develop a complete measure of samadhi. [Initially] we should choose an image that is soothing, relaxing, and easy to focus on. (Some traditions use walking meditation to begin each session, and focus on the feet sensations, connecting relaxed breathing with the body in this way.) The image should not stir up thoughts and emotions or contain any special significance or meaning. A mere white point or dot will suffice . . . The citta gathers together on this single spot. We change the image or alternate between images according to our requirements. We can change from one image to another . . . manipulate them, to play with them . . . As we do this we are developing our ability to master [intensify] the mind [and Heart] in increasingly subtle and powerful ways . . ." (Buddhadasa)

It is unfortunately true that many people actually go to sleep at some point during meditation. They have remarkably learned to sleep sitting in the lotus position, which is a feat I cannot accomplish. In Buddhism this is considered part of a delusion, or even an aversion to taking on sensitive areas of our lives that involve suffering. There are steps to take, including standing up, keeping the eyes open, walking, of course preparing by getting plenty of sleep beforehand, and simply taking a break and washing your face with cold water. It is not skillful to fall asleep, unless our meditation is being used prior to sleeping in bed with the very intention of calming the mind to contemplate insomnia to prepare for sleep. That works for me sometimes, and I rationalize that by using those times during the night when I cannot sleep to meditate, it is sort of a tradeoff. I never suffer from insomnia; I benefit from it in this way and find myself fully rested in the morning. My mind will have tracked through all the stages of short waves and long waves, the technological functioning of sleep, and achieved proper physiological and neurological conditioning. We can think of sleep as a kind of conditioning analogous in the same way we have used the breath as a body-conditioner. Sleep is our friend, as long as we keep it in perspective and corral it into the times when it is appropriate and useful.

If we are sleepy or groggy, (torpor) we can't do the work described here. We should use our best, most productive moments during the day for meditation, because of the significant, potential impact it has for our lives. This effort is key to developing a calm mind, and answers the promise to which we alluded in chapter one.[38] With this conscientious effort, the

---

[38] "Because we can now control the mind more than before, the citta automatically grows more subtle and refined by itself (and corresponds to what we call our feeling Heart place.) The citta becomes more and more calm until eventually we are able to calm the mind completely . . . in only a matter of minutes. The fourth technique is controlling the mental images as we wish . . . We observe the calming process while practicing this step . . . Concentrating everything on this one point is the fifth of our skillful means . . . In Pali this state is called ekaggata,

Heart is poised to unfold its truths. This is the process that we can expect to use to our benefit for the rest of our lives, so it makes sense to become adept at setting this up correctly.

What would constitute a mental image or object? It is easy after so many years of holding images and objects at my guarding point to forget about this fundamental question, but there was a time when this question was a real issue for me. A mental object is one which we hold to study or contemplate, most often; however there are other sorts; concepts or issues of suffering that beguile us. "You can close your eyes and 'see' it, you can open your eyes and still 'see' it." This may be a struggle to begin with, and this gradually becomes easier as watching your breath and guarding becomes more refined.[39] There is a corollary that is not obvious; if you have a strong image you are perhaps already well refined! One purpose of an icon is to provide an image readily to hand, and this image will ideally carry a meaning that encourages the meditator to work on eliminating suffering relating to one or more of the defilements, for example, or any other aspect of one's life that needs work. I find that it is more effective to choose simple images, consolidated images, such as an emotion or one pain that relates to some activity or relationship I wish to evaluate.

This is of course where the art of meditation comes into the picture, learning to choose worthwhile objects in a skillful way comes with experience, and eventually we notice how effective our effort in obtaining some resolution is; which is most often to reduce, and/or prevent suffering. In this process of deciding and meditating obviously the object needs to be something

---

which means 'to have a single peak, focus, or apex.' Everything gathers [intensifies] at this single focus . . ." (Buddhadasa, 1988, pp. 50-55)

[39] "If we create a mental image (nimitta) at the guarding point, the breath will be further refined and calmer . . . You can close your eyes and 'see' it, you can open your eyes and still 'see' it. The image is like an hallucination the mind creates by itself to calm the breath . . . The breath, indeed all the faculties, must be refined in order for a mental image to arise. The breath must become finer and calmer until the image is created." (Buddhadasa, 1988, pg. 50)

that is relevant to our present lives. I recall deciding what my college major should be and what courses I should take. I discussed the possibilities with several adults I respected, my brothers and other family members before I decided. Had I been a Buddhist I would have used my Refuge privileges to consult Sangha members and taken this question as an object for meditation. I would still have consulted my brothers, etc., and probably would have reached the same conclusion (to major in Economics). But perhaps my confidence level would have been greater had I derived the conclusion at least in part by having used meditation skills. I stayed with my original major through graduation and still feel satisfied. Now I do use meditation skill even for minor questions which do not require any consultations. Otherwise, I do both, talk it over, and mediate on the object of my decisions. I tend to use this acquired meditation skill of guarding etc., to work on issues that are in front of me, not behind.

We come to understand that the breath is a tool, of course it is impermanent, incidental, not inconsequential but subsidiary to the main intention of meditation. So developing and having this skillful guarding point is a capability that enables us to succeed in our mundane lives as well as in our religious objectives, as it were. I wrote a poem once about the importance of being on surfaces, something we all take for granted, rather than sleeping in trees or being suspended in the water in some way. We are a species of land-dwelling animals, and many of us are afraid of heights and don't even like being in tall buildings. Locating our breaths at a single point and watching or guarding is somewhat unnatural, contrary to the way living on a single point or surface is very natural. It may seem more natural to chase our breaths rather than see it pass by this guarding point, but as long as it doesn't cause vertigo or disorientation, it is somewhat easier to learn to do than swinging through a rain forest on vines.

It is taught in the Mahayana tradition also by the Vietnamese monk Thich Nhat Hanh, that "When you get angry with someone, practice breathing in and out mindfully."[40] In the next chapter we begin to deal with emotions and how meditation can be used to eliminate the mistakes we make based on following our extreme emotions. Use these first four steps of Anapanasati, especially guarding, in this way to also contemplate and develop the compassion you need in your life. When we do this successfully we become very peaceful, our breathing is calmed, refined and even tranquil. "You're meditating not for the sake of the breath, but for the sake of awareness, so stay with that awareness."[41] But the breath is a useful measure of our peace and progress. With our enlightened awareness we see it, and read valuable information. When it becomes subtle, this is a real phenomenon that permits and leads to the experience or 'piti' and 'sukha' and then on to jhana (Zen).

The promise of Buddhism is to develop our lives into meaningfulness and even serenity. This development of calmness in our lives is an achievement of its own that is worth the effort.[42] Is that enough or must we seek repeatedly

---

[40] "Compassion is a beautiful flower born of understanding. When you get angry with someone, practice breathing in and out mindfully. Look deeply into the situation to see the true nature of your own and the other person's suffering, and you will be liberated." (Hanh, pg. 153)

[41] "When the breath becomes more refined, that shows that the mind is refined. Even if the breath becomes so refined that it disappears—at the same time that you're aware that it's disappearing—don't be afraid. The breath disappears, but your awareness doesn't disappear. You're meditating not for the sake of the breath, but for the sake of awareness, so stay with that awareness. You don't have to worry or be afraid that you'll faint or die. As long as the mind is still in charge of the body, then even if the breath disappears, you won't die. The mind will dwell with freedom, with no agitation, no worries, no fears at all. This is how you focus on the breath." (Boowa, 1996)

[42] "One whose senses have attained calm\ Like horses well trained by a charioteer,\ Whose pride has gone, who is free from defilements—\ Such a one even the gods envy.\\ Calm is the mind\ And calm the speech and actions\ Of such a one, perfectly calm,\ Who is freed through right knowledge." (Dhammapada, vs. 94, 96)

to fulfill the promise of Zen, to experience jhana, or should we have a more modest expectation? No question about it, if we progress toward the absorption leading to jhana, we will have achieved phenomenal progress toward relieving suffering.[43] The experience of jhana is a beacon, a guiding light perhaps, a tool, not an ecstatic way of life, but instead an ideal of calmness, introspection and peacefulness. We will prepare and earn that by creating a certain rectitude in our lives, and we will perhaps have progressed more than once through the study of Purification which begins in the next chapter. Having a calm mind is a foundational assumption of making progress toward the serene experience of jhana, and having facility with holding to a guarding point is a good indication that we can calm our minds. Again, the objective of studying our breath and altering our breathing is not to excite or alter our body's chemistry in a way that will excite, create hallucinations or visions, which can be done, but quite the opposite: to prepare for a serene mind and calm body that will pre-dispose us to the experience of jhana, which is a calming and less than exciting experience. With all this introductory explanation, we should be ready for some serious work.

---

[43] "Hence, in conclusion, are we not right in drawing the inference that the practice of Dhyana is the true gateway to Supreme Perfect Enlightenment? Is it not the Noble Path that all followers of Buddha must follow? Is not Dhyana the pole star of all goodness and the Supreme Perfect Enlightenment?" (Goddard, pg. 441)

PART II
Pure mind

Chapter Five

Recognizing Suffering and Piti

Key Words:

Purification, compassion, moral training, Piti (5 types), clarity, defilement, Five Precepts, recognition, vinaya, cleansing, emotional tone (vedana), art of living, contentment, Insight, impermanent (aniccam), self-deception, Mahayana, bhoga

Why Should I Meditate?

We can learn in meditation to control our emotions, reactions and feelings because these are influenced by self-awareness. All our emotional states or repressed anxieties are the proper objects for meditation because we can overcome the debilitating effects of these pains and problems. We gradually learn the *art of living*—by becoming more skillful with our meditation practice. In meditation we calm our random and irrelevant thoughts, then we allow our sub-conscious mind to come into plain view. One intention of meditation is to examine and recognize Piti, to see how it relates to a sense of joy; if it does. We learn how to get to a neutral point or calming before we proceed to substantial and positive happiness. When we evaluate our emotional status (an essential element of human nature) we see that our mental natures need what amounts to psychic nourishment. We can contemplate spontaneous thoughts and examine those briefly but thoroughly to see any message from our Hearts. Piti is often a pleasurable experience, a reward we feel frequently, but in meditation it is a mining of our emotional psyche, then we have to purify the raw material. As we calm the guarding point, our breath nearly vanishes, then we introduce tasks (objects) or negative emotions at this point. When we deliberately proceed to Sukha (joy, happiness) we study how to make it more facile, more beneficial for our lives. When happiness occurs as satisfaction, it is the triumph of the Heart over the confusing and too complicated world. The art of meditation is to proceed like a painter uses his/her easel, palette, paints, brushes and ideas to create, perhaps not a masterpiece, but to be in the process.

The concept of purification is fundamental to Buddhism in the same way that compassion and meditation are. I have often heard it stated that Buddhism is an ethical teaching, and when we consider the path to Purification, along with the Precepts and focus on overcoming Defilements, then certainly this is a true statement. Even with the emphasis on mindfulness training and meditation, we cannot neglect the ethical and moral training passed down from The Buddha. That is, after all, the message of his famous, often quoted, first sermon. It is no wonder then, that the major part of this book is devoted to explicating and untying the knots that might otherwise prevent purification from enhancing our lives. Every successful, persistent religion concerns itself with the rectitude and behavior of its adherents. (Is the word adherent, derived from the word Arahat?) Purification is a metaphor in the sense that it literally relates to the separation of coarse or foreign materials from the pure mineral such as dross from bronze, chaff from wheat (or rice) or cleaning and carding wool before weaving. The idea is to eliminate behaviors that are destructive and harmful (defilements) to ourselves and others—and to retain good behaviors; and for Buddhism, preventing the suffering we might easily avoid by adopting habits that are skillful and compassionate. We have to at least try to live with the best rectitude we can muster, if for no other reason because that karma will bless us in the future with happiness.

The first step in this purification process, as recited earlier, is "recognition" ("this is", direct knowledge), which mostly refers to acknowledging the truth and details of the Four Noble Truths: first, life means suffering (also translated as unease, stress, pain etc.). "Vision arose, insight arose, discernment arose, knowledge arose, illumination arose within me with regard to things never heard before: 'This is the noble truth of stress.' Just as if we wish to solve a math problem, it is the case that we have to know all the details and then decide upon a method; in order to end suffering we have to know about it, we have to develop direct knowledge of what it is in all its subtle levels, determinants and aspects. We have to learn to *recognize* it for "what it is" when we see it in ourselves and others so we can proceed to apply the appropriate methods to eliminate it.

Can we become free of suffering? Yes, that is the promise of Buddhism as we will discover, but recognition (direct knowledge) as the first step on the path to purification, is for the most part synonymous with eliminating one, and often more of the causes of suffering that are within our control.

When we begin our involvement with Buddhism we learn very quickly about the basic Five Precepts that teach about not killing, not stealing, etc. Of course there are many other teachings and for monks, there are numerous precepts and disciplines, *Vinaya,* that control the clothing, hygiene, diets, behaviors (usually 227 precepts for men, more for women) and even the emotional status of those who live in monasteries. Our emotional status in a more general way is often influenced by our own self-awareness and control, and how well we deal with and are affected by other people around us. Most often the emotions we deal with come from issues and complications from which we have suffered. We have all had many experiences by the time we are old enough to seriously investigate Buddhism; we will have had a lot of interesting and challenging interactions with school mates and family members. We are like walking and breathing libraries of human potential and interactions. Many of the negative experiences and the emotional consequences of those we have likely suppressed or ignored. How do we get hold of these issues (recognize) so we can work them over (using direct awareness and self-awakening) and eliminate the load they have (unbinding) as determinants of suffering? In an important way, Buddhism is more directly concerned with teaching us how to recognize our emotional tone and the status of our Hearts, than it is about specific conducts or karma we might choose. The rationale of Buddhism is to help each of us learn how to follow a pure line of behavior in order to be happy, to eliminate and avoid suffering, so purification becomes more than anything (not a sacred commandment) a pragmatic solution to improving our lives. When we *recognize* this fundamental truth, when we acknowledge our personal responsibility, we are likely well on our way; but here I've given out the secret, and now it remains only to act on it!

So once we have concerned ourselves with and learned from observing our bodies, breath and minds, once we have developed these basic skills, we concern ourselves with improving our emotional status. This may seem like trying to deal with the horses after they have escaped from the barn or the cats when they are out of the bag, but of course there is a lot of advice about how to act and behave in order to also *prevent* emotional problems and reactions. On any given day when we might begin meditation, we will have had many years of life and numerous emotional issues from both past and present that affect our thinking; we can deal with these issues one at a time as an object that imposes itself on our consciousness. When we notice our own inappropriate thinking, which often happens in the normal course of our lives, grab it and begin to deal with it. No time like the present. In Buddhism we ought to deal with this reality that confronts us as a beginning point. We are bound to have experienced the death of friends or family members that has left us sad or depressed; perhaps we still carry this impact like a secret wound. We may have experienced discipline or arguments with family members that leave us sad or angry underneath the surface of our lives. We might be carrying the baggage of a divorce or separation, and these past and present emotional confrontations may become a devastating burden. All these emotional states or repressed anxieties are the proper objects for meditation because we can overcome the debilitating effects of these pains and problems when we recognize them and when we can get to them. Buddhism offers the framework where we can deal with all manner of these kinds of issues, not as theoretical generalizations, but as real-life, real-time problems.

As we progress through our lives we continue to encounter or create complications that have emotional impacts, and these can be the proper subject for our meditation effort from day to day as well. We can bravely make these issues the objects for our practice in the context of "guarding our breath" as a technique to alleviate any negative impact on our lives. There is no point in getting bogged down in discussing specifics, although I will suggest some examples, in fact Buddhist teachings can be seen as mostly generalizations of how to proceed with any number of details of our lives. We gradually learn the *art of living*—by becoming more skillful with our meditation practice, by learning to recognize what is suffering and what is not—as we apply the techniques we have learned to many different emotional and social situations that arise. The only way to be free of these conditioned details is to be fully conscious of these, and meet these complications directly.[44]

---

[44] "The only way to be free of our conditioned patterns is through a full, conscious experience of them. This might be called 'ripening our karma,' what the Indian teacher Swami Prajnanpad described as bhoga, meaning 'deliberate, conscious experience.' He said, 'You can only dissolve karma through the bhoga of this karma.' We become free of what we're stuck in only through meeting and experiencing it directly. Having the bhoga of your karma allows you to digest unresolved, undigested elements of your emotional experience from the past that are still affecting you: how you were hurt or overwhelmed, how you

In the fifth step of Anapanasati we learn to examine our feelings or feeling tone—emotions that reside in our Hearts and memories. Access to these emotions and more importantly, the development of productive emotional experiences during meditation, comes when we have developed a calm mind based on the proper utilization of our breath. "(Contentment—piti) arises from . . . samadhi . . ."[45] What is happening when we have these mental states of Concentration and Mindfulness? Usually we are sitting in a quiet place for the purpose of relaxing and being at peace. This occurs when we calm our random and irrelevant thoughts, and we allow what is often called our sub-conscious mind to open into plain view. This kind of calming, single-pointed focus can be seen as the first step toward developing a capable mind and finding solutions to the complications of our lives. That is when our real work of recognition begins to produce results. Once we calm our minds and Heart and experience contentment, we open the door of our creativity and intuition that can point to our own problems, etc., so we can identify problems (objects) and then find the solutions. We move then from the general to the specific. One approach is to consider each problem we recognize as a koan, and proceed to solve the puzzle.

The solution to the most complex emotional problem can seem at first too simple or feeble. We might be told upon sharing our solution: "That goes without saying . . ." or that it is trivial, or "everybody already knows that." These statements may be true, because what might be confusing or obscure to us can be well accepted truths for others. This should not be

---

defended yourself against that by shutting down, how you constructed walls to keep people out." (McLeod, (Welwood) pg. 133)

[45] "The first two steps of this tetrad take piti (contentment) and sukha (joy) as the subjects of our detailed examination and study . . . Once the body and the body-conditioner, and the breath, are calmed, . . .sankhara [conditioned]—feelings of piti and then sukha appear . . . proportionate to the extent of that calming . . . (contentment - piti) arises from our [having] successfully inducing samadhi in the previous steps [of meditation. . .]" (Buddhadasa)

discouraging, but reassuring, we are obviously on the right track when we discover, state or recognize obvious truths. These kinds of inspirations when they occur are a kind of catching up, but no less important for that fact. When I write poetry, I often notice later that much of it is, if not hackneyed or trite, at least common place, what seemed to me at the time to be noteworthy or, if not profound, at least worth recording. That is usually the experience of those who indulge in marijuana or other drugs (so I am told) who have some exciting inspirations they record, and later notice that the numinous significance is not so apparent from the mere recorded message. The words and phrases recorded are banal and trivial. The emotional absorption or enthusiasm was not part of the content in those cases. Likewise for poetry, not everyone is at the same level of ecstatic association with the author at the time the creativity was fresh. I tend to be reluctant to share my recent poetry, because I notice later that it is not quite as interesting or brilliant as I thought it was. Being overwhelmed by immediate events is perhaps one aspect of the social conditioning we have accepted, it is related to the emotion of piti under consideration in this chapter, and being under-whelmed in retrospect is often the rational activity of hindsight. Thus it is usually a good idea to do proofreading after a certain passage of time, in that way we get a better perspective and a bigger context for what we thought was initially significant. This is a technique that has stood the test of time in my experience (including for this book). Seeing clearly and objectively in the moment is a real skill, and one that ought not be trivialized.[46] In saying this I run the risk of creating inhibitions and writer's block, but as long as we can be patient and understanding to others who share with us their inspirations, we can be patient

---

[46] "The key—the how of Buddhist practice—lies in learning to simply rest in a bare awareness of thoughts, feelings, and perceptions as they occur. In the Buddhist tradition, this gentle awareness is known as mindfulness, which, in turn, is simply resting in the mind's natural clarity . . .[a place in the Heart.] Simply looking at what is going on in our minds actually changes what was going on there." (Mingyur)

and understanding for ourselves. Consider how many years it took Walt Whitman to finish his inspirational work *Leaves of Grass.*

It might take more than one meditation sitting to succeed in finding a solution to any given problem, and it might be useful therefore to break the problem down into the smallest component parts. It may not be intuitively obvious that we have to get to some neutral point or calming before we can proceed to a more substantial and positive happiness, but that is the traditional teaching of Buddhism and there is a good deal of wisdom that can be found in this teaching. Piti is often thought of as contentment, but in reality it is an energetic and often active mental state. It is like the feeling of delight or pleasurable anticipation we might have when a friend invites us to join him/her for an interesting concert or outing. This emotion of pleasure, anticipation and perhaps a positive nervousness is energetic, and is usually accompanied by some apprehension or second guessing; in any case this is an example of what might occur during a meditation sitting that we might call Piti-jhana. This is not anxiety, which can be a stumbling block or source of futile suffering all of its own type. It is often an energetic *recognizing* of a problem and having direct knowledge before we have a possible solution, often we are dealing with it in constructive stages, not being overwhelmed by it before we even get started. Or it might be that feeling of relief from finding a solution to an emotional entanglement, in the way we might cheer for ourselves: "Yea, I did it!" Or we might experience the feeling of sadness or grief, or the very emotions associated with past sadness or grief at the time it occurred (an empathetic recollection). Recognizing these emotions for what they are is a kind of direct awareness, and knowing Piti-jhana in this way will lead to a more long-term benefit, instead of just momentary relief. Again, hold the rewarding thought or transitory solution at the guarding point until you see it as clearly as you can be mindful of the movement of your hands.

The intention of step five is to examine and recognize Piti, to see how it relates to a sense of joy if it does. Or we can just as readily notice that this energy is associated with a negative emotion, remorse, dread, emotional pain and curiously we can be having the same kind of mental signs and physical symptoms as we might associate with a positive emotion. And moving beyond the calmness we initially created we become receptive to whatever messages are there. When we get the sign or notion, positive or negative, we take it likewise to our guarding point and examine it for insight, and deal with it like a segment of our secret emotional lives. It is not my intention to describe every possible scenario, but merely to verbally paint a picture so that when this experience happens, we recognize it for what it is and keep it as a productive experience in some way. It may seem curious that we can do our best work when we initially feel contentment, but that is what it takes to expect to be excited and energized in a positive and friendly way. It's like we have to be quiet in order to hear the whispering of our Hearts, then we can be healed. We have to study how this Piti works and then we can go there over and over like a repeating cycle of cleansing.

As we have learned, much of what we do in meditation is watching the thoughts that occur while we are using our breath, our minds will be active and creative.[47] I have this image of a raccoon picking up its food, dipping it into water before it eats, fondling the food before it bites it. Perhaps such an image can be useful to explain how it is we might deal with emotional issues. When we feel joy or positive excitement, Piti, we have to remember that even these useful and *enjoyable* emotions are impermanent and not fundamentally satisfying. We want to look into our ambitions and desires, our victories and our challenges, our attachments and our cravings especially, with

---

[47] "Simply sit up straight, breathe normally, and allow yourself to become aware of your breath coming in and going out. As you relax into simply being aware of your inhalation and exhalation, you'll probably start to notice hundreds of thoughts passing through your mind. Some of them are easy to let go of, while others may lead you down a long avenue of related thoughts. When you find yourself chasing after a thought, simply bring yourself back to focusing on your breath." (Mingyur)

equal perspicuity, and a certain kind of suspicion. Contemplate as many of these individual thoughts one at a time, to the extent possible, and examine those thoughts briefly but thoroughly to see if there is a message from your Heart. If not, move on to the next thought in a process of calm, systematic elimination. Remember that it is in our Hearts where the sadness and weight of past suffering might linger mixed with the positive emotions of our more recent successes, rather like a stew. If you find an issue that sounds a gong, you can hold it; remember it to perhaps work on later with the technique of direct awareness.

What we are working with in our evaluation of our emotional status is one of the essential elements of human nature. Some people may call this our spirituality or buddha-nature, others may think of this as our psychic nature. In the same way our bodies need food, clothing, housing and medicine, our mental natures need what amounts to psychic nourishment. "There are the mental and spiritual aspects of life which must be attended to . . . that cajoles the mind into a state of normalcy and happiness . . ."[48] As we learn to appreciate the richness and diversity of our own Buddha-nature, we gain an insight and appreciation for the genius and complexity of all of human nature. In addition, as we proceed with this examination of the signs and details that relate to Piti-jhana, we can think of it as a housekeeping practice that sets our Hearts in order. This demonstrates that Buddhism is, in addition to being a religion, an ethical teaching, a philosophy; it is also a spiritual training.

---

[48] "If we were to assume a worldly point of view, there is yet something else to be learned about `vedana`. It is something called `piti` (joy) and `sukha` (happiness), which are necessary for. . . human beings. . . the physical body, but it is not sufficient to have only the four requisites [food, clothing, housing and medicine,] there are the mental and spiritual aspects of life which must be attended to. . . [these two Piti and Sukha] can be said to be the factor that cajoles the mind into a state of normalcy and happiness. . . " (Buddhadasa, 2536, pg. 125)

Gradually with each succeeding meditation session I have noticed a pattern of seizing on a few serious thoughts or emotions, watching or guarding these as objects of meditation, seeing the negative consequences dissolve like an itch that disappears, and ending the session with a sense of success, a sense of accomplishment that can hopefully energize my life. Piti has often been thought of as a pleasurable experience, a reward, but it is better to think of it as mining of our emotional psyche, a series of steps in a process of recognition, then we have to purify the raw material. The details of jhana experience are rather sketchy in popular Buddhist literature. It is only after several years of taking bits and pieces of advice and experience of a few others and applying this to my own circumstances, that I have noticed what are described as the signs of joy, and that these contain both the potential for healing and the signs of residual emotional sadness. I have alluded to the fact that Piti can be joyful or sad, interesting or worrisome, because it also contains as any dialectic, its complement, both positive and negative aspects as weaknesses. It is often just as important to experience the troublesome and joyful emotions in one sitting, because these can be expunged and/ or be learning experiences. A comprehensive analysis from a knowledgeable Thai source follows: "The wholesome Piti has to be strengthened fully. As one constantly concentrates on a suitable meditation object without the wandering of the mind . . . five types of Piti [may arise, so the time honored teaching suggests:] a. Khuddaka-piti is a slight degree of joy [khutthaka—small] which can sometimes raise the hairs or 'goose bumps' on the body. [What is the immediate source of this emotional experience? Is it coming from some suppressed fear or a victory, from the memory of an antagonistic person we must confront, or from a positive change in our lives? So many possibilities! When in our lives did we ever have that emotion, and perhaps like a detective, we can point our attention toward the real source of this energetic emotion.] b. Khanika-piti is a momentary joy [temporary] like a flash of intermittent lightning. [When have you had this kind of emotional Aw-ha moment? We ask the same questions as for 'goose bumps'.]

c. Okkantika-piti is a flood of joy [okantika—intermittent] which descends on the body and breaks like the waves of the ocean on the beach. [For a mathematician this could be that moment of understanding and being able to repeat a proof. What other positive or negative experiences have we had that create this emotional expression?] d. Ubbega-piti is a 'floating' joy [bubhekha—violent or rocking] literally lifting the body to the extent of raising it above the ground. [This could be when you get the big picture of a political concept, and you felt you could be part of the solution. Perhaps you experienced this as a result of Step Four as you practiced guarding an object with your breath?] e. Pharana-piti is a suffusing joy which pervades the whole body like a flood that overflows a small tank. [This latter can be accompanied by a sense of warmth, or it might be like the joy in your Heart from love and security you feel with a child or mate.]" (Ussivakul pp. 34-35)[49]

I find that it is easier to remember and deal with the negative circumstances when I associate these at the same time with positive emotions. When I experience these categories of emotions and signs (I seem to get the lightening, "aw-ha" more than the others) then I analyze the positive emotion as the other side of the coin, I proceed to hold it in the light of vipassana at the guarding point. Once we get some information from our emotional experience of Piti-jhana, it may be that the only way to learn is to take it back to the guarding point and try to develop some insight and turn the negative into a positive learning experience. We are often told that even the most negative experiences, may have a silver lining. "It is all for the best." we are often told. I call this a "turn around." When these significant experiences manifest, we should not take them lightly. These steps are abbreviated here and are parallel with more elaborate explanations of jhana that I have read based on informed and personal experiences. The reader will need to keep this taxonomy available for future comparison.

This is all something of a study, as we review our memories and emotions, we are observing how this Piti-jhana works in

---

[49] Also found in (Wee, pp. 34-42) and (Buddhadasa, 2003, pg. 139)

our minds. But it needs to be personal, not academic. "We need to apply the real `Piti` that comes from our hearts or minds . . . in order to use it as the mind-object of contemplation."[50] We have to cure our own ignorance, and the apprenticeship is the time we spend in meditation guarding our breaths. Keep it simple is a useful admonition. "Better than a thousand verses\ Made up of useless words\ Is one word of verse\ Which calms you to hear it."[51] Consider the mantra "Mu", and how that is used in Zen practice.

It is best not to become too preoccupied with distinguishing these five states one from the other, nor to strive for these experiences, nor even to overly analyze these. You can't force these sensations, but just accept these signs effortlessly as the result of guarding your breath until it becomes very peaceful. If we know about these stages conceptually we can make better use of them. When we use the application of this technique to deliberately contemplate a subject or recent experience, we set up our minds-eye to be ready for work. As we calm the guarding point, our breath nearly vanishes from view, and then we introduce tasks or negative emotions to this point.

I have used this process to examine my emotions and the on-going details of my life during and after a divorce. The separation of a once dear companion is always a complex affair. It is a mixture of nostalgic recollections, there is regret

---

[50] "The important principle in the stipulation [to know especially well only about `Piti`] of the contemplation of the mind [cittanupassana-satipatthana] is to apply the real thing, not using knowledge from the memory from books or sound from elsewhere. It will not do. We need to apply the real `Piti` that comes from our hearts or minds. . . in order to use it as the mind-object of contemplation. We have to bring about the arising of `Piti` . . .from the last step of part one; [step four of Anapanasati.] . . .so that we may learn more about it, what its characteristics are, how its influence is and how its impact on the mind is." (Buddhadasa, 2003, pp.137-139)

[51] Also "Better than speaking a hundred verses\ Made up of useless words\ Is one word of Dhamma\ Which calms you to hear it." (Dhammapada, vs. 101-102)

from not having the emotional support continue, some anger from the details, self-blame, concern about the social stigma, and relief from the ending of quarreling . . . so many morsels of emotional bread to digest and ponder one at a time. I have learned that you can love someone and not be able to live with that person for many reasons. This kind, gentle examination during meditation can lead to healing and learning gains. "If it doesn't kill you it makes you stronger." I think it is important to be comprehensive and objective in this process of emotional scrutiny, as well. I honestly try to notice my own faults and "blame" in turn. I feel the emotions and notice any signs or images if and when they occur, and think about each later when I review and protect any insight.

These are conceptual stages—or an attempt to describe and differentiate what is often referred to as jhana (Dhyana). These are often subtle experiences, and most thoughts don't rise to the level of joy or Piti-jhana as dramatic images. Some people who are "emotionally available" may have a facility with the calming and affirming emotional states leading to contentment. Some people may have one of these experiences once in their life as an epiphany, and then use this as a resource, not to be repeated. It is not difficult to see a parallel between step five with steps one and two of Anapanasati. We examine our emotional state the same way we studied our breath. Another parallel that our emotions condition our minds will be discussed later.

I find it helpful to identify experiences in my ordinary life described by each of the five signs of piti, and examine what was happening to see if there is something to learn, not unlike that pesky raccoon. When did I experience goose bumps in association with an emotional experience? When a sense of lifting or floating above my body? A flash of lightening or creativity? I have had all of these experiences in my ordinary life before I began seriously a practice of meditation, albeit as exceptional experiences, not often. So I have some basis for comparison.

When I meditate I seem to be more reserved and these signs don't occur so often. I am reminded that even the most significant routine biography can be condensed into an interesting two hour movie. Perhaps my emotions are suppressed instead of being readily available. I still tear-up during dramatic moments of cinemas, so I know that I am not emotionally dead. I don't seem to have strong empathetic reactions when I achieve insights; perhaps I have that to look forward to. I do have success with insight, but it is most commonly a cerebral experience or best described as a creative intuition in my Heart. I know people who report more facility with these empathic states, and I believe it is a useful reality. I admire this attribute, and work on cultivating it. Perhaps if I were severely hungry or sleepy I might stimulate these experiences, as with enhancing a neurotransmitter—chemical reaction during sever ascetic practices. Or would this just be some kind of self-deception?

The point is that we must each work through and examine these images and emotions for ourselves, and develop our own techniques and cycles. But we can know that our lives are on the mend when we have these experiences, or at least a realistic hope.[52] Piti-jhana can be thought of as a preliminary step that helps us overcome emotional obstacles, that helps us essentially burn off defilements and find contentment by eliminating suffering, and this helps us change our lives—or otherwise what value is it? There is no particular virtue in developing Piti-jhana into an ecstatic trance state, which seems to be a goal or pattern in some of the Hindu-Guru

---

[52] "Piti is not peaceful . . . There is a kind of excitement or disturbance in piti; only when it becomes sukha is it tranquil. Part one of the second tetrad (step five), 'experiencing piti' consists of contemplating piti every time we breathe in and breathe out . . . Find out what this feeling is like. Fully experience it [don't expect it to be the same each time.] . . .This is the essence of the practice of step five . . . we study and observe the power piti has over the mind . . . i.e. it can grow into pride and self-satisfaction. What is our contentment about? Finally, we realize that piti stimulates the mind in a coarse way; it lacks a refined and subtle effect like sukha . . . [which can exult in our Hearts.]" (Buddhadasa)

practices. I have observed these and the stated goals are egoistic and seem to encourage self-gratification instead of in any way reducing suffering. In a very crude way, this can be thought of as spiritual masturbation. The emotional reactions are real but directed toward a very different intention, or these become an end in themselves. Often this occurs in a cult and leads to indoctrination or brainwashing, and accumulation of wealth and power by the guru. It becomes another way of experiencing sensual pleasure, perhaps superficially like a failed tantric practice.

But again, this is perhaps an individual matter that we can evaluate for ourselves.[53] This instruction comes from a monk with many years of experience. His teaching, along with the example of his modest life, leads to rewards that are natural and available to everyone with practice, and based on following these simple instructions. Big consequences can come from what initially seemed like a very simple technique. For example we say: **May this merit be shared with all mankind alike to promote peace and relieve suffering!** "It is merely the feeling that arises by the law of nature [the Law of Causes and Effects.]"[54] The images that come in the form of Piti can signal negative emotions, and when these are subjected to direct awareness without the development of "concoctions", instead the use of vipassana, they can turn into positive Sukha-jhana. So just by looking at and focusing on (having direct knowledge)

---

[53] "We study and train, pause and observe warmly as we experience piti in the mind." (Buddhadasa, 1988. pg. 59)

[54] "If `piti` is being restrained, it can be turned to become `sukha` or happiness. `Piti` is the active joy that has not yet become `sukha`. It is the joy [and at times sadness] that is still subjected to distraction. It is the satisfaction that is derived from the success in accomplishing something [like solving a contemporary emotional problem.] . . . When unrestrained, `piti` can lead to distracted thoughts; so we have to restrain it till it turns into `sukha` and the concoction (and manipulation) of the mind goes on. . . .know the `joy` that is still shaky and coarse. . . It is merely the feeling that arises by the law of nature [the Law of Causes and Effects.] " (Buddhadasa, 2003, pp. 143-145)

our negative feelings we can change the day from cloudy to partly sunny?!

This discussion of piti-jhana may sound repetitive but in reality it is preliminary and cursory, and is intended as a target or goal, useful as we begin to meditate so that when we actually feel any of those sensations or signs we might recognize what has truly happened.[55] This caution and apology is appropriate for anyone trying to describe or read about the experience of jhana, which might be different for each successful meditator. Instead, what is experienced might be best explained by some kind of abstract poetry (i.e. *Bhagavad Gita*).

The actual experience of meditation is to alternate between Concentration which is one-pointed calm meditation with no specific agenda, and Insight—mindfulness, which is when we endeavor to examine our thoughts and emotions and eliminate suffering. We can subject our emotions or mental objects to this back and forth awareness as we might polish a furniture surface. In this way the experience of piti-jhana is almost subsidiary or optional to the practice of meditation.[56] It is perhaps useful to identify the scope of this practice of Insight meditation. Although it seems enough to say that we can use the previously described techniques for any

---

[55]   "If anyone thoroughly understands what has been said here about Dhyana, s/he will appreciate that its practice is not an easy task. However, for the sake of aiding beginners to clear away their ignorance and hindrances and to guide them toward enlightenment, we will aid them all we can by explaining the practice of Dhyana in as simple words as possible, but at best, its practice will be difficult . . . Those who are really seeking Truth, but are more advanced, should not look upon this book with contempt because it is written simply and for beginners." (Goddard, pg. 441)

[56]   "They [meditators] should be humble and prudent because of the difficulties they will encounter when they come to its practice. It is possible that some will be able to digest its teachings with great ease and, in the twinkle of an eye, their hindrances will be abolished and their intelligence will be boundlessly developed and so will be their super-normal understanding, also . . . " (Buddhadasa)

emotional experience we encounter or choose to evaluate, even something as mundane as boredom or as special as friendship, and these are amenable to this examination—the index of our "thoughts and emotions" is surely a rather large collection.

On a historical note, the experience of Piti-jhana has been very significant with the expectation that images would be present to signal the arrival of Piti. "It is quite enough for us to work till just `piti` [of any sort] arises for that will be enough of an achievement."[57] This involuntary effort of experiencing spiritual images can lead to the subsequent experience of tranquility, but this is not the only path, and Sukha-jhana is worth working for and a most desirable objective, one way or another.

The reader will have noticed by now that in each chapter I have summarized the reasons for meditating that are described in the context of the discussion. I found another more generalized summary of the kind of objects or subjects that are most often the concern of meditation. We can find ourselves engaging in meditation according to this other more intellectual schemes, but again, that is not necessary either. This list of "ten heads" or agenda constitutes what can be thought of as a theory of meditation, as a set of goals for meditation, it is informative but not comprehensive, and when viewed at one sitting it is a bit daunting. How long will it take

---

[57] "The old style of `vipassana` meditation gave much importance to `piti` so much so that the word `Phra` [brother] had been added to the word `piti`. Thus it became `Phra Piti` and the meditators had to perform an invitation rite to `invite` Phra Piti to appear in the mind while meditating. If `Phra Piti` did not appear, it would then be a matter of guessing or speculation. If it really appeared in the mind in whatever form, there would be much satisfaction and the practice would be considered a success. . . it is quite enough for us to work till just `piti` [of any sort] arises for that will be enough of an achievement." (Buddhadasa, 2003, pg.139)

any one of us to work through all of these issues?[58] How is this related to other religious events and practices such as for Christians, being born again? Do we need to accomplish all these agenda items before we obtain purification? Or is the journey, (jihad) pursuing the path, the very effort on a continuous basis an important process or achievement? These are more koans about process, rather than questions derived from contemplation.

After rereading this explanation I had a kind of drowsy vision of walking along a path carrying an air blower, and blowing away all the leaves and debris in front along the path, and walking along on this clean and well defined track through the trees. This involuntary vision is a good analogy of what we might do with Piti-jhana to purify our life path. We are able to see clearly, recognize, acknowledge our suffering, but we know also that this is just the beginning of the "twelve permutations".

We have become well acquainted with the word 'aniccam' or impermanence, and these concepts figure prominently in Buddhism in a very general way as a clue to how we should view the world. Thusness: "It is the way they are."[59] During

---

[58] "The Ten Heads: 1. External conditions. 2. Control of sense desires. 3. Abolishment of inner hindrances. 4. Regulation and adjustment. 5. Expedient activities of mind. 6. Right practice. 7. The development and manifestation of good qualities. 8. Evil influences. 9. Cure of disease. 10. Realization of Supreme Perfect Enlightenment. These ten headings indicate the stages [or categories of topics?] of correct Dhyana practice . . . [When] these ten stages are faithfully followed the mind will become tranquil, difficulties will be overcome, powers for concentrating the mind and for gaining insight and understanding will be developed, and in the future Supreme Perfect Enlightenment (anuttara-samyak-sambodhi) will be attained." (Goddard, pg. 441)

[59] "It is the establishing point of a perspective known as 'Dhammathitinana' which means 'the insight to realize the existence of things in the context of their natural existence [state.] In other words, it is the truth of things which exist as they commonly do. It is the way they are." (Buddhadasa, 2008, pg. 287)

75

the time of this writing, I found out that a brother-in-law of mine, Virgil, died in Texas at the ripe old age of 98. He has always been 33 years older than me, obviously, but when we were both younger, he never seemed to act that way. He was always mature and responsible, but that was the cover of his youthfulness. He came to mind when I reread " . . . the journey, (jihad) pursuing the path, the very effort on a continuous basis is an important process or achievement." He was a testament that the process of living has its own rewards. He liked to keep, breed and milk goats, and pitch horseshoes, go figure? His life and process lasted for a long time (he was Mormon not a Buddhist), but as with the lesson of impermanence, the achievements he made in his life are mostly in the Hearts and minds of his family, ephemeral, certainly some of them are with me. (We revisit aniccam in chapter thirteen.) In my mind his most significant achievement is to have loved and supported my oldest sister, Lila. Physically they were an odd pair, he was rather short and slight, she of average height and large, but somehow spiritually they must have matched and supported each other in so many ways.

As suggested in the beginning of this chapter: " . . . in fact Buddhist teachings can be seen as generalizations of how to proceed with any number of details of our lives." Certainly the ten topics suggested above are useful conceptual guides, but the art of meditation is for each of us to proceed, again, like a painter uses his/her easel, palette, paints; with brushes in hand, creative ideas can be expected.

A few words of review and closing words about piti are found in the Mahayana tradition. "Every time you feel lost, alienated, or cut off from life, or from the world, every time you feel despair, anger, or instability, depression, practice going home. Mindful breathing is the vehicle that you use to go back to your true home [your Heart.]" (Hanh, pg. 99) Thus, as sophisticated as Buddhist teachings can be, getting back to basics is in the end the essential message. Negative emotions afflict us all at one time or another and we use the same pathways and neurons as positive Piti-jhana to indulge these experiences. These are the trappings of and most likely the tailings initiated by contentment, as we begin the process of purification, so they can be overcome. The next step, Sukha-jhana, is closely connected.

Chapter Six

Recognizing Causes and Sukha

Key Words:

Sukha-jhana, happiness, hindrances, tranquility, addictions, bottomed out, craving (tanha), empathize, refuge, citta-sankara, attachments, ignorance, assatha.

Why Should I Meditate?

In meditation we can expand our Hearts and solve the puzzle of how to give up "I, me" and the tendency to develop our egos. In meditation we relax our mind while watching our breaths with "peripheral vision" of our mind's eye and deposit resources into our Heart that we can use later. Our meditation is both to purify our lives, and expand our capacity for compassion and virtue. We learn to taste the tranquil flavor of Sukha with in-out breathing, like imbibing an elixir of pleasure and comfort. The momentary peace and tranquility from altered states of consciousness are a counterfeit to calm happiness that can be derived from simple meditation. Examining Piti and Sukha leads to positive results from meditation. Intelligent un-control of meditation is how to go about recognizing simple truths, and discovering and benefiting from the presence of Sukha in our minds. In meditation we overcome suffering by eliminating or modifying desire, passion . . . craving and clinging. Whatever issues the mind forms, we observe them, if they're good, they vanish; if they're bad, they vanish. This is why we investigate them. During meditation we can examine the details of our heritage that influence us for better and take advantage from these.

One of the most powerful pedagogical devices of Theravada Buddhism, as I have found it in my visits to Thailand, is the focus and explanation of the Heart and its meaningfulness. As we will see, the Heart (as a skillful allegory to live with) is what controls the details of our lives once we have gone to the effort of developing it to be compassionate and virtuous. This is the home of purification as we are taught in the Satipatthana Sutta; this is the solution to the puzzle of how to give up "I, me" and the tendency we all have early in life to depend on or develop our egos. We can be victims of Heart-ache, or a black-heart, or we can develop this capacity into a comforting ideal, a warm-heart, that is the fountain of love for our families and ourselves. It is a lot more pleasant to live with a Heart full of love and kindness, to recognize this as part of the Art of Living, than to have a hard-heart, a broken heart, or a cruel, sad heart full of revenge or greed. The healthy, positive Heart that thrives on Piti-jhana, also knows the joy and pleasure of Sukha as the calm, emotional extension of that success.

Our self-conscious practice is recognition of our partnership with the ancients along the path of purification.

One simple way to recognize the relationship between our expanding happiness and the emotional victory of utilizing Piti-jhana is to think of it as being derived from a healthy, buoyant Heart. Finding Piti, at even the most basic level as we learned in the last chapter, at best an active contentment, is a good place to start. Now we turn to recognizing and contemplating the causes of a more tranquil kind of joy and even relaxed bliss, and instead of just utilizing our refined Hearts, we actually follow the path of developing our direct knowledge and expanding our Hearts. That is a useful and skillful goal—studying and experiencing Sukha. In the emotional state of Piti we made withdrawals from our Heart bank, so to speak; now as we relax our minds, guard our subtle breaths, watching them, again with "peripheral vision" of our mind's eye, as they come and go, we put back and deposit resources into our Hearts that we can use later to both purify our lives and expand our capacity for compassion and virtue. The Buddha's dhamma was one of the first teachings to claim and hold as a priority that this profound purification could actually lead to blessings in this life; in fact that was the Buddha's focus!

I have often heard people explain how they are invigorated or recharged by having taken a hike, vacation or trek into a nature preserve or wilderness area with a particularly scenic view. The views and the pristine environments share their peacefulness without in any way being depleted, and we can derive strength, energy and blessings from this. I commune with nature everyday one way or another, never satiated, but never disappointed. I especially enjoy standing under old growth trees, and touching these stalwart reminders of the Law of Cause and Effect, and I see all around the causes of life, clean air, diverse organisms and a connection to bye-gone epochs. We are challenged in Buddhism to recognize the causes of suffering, stress etc., in the same way the Buddha did. "Vision arose, insight arose, discernment arose, knowledge arose, illumination arose within me with regard to things never heard before: 'This is the noble truth of the origination of stress' . . . (Appendix II) Communing with nature helps us achieve this direct, "this is", knowledge.

If we can consciously expand our Hearts in this way, we achieve an equivalent tranquility to what some practitioners can achieve by sitting in meditation (and vice-versa), and we can share the benefit of both blessings with our family and Sangha members just by sharing our peace of mind. These sensual pleasures are innocent enough and temporary, and will not be a hindrance to meditation, nor lead to suffering when we know in advance the insatiable, essentially impermanent and fleeting (because we will want to and can do it again) nature of the experience.

Eventually in step six of Anapanasati, we proceed deliberately to Sukha (joy, happiness), like imbibing an elixir of pleasure and comfort, and we study this process so we can make it more facile, more of a benefit for our lives. This, when it occurs, is the triumph of the Heart over the confused and complicated mind. Continue the technique of breathing normally and meditate, relaxed, content, and follow what for many people is tranquility, shinay, or Concentration meditation. We practice recognizing our painful, pleasant and neutral feelings.[60] For many traditions, serious meditation begins and ends here, but for the persistent and dedicated practitioner of Buddhism there is more. This kind of self-examination and investigation of our minds is very useful even though it may seem simple, it is profound and skillful, and has been described repeatedly as part of every meditation protocol, if you will.

There are residual formations in our Hearts as well, and every so often we should make a special effort to clean house, and "probe on down right there" into our Hearts and as we become more adept, we see that we are eliminating more causes of suffering. "Matters that passed months and years ago, we warm up and serve to torment the mind, to oppress and coerce it, because of our delusion, because of the fact that we aren't up on the tricks and deceits of this

---

[60] "And how does a monk remain focused on feelings in & of themselves? There is the case where a monk, when feeling a painful feeling, discerns that he is feeling a painful feeling. When feeling a pleasant feeling, he discerns that he is feeling a pleasant feeling. When feeling a neither-painful-nor-pleasant feeling, he discerns that he is feeling a neither-painful-nor-pleasant feeling." (Satipatthana)

sort of defilement."[61] How can we correct a delusion when it is integral to whom we are and it is the way we think? How do we gain direct knowledge of the most subtle causes of suffering? We have to question and challenge the way we normally think as a matter of course. Some of this instruction is repetitive from the last chapter, but the same teaching, as a principle of action, applies to the emotion of Sukha-jhana as to piti-jhana.

There is a caution that we must recognize along the way while developing our Hearts. As we study the causes of our suffering and learn from our emotions, we must remember that we are basically "playing with fire". We are telling ourselves that we are vulnerable but strong, we are innocent but capable, we are alone but united, we are humble but we can be successful. So even if we had to bottom out, or somehow get a shock to come to this place of humility, now we are there. We can grow just like those old growth trees. We all need external help, more than just reading a stack of self-help books like this one. We may not need therapy or counseling to succeed, but we do need a vision and frequent, even continuous loving support. Taking Refuge in Buddhism offers this help even when all else fails, so there is no particular gap, even if we are living alone or isolated, no high-wire without a net; that is another meaning of Refuge.

---

[61] "Sankhara refers to the thought-formations in the mind—good thoughts, bad thoughts, this issue and that. They keep forming all the time. Each of us falls for his or her own issues. Even if other people don't become involved with us, the mind has to paint pictures and form thoughts, past and future: a big turmoil within the heart. We get infatuated with this preoccupation, saddened by that one. Matters that passed months and years ago, we warm up and serve to torment the mind, to oppress and coerce it, because of our delusion, because of the fact that we aren't up on the tricks and deceits of this sort of defilement. This is why we have to investigate them. Whatever issues the mind forms, if they're good, they vanish; if they're bad, they vanish—so what sense or substance can we gain from them? Wherever they arise, probe on down right there." (Boowa, 1981)

How can we encourage this same result to come for others, beyond the mere act of sharing merit at the end of our meditation sessions, so they can accept the kind of help Buddhism offers?[62] And there are certainly a lot more people who simply drop out, or practice so seldom that they make no significant changes in their lives—than the total of those who begin at one time or another to meditate. Even the positive emotions of Piti (and Sukha) as discussed in the last chapter and elsewhere can be thought of as hindrances if we become preoccupied with these as a sole motivation for our practice. Going further, at the extreme of this search for happiness is the destructive activity of drug and alcohol addictions—self medications. Using artificial means such as wine, beer or marijuana, to achieve "happiness" is not part of any Buddhist tradition that I am aware of; not like the Native Americans in Southwest USA who used (and still today use) peyote for their religious rituals. The Dalai Lama is such an inspiring leader, but not everyone follows his wholesome and joyful life pattern.

As we saw in the discussion of Piti, the momentary peace and tranquility that comes from altered states of consciousness are a counterfeit to the beneficial and calm happiness-joy that can be derived from skillful, well-schooled meditation. But for many, meditation may seem like a lot of work, boring or just an intellectual mind trip. It is easy to recognize how the hindrances of ignorance, cynicism and laziness can play havoc on the lives of so many people. Are there more people who die from preventable causes in a ten year period in the

---

[62] "Human problems come from `vedana`[emotions and feelings.] We become the slaves of `vedana` and are dragged and driven [cajoled] by it to do all sorts of things, sometimes shockingly evil things. For one to be a wise [wo/]man or a bad character, it all depends on one's own `vedana` which motivates one to do things as one desires. A bad character may steal or rob just to get the money to buy the `vedana` that means happiness to him. Even a wise man may seek merit [boon] in order to get an increasingly clean and pure `sukha-vedana` or happy feeling. Therefore `vedana` is the driving force behind all the actions or deeds." (Buddhadasa, 2003, pg.133)

West, than are comforted and blessed with the Sukha-jhana from meditation in Buddhist disciplines? I suspect so. Then think of all the pain, loss of life as collateral damage, and so much suffering involved with narco-trafficing.

As suggested, many people come to meditation and Buddhism after they have "bottomed out" for a lot of different reasons. People who have overcome serious and debilitating experiences seem to be the best advisers and mentors for young people. I have avoided those extreme negative experiences for myself, although I have gone through the training and group activity of Al-anon as a vulnerable co-dependent, heard about so many tragedies and experienced a few of my own from that perspective. We all experience cravings, whether chocolate, alcohol, food, fame, sex, possessions, (I seem to have too many books).[63] Perhaps someone who has had that experience of craving and recognized the error of their ways would be in a good position to discuss all that and warn people away from unwise cravings. Many monks have achieved that kind of turn-around in their lives, that's what the Buddha did. I can see, after the fact, that my own craving for pleasure and satisfaction of `vedana` was at the source of my co-dependent issues. I believe that **taking good advice** before succumbing to such experiences is one of the meanings and benefits of Taking Refuge in the Buddha, but it is always easier said than done. I remember a science teacher in my high school who always said: "A word to the wise . . ." before he gave us advice or as he was warning us about questions that would be on an upcoming test. We all thought he was very annoying.

In the second part of this second tetrad—or step six overall—"experiencing Sukha" we contemplate Sukha (happiness, joy) with every inhalation and exhalation. We learn about the meaning of being calm and tranquil.[64] I find

---

[63] "Vedana` is the bait of `tanha` or craving. It is this craving that brings people under its power and makes people do or act unwisely. It uses `vedana` as a tool or lure." (Buddhadasa, 2536, pg.133)

[64] "We focus on Sukha as arising out of Piti. . . .however, Sukha does not stimulate or excite; it calms down and soothes. Here we contemplate

in various texts that the same English words get used at different times to describe Piti and Sukha. It was only after my own experience of each kind of emotional tone that I can clearly distinguish between these feelings in my life. The distinction is useful, the vocabulary is not so important as the understanding, not unlike the feeling and rush of emotion of almost falling out of a tree, and the relief from catching myself safely before I fall. I am afraid of heights, but am capable of controlling that fear in a useful way as a helpful warning to be careful. I have a variety of physical symptoms, rapid heartbeat, tightening in the chest, sweating (perhaps this is an adrenaline rush?), and higher body temperature, but I am not completely disabled. Sukha-jhana is the relief I feel when I am back comfortably walking on ground level, if I have achieved my objective. Can I just feel sukha when walking around on the ground knowing that I am not standing precariously on a cliff somewhere? Parachutists and skydivers have to go to more serious extremes to get this sense of relief perhaps, but we don't need the adrenaline fix since that is just another kind of addiction.

Suffice it to say that examining both Piti and Sukha leads to positive results from meditation. Elsewhere I have written about two different levels of happiness, one that is characterized by sensual pleasure or momentary entertainment, not unlike listening to a favorite song; and the more subdued happiness we get, for example, from knowing we have worked hard over a period of four or more years and obtained a college degree in the subject of our career choice. When we understand this difference and study our minds we can carry this happiness into our daily lives and "feel saturated with happiness . . ."[65]

Sukha as the agent that makes the citta (the Heart and thoughts) tranquil . . . Usually Piti obscures Sukha, but when Piti fades away [as during the five levels described above,] Sukha remains. The coarse feelings give way to calm. Taste the tranquil flavor of Sukha with every inhalation and exhalation." (Buddhadasa, 1988, pp. 59-60)

[65] "This work is fun to do; it is a most enjoyable lesson . . . If Piti [persists or] interferes, the contemplation of Sukha is ruined and real tranquility

When do we feel this kind of relaxed happiness or tranquility otherwise? It is not just a reward for college graduates certainly; it is a rewarding tranquility that anyone can obtain, perhaps after having completed a volunteer service project. Perhaps when we commune with nature (or with Buddha—as with reciting Bud—dho) for a weekend retreat, or can it be just a special moment?

Those aha moments when the light flashes on in our heads and we recognize a key understanding of the dhamma, etc., perhaps that is comparable to Piti-jhana. And when we absorb that new truth and let it blend pleasantly into our lives, then we can compare that to a Sukha moment. It can be that simple, but rewarding, to distinguish between the two, and when we do, we ought to write a poem. Can we discover a mnemonic or visualization that will enliven these feelings as we begin to meditate? The breath is neutral, but we can develop associations with gongs or incense, and we can create our own fetishes that are productive of positive emotions, i.e., counting beads. I have had many such moments as I have been writing lesson and study books such as this, because organizing the teachings and hearing the voices of wise teachers in both written and spoken words, has given me many moments of tranquility as well as many new understandings. I have shared many realizations in these pages which have been satisfying and peaceful, as with sukha-jhana.

The instructions that come from the Tibetan monk are valid again here, about "bare awareness" and seeing the details of our lives correctly and objectively.[66] This describes intelligent un-control of meditation, and a very clear explanation of how to go about recognizing simple truths, and discover and benefit

---

will not arise . . . We should not let any other feelings interfere . . . We should feel saturated with happiness, [and peaceful] certainly a wonderful way to meet with success in the practice of step six." (Buddhadasa, 1988. pp. 57-61)

[66] "The key—the how of Buddhist practice—lies in learning to simply rest in a bare awareness of thoughts, feelings, and perceptions as they occur." (Mingyur, pp. 43)

from the presence of Sukha in our minds. Our piti-jhana is usually attached to some outcome or event, but sukha-jhana can be open ended, and a state of receptivity rather than one of recent achievement. I have traveled as a tourist to the ancient city of Sukhothai and seen the relics and archeological remains of this once thriving (Khmer-Mons) Buddhist/Hindu community named for the tranquility under consideration here. Once you are in tune with the practices and significance of this culture, you can't help but empathize with the happiness and hopes, the sadness and tragedy of those people, and then recognize their triumphs of course. I walked around the temples and artifacts and let my immediate experience flow naturally as I tried to visualize and absorb the details, and still think about it five or more years later as I add meaning to my memories bit by bit. Each time I travel to these artifacts and observe and experience these relics, I relate more strongly to the sense of sukha-jhana.

That is perhaps the most beneficial result of being a tourist that cannot be gained from any other activity, the sense of empathy and reality that I gain from being there in the middle of the crumbling record of so many other people's lives. You can't get the same kind of emotional connection just from reading travel or coffee table books. I wrote about this modest accomplishment of recognition in relationship to the development of purification in the first chapter of the book on *Higher Truth*. It is worth repeating here. "Think of those raised from childhood in Buddhism who make their well-practiced gestures, what is going through their minds? How are their Hearts affected by their rituals and religious practice? Their thoughts might be quite different than what is in the books, or in the mind of an eager novice. For me as long as I have been practicing, each event of bowing is a very self-conscious practice, it is an emotional experience that reaches into my Heart; I am a bit nervous as if I were bowing on a concert stage [Piti?] with hundreds of people watching. I see my surroundings and myself not only with my own eyes but as if each bow was my first innocent gesture of faith watched by the collective eye of humanity even when I am alone. For each of us this is a unique experience, and we will learn to be consciously aware [Piti?] of this mental sensibility. For example, when we make these gestures—as we are mindfully somewhere along the pathway to purification—this can simply be a renewed commitment [Sukha?] to pursue our chosen path." (*Bodhicitta: Higher Truth*, pg. 21) My self-conscious practice is clearly an example of *recognition*; it seems to demonstrate a kind of sincerity of purpose regarding the first frame of reference along the path of purification. Perhaps this is another example of Piti, it is certainly not a sense of tranquility until it passes and I am absorbed internally in reflection about the intention of my devotion and meditation. Sukha does not follow for me until I am removed from the environment of the public temple, until I can sustain the peacefulness and commitment during those isolated moments of reflection that come with my private practice in my home.

Making these distinctions and studying the ways we experience vedana is informative I believe. We can engage in our culture in so many ways, watching movies, reading poetry, listening to inspiring music, etc. and learn about emotions and become more sensitive in our social interactions. Our emotions condition our thoughts, and we have to be in control of this conditioning in the same way that we are in control of our breath, and the way we use breathing to condition our bodies.[67] I don't expect anyone to get it all the first time—I am reminded of the way it took me many years to realize the significance of Dharma after I first heard about it. I initially heard misrepresentations about trances and ecstatic

---

[67] "When Piti [fifth step] conditions a thought, that thought is coarse [raw satisfactions and pleasures] . . . when a thought arises through Sukha [sixth step], that thought is calm [singular] and tranquil. Thus we realize the way that Vedana (emotions) condition thoughts—'conditioning [preparing] the mind [to know the Heart sounds.]'—to have an 'understanding of the citta-sankhara sufficiently' . . .It is an art, a spiritual art of controlling Piti and Sukha so that they benefit our lives. This is the secret that we ought to know concerning Piti and Sukha." (Buddhadasa, 1988. pp. 57-61)

experiences, and other false information. But eventually I got it as I do, now I recognize this simple and clear distinction between contentment and tranquility. It is sufficient for now for me to know that there is this basic distinction, and that Sukha is actually the reward, the blooming flower of meditation; also called the fruit of meditation. This is what anyone might look forward to.

> When I feed the birds
> all the bushes come alive
> with a special fruit.
>   I.J. Hall, February 22, 2012

We studied and learned how the body was conditioned by the breath, and this happens whether we try to control it or not, both positive and negative respectively. Now we learn how the emotions are conditioned by the breath using Piti, an energetic form of happiness, to condition the Heart (citta-sankhara) and prepare the way for the tranquility of Sukha, to move us to a level of progressively greater compassion and purification—and how this conditions our minds in a chain of events. Compare this following description of jhana with these brief notes—"a slight degree of joy"—in the previous chapter about the first state of piti-jhana and the contrast that is made to Sukha-jhana. "Your mind is filled with rapture, bliss, and one-pointedness . . ."[68] I

---

[68]   "As [we] enter the first jhana, something remarkable happens. There is a total break with normal thought and perception. Your mind suddenly sinks into the breath and dwells. The breath is still there, but it is no longer a 'thing,' just a subtle thought, much like a memory or an after-image. The world goes away. Physical pain goes away. [We] do not totally lose all sensation, but the physical senses are off in the background. Wandering conscious thought stops. What remains are subtle thoughts of good will toward all beings."
"Your mind is filled with rapture, bliss, and one-pointedness. 'Rapture' or 'joy' [Piti] is like the leaping elation you feel when you finally get what you have been after. 'Bliss' or 'happiness' [sukha] is like the rich, sustained satisfaction you feel when you have it. Joy

have experienced jhana that comes in essentially two levels, the active first opening of the sixth sense or mind/heart to this blissful state, then a peacefulness that is calm and pure. Thus Piti-jhana utilizes the Heart to generate an experience, and Sukha-jhana can peacefully help our Hearts grow. When we do good and are generous both with our resources and our time we can justifiably feel good. "If a person does good,\ [S/He should do it repeatedly;\ [S/He] should set his[/her] will upon it:\ It's pleasant to accumulate good." (Dhammapada, vs.118)

We need to recognize and be aware of the development and characteristics of Sukha-jhana at least, which is the goal of following this chapter. But we can't let ourselves be stalled in this momentary pleasantness when indeed we need to focus on the causes of suffering that we can overcome![69] Oops, if we allow this hindrance or "deadlock" to dominate, then we

---

[contentment] may be physical, like hair rising all over your body. It may be momentary flashes or waves that shower you again and again. Happiness [tranquility] is more restrained, a gentle state of continuing ecstasy. . . Happiness is like relaxing in the shade of a tree. . ." (Gunaratana, pp. 104-105)

[69] "Step two [Six] requires our contemplation on `sukha` or happiness. It is something that is useful and ought to be sought after. . . In our life, we may develop `sukha` in this way: practice till `piti` arises and restrain it to allow it to turn into `sukha`. . . we need to examine `sukha` and see what characteristics it possesses, what it is like. . . and how it functions. The purpose is to discern it more clearly and see how it controls and leads the mind [Heart] by its own power. . . `Sukha` has `assatha` or charm of its own. It can control the mind a great deal because it is a happy feeling. It leads to a satisfaction in happiness to an extent that further practice may not be possible. . . The mind does not incline towards `vipassana` because `sukha` has too much charm. Therefore do not be deluded [obsessed] by `sukha` till it becomes the enemy of `vipassana`. . . Meditators tend to get adhered to `sukha` because it is a kind meditative delight or happiness and there is always a chance to get deluded by it, leading to a deadlock in progress. . ." (Buddhadasa, 2003, pp. 147-153)

will fail to use our meditation periods for active contemplation and further purification to remove "defilements". There is a lot of work to do during meditation, and if we seek only after the tranquility of Sukha-jhana, then we will retard our effort to eliminate ordinary suffering, which should be our main task.

When we recognize that the origin of suffering is *attachment*, what we are suggesting is that this attachment is only one of the determinants, but a useful one because it is one we can control in our own minds. Here is an insight that I have achieved, perhaps not so special, but hey, it is mine and I can boast a little too. I finally understand why Buddhist monks and ancient teachings emphasize the elimination of craving and attachment. This is the recognition of Nirodha. Consider the following story.

We might suffer as a result of being born into a family with alcoholic parents, and live out all the sad stories that attend that lifestyle. We are somewhat less in control of that; it is so difficult to move away from ones family, no matter how abusive or destructive that group might be for us. Thus when we say that the origin of suffering is attachment to transient things and the ignorance thereof, it is to suggest a possible cure for suffering, something we can control right here, right now. Contrast that to a student who has moved away from that confusing family situation to go to college perhaps; and just changing the environmental determinant will likely remove some of the suffering experienced in the past. When we start such a new life, we can become a new person, a rebirth so to speak. Although a lot of students take up the pattern of alcoholism in a college environment that encourages these behaviors, they don't need to, many don't. We thus lose at least part of the attachment we once felt toward the destructive environment of our childhood, and as long as we don't replicate that environment in our own adult lives, we have successfully eliminated a source of suffering by eliminating our attachment. Put this together with the teaching that in order to reduce or eliminate suffering it is often sufficient to eliminate just one cause or determinant, and here we have the element of attachment readily at hand.

But that's not the whole story. We have attachments to many smaller incidents and material objects in our lives, e.g. stylish clothing, jewelry, shoes, or modern art. Transient things do not only include the physical objects that surround us, but also ideas, and—in a greater sense—all objects of our perception. And attachment is one way of relating to these details of our lives, such as the way we might feel toward the new car we would like to have, and when we get it we are proud and compulsive about its care. One kind of ignorance is the lack of understanding of how our mind is attached to impermanent things, even to the loves of our lives, or new cars. Some of the reasons for suffering are: desire, passion, ardor, pursuit of wealth and prestige, striving for fame and popularity, or in short: *craving* and *clinging*. This brief list taken from the internet, presents some of the mental activities that *we have control over immediately*, or at least over time during repeated meditations. Because the objects of our attachment are transient, their loss is inevitable, will suffering necessarily follow? Unless we are prepared with a good mental attitude for this loss, we can expect some kind of suffering. The Buddha would have hoped we could prepare for, and avoid suffering in this way; why else would he have warned us about it in the first place?!

One object that is an "attachment" includes the idea of a "self" which is a delusion, because there is no abiding self, no eternal spiritual entity residing in our bodies that can possess those objects (and the rest of us is constantly changing). Our lives were caused by so many chemical and human relationships, and so much active living, karma, by so many generations of ancestors. We may feel kinship, but that does not have to lead to debilitating attachment. So "craving" in all its forms is a determinant of suffering that we carry with us, it is portable, thus accessible to "bare awareness" at any time skillful meditation can happen. That is the rest of the story: we can have immediate and skillful control over our craving, clinging, direct knowledge of attachments and minimize the impact of these, thus eliminate suffering, poof! without making other gross changes in our lives. We can still love, cherish, and hold sacred our closest relationships, knowing in advance the impermanent and unsatiating nature of these, and that they are, paradoxically, not essential for our personal identities or existence.

Most of my ancestors were early Mormon pioneers in the West of the USA, and that was a huge determining factor for my life, not one that I can control. But now that I travel to learn, I have hopefully overcome the parochial tendencies (a kind of clinging) I had due to living in a closed and sheltered environment. I believe in retrospect that the benefits out-weigh the negatives. When I left home for college I stepped through the threshold of this new, expanded lifestyle purposefully. We all have in differing details a heritage that somehow influences us for better or worse. However, what we call "self" is just an imagined entity, (comparable to the allegory of our Heart) and what we are, instead, is merely a part of the ceaseless becoming of Universe. I don't feel like the same person I was then, I have had so many rebirths. That sounds a bit lofty, like what can I possibly learn from the big dipper? When I come back to Earth I recognize that I do have talents and I am obliged to use these in order to contribute to the society of my species, to the benefit of my family and to exalt my own life to the extent I can. And it is the same, more or less for everyone.

When we think of this matter of choice and freedom as a blessing, it is only a reality when we act well and earn this. "Do not speak harshly to anyone:\Those spoken to will answer back.\ For angry speech is painful:\ Retribution may reach you." Once we gain it, we can participate with millions of Buddhists who preceded us and carry lightly this message of tranquility; and when we share our direct knowledge about sukha-jhana faithfully, we can benefit from feeling Sukha-jhana without developing attachments.[70]

---

[70] "If, like a cracked gong,\ You don't let yourself make a noise,\ You have attained nibbana:\ There is no arrogance in you.\\ Neither going naked, nor matted locks, nor mud,\ Nor fasting, nor lying on the bare ground,\ Nor dust, nor dirt, nor striving in squatting posture\ Can

Chapter Seven

Recognizing Nirodha

Key Words:

Realization, dukkham—unsatisfactoriness, anatta—not-self, second jhana, superstitions, visions, reliving, voidness of attachments, tranquility, bare awareness, vitakka—vicara.

Why Should I Meditate?

In meditation we recognize the causes of suffering, how this is overcome (ceases) and the causes of our own existence. We learn to relieve suffering and be at ease [tranquility,] contemplate what's happened in the past, present, and in the future. Meditation can lead us, like a monk holding our hand, through our personal history of growing older (aging). Meditation is undoing problems of birth, aging, illness, and death. When thoughts drop away, you experience your entire body and mind filled with joy and happiness. When the

---

purify the mortal who has not gone beyond doubt.\\ Even though you wear fine clothes, if you live peacefully,\ Calmed, controlled, disciplined, living the holy life,\ Laying aside the rod in dealing with all beings,\ You are a Brahmin, a wanderer, a monk./" (Dhammapada, vs.133,134,141,142)

mind is ready it glides beyond second jhana; but only if you relax and let it. We should replay emotions of pleasant and dreadful experiences and expose these to 'bare awareness' to learn from these. This reliving helps get rid of defilements and suffering, and makes meditation personal instead of a theoretical exercise. Wonderful experiences occur when we rest our minds in meditation. Often during meditation a great deal of "complex" but submerged psychological material arises into consciousness—we can use this like nutrition to eliminate craving and attachments. Once we regulate the feelings, we have a chance to keep our life on the correct ethical path. Nirodha is about extinguishing clinging and attachment, because we lose craving and we don't "go there". In meditation suffering can be overcome through mental activity, by removing one aspect of a particular suffering. We practice the spiritual art of controlling piti and sukha to benefit our lives, as we would a symphony.

What does it mean to develop a pure mind? That is after all what we are working on in these middle seven chapters. We learned in the very beginning of *Bodhicitta: Higher Truth* that purification is related to following the twelve permutations or spokes of the proverbial wheel of Dharma, the very first teaching of the Buddha—the *recognition, encouragement and realization* of the Four Noble Truths of our lives and overcoming defilements. We do this as we change our lives for the better and eliminate hindrances, all part of a very complex religion, and the ten thousand aspects of Dharma. But does it simply boil down to watching the breath and mindfulness at a guarding point in meditation? In the seventh step of Anapanasati we review " . . . aniccam (impermanence), dukkham (unsatisfactoriness), and anatta (not-self)" until we see these directly with clear, relaxed understanding.[71] That

---

[71] "We have discovered that piti is a foe [agitation] of vipassana, whereas sukha, happiness-joy, is a friend, a supporter. Vipassana means 'seeing clearly" having direct insight into the truth of aniccam (impermanence), dukkham (unsatisfactoriness), and anatta (not-self). We must acquire

is the spiritual art of Buddhism. As before, Piti is the foe of Sukha, not because it precedes Sukha, but because Sukha is perhaps tentative, ephemeral, and we can easily lose that sense of peacefulness and lapse back into the more energetic level of Piti with a sense of pride of accomplishment. When we think, "I made it, I have experienced jhana!" it disappears and eludes us just as quickly as it began. There is, then, such a thing as too much mindfulness, but a pure mind can sustain the tranquility we all deserve to feel.

If we wish to experience Sukha on a sustained basis, or repeatedly, since it is a precarious mental state, we have to prepare our mind to be selfless and humble. In the same way we can lose our first conscious experience of jhana, we can interrupt or prevent our experience of the deeper level of spontaneous, un-willed tranquility. "Only with full awareness can you maintain it."[72] Even so, we will retain these victories in our memories and benefit from the changes in our lives so we shouldn't feel any disappointment when our mind changes from state to state. This experience of jhana can come and develop with practice (that's why it's called Practice) but it may not come very often, perhaps this tranquil state will come

---

the ability to regulate piti and find sukha. We contemplate this fact [with calm emotions] in the mind [and we visit our Hearts,] every time we breathe in and breathe out. This is step seven." (Buddhadasa, 1988, pp. 61-64)

[72] "The attainment of the second jhana does not take place by wishing or willing or striving. When the mind is ready to attain the second jhana, it automatically lets go of the first jhana. You don't even have to wish to go to the second jhana. When the mind is ready, it glides into the second jhana by itself. But only if you let it. . . The moment your thinking or subtle thoughts vanish from your mind, you are aware that you have entered the second jhana. But as soon [paradoxically] as the thought, 'This is the second jhana,' appears in your mind, you lose it. Try again and again until that thought does not appear. You can stay with the awareness of second jhanic experience without the concept 'this is the second jhana.' This is a very delicate balance. Only with full awareness can you maintain it." (Gunaratana, pg. 143)

only once in a lifetime, then it will be a cherished memory, like winning the gold medal in the Olympics.

In meditation we should not expect to feel an ecstatic swoon or trance state.

Buddhist teachings are based on the psychological status and make-up of human nature, a credit to those ancient savants and The Buddha for having made these observations and conclusions without the benefit of modern science. We each get to measure our psyche against the general teachings that have evolved over the years. However, at a more general level, we naturally require the satisfaction of happiness and at least occasionally the comfort of other human understanding. This is not the experience of jhana, but the comfort that is known by a small child who falls asleep in his/her parent's lap. We are acquainted from an early age about the physical necessities of life, food, clothing, housing and medicine, but Buddhism recognizes that there are spiritual needs that are just as important. "Without the nourishing of 'piti' (joy) and 'sukha' (happiness), human beings can hardly survive."[73] This is the rub according to Buddhism, this need for happiness and "spiritual factors" can lead us astray if we head in the wrong direction and follow a charismatic leader giving empty promises along a selfish path. But we ought to be heartened by the Buddha's promise that stress, suffering etc., can be eliminated and cease, we need no other. "Vision arose, insight arose, discernment arose, knowledge arose, illumination arose within me with regard to things never heard before: 'This is the noble truth of the cessation of stress' . . ." (Appendix II) This

---

[73] ". . .mental and spiritual aspects of life which must be attended to. The mind needs some nourishing factors to support its state of well-being. Therefore the spiritual factors can be regarded as the fifth requisite of life." (Buddhadasa, 2008, pg. 125)

Irv Jacob

was part of his enlightenment; we have it for free and can use it to our advantage.

We are all vulnerable to some kind of emotional grasping. This is what gets us doing all the things we might later regret—and which cause suffering—and motivates us, ironically, to do the good deeds in life and essentially follow the Eight-fold Path in an inspired way as well. So this very search for happiness has a dialectic nature, a two sided coin, and two opposite and contradictory outcomes so this direct knowledge can be illusive. Our effort to find happiness-joy can succeed " . . . When there are proper things to cajole the mind [nirodha,] there will be happiness, but when the cajoling factors are of the wrong kind, mental defilement arises."[74] Are we constantly on this precarious balance? This explains the teaching of many Hindu gurus that life is an illusion, yet the "inspired way" is in plain view and is perhaps simpler, and involves having compassion and gaining peace of mind. That is the promise of Buddhism. The koan that precedes this

---

[74]   This search for pleasure ". . .cajoles the mind into a state of normalcy and happiness. Without it the mind will be in a restless and agitated state. It will be abnormal and mentally ill. It may be even insane. . . Therefore there is a part of it which needs something that seems to be delusive, to make it feel satisfied, assured, safe, and contented with life; or at least it has to be something that amuses the mind. . . Fame, honour and power. . . and 'merit' (or 'boon' in Thai). . . is something which makes us happy and contented. . . It is therefore a fifth requisite for it cajoles, coaxes or leads and supports the mind. It is thus a spiritual factor. It is 'vedana' or feeling. . . When there are proper things to cajole the mind [nirodha,] there will be happiness, but when the cajoling factors are of the wrong kind, mental defilement arises which can come in the form of sensual desire. . . Food, clothing, housing and medicine are the four basic requisites of life but these requisites too, when [they] get mixed up with abusive or wrong purposes, can be the baits that lure people into delusion and even insanity. . . 'Vedana' is also known as 'citta-sankhara' for it conditions the mind to allow 'piti' (joy) and 'sukha' (happiness) to arise." (Buddhadasa, 2008, pp. 129-131)

lesson is to understand the virtue of boredom; that is when we are experiencing a naïve form of preparedness for meditation. When we are experiencing this in meditation, we should consider it as a triumph against sensual stimulation.

With this theory of suffering in hand we can do a review of our lives in both directions, that is, we can look back at when we suffered as a result of seeking fame, power or merit, and see how our emotions led us or cajoled us into problems that we later regretted. Or we can look at our history of emotional demands, reactions or needs for happiness and see how that has predisposed us (and how that is affecting us today) to do things that are positive and beneficial. The psychological theory is open ended for us to apply in real life, and recognize how it works in our lives. We can learn these lessons from experience or from accepting the good advice from those who have already "been there, done that." This can be considered as comparable to Taking Refuge in the triple gem. In every society and culture there are wise people who have learned from experience and who are inclined to share their wisdom, and certainly corrupt leaders who manipulate people to satisfy their own ends.

Being willing to help others is sometimes a risky business, and there is a caution. I have had the experience of being ridiculed or diminished by people when I have tried to share these explanations and Dharma teachings with them. "Who are you to say all this?" "Do you live this?" "Has it made you a better person?" or "You are a know-it-all, I don't want to listen to what you say!" These are different kinds of petty, ad hominem reactions, complaining about me rather than looking at the message. If someone is disturbed by the message it is almost a natural reaction to "kill the messenger", at least figuratively. Instead, we can easily take the advice we get and evaluate the content of that, and disregard the source, even The Buddha. Thus we don't let our own emotional hang-ups interfere with our self-improvement and we conscientiously seek to obtain direct knowledge. Since that is probably too much to ask from many people, even when we try to avoid any personal criticisms, just describing better or appropriate behaviors can imply criticism. So we adopt ways to make sure the messenger is somehow welcome, and learn to be empathetic not critical.

How do people who are not Buddhists get this kind of essential and positive nurturing? Certainly other religions offer ethical teachings (saints) and "cajole" members into developing the spiritual aspects of their lives. For people who are deliberately not involved in any particular religion, they can achieve happiness (or seek it) through the pursuit of art, or find it in meaningful personal relationships, or wander around searching for it—this is perhaps, at least temporarily, the most common experience. I confess to having done some of each of the above, and perhaps more wandering than I care to admit. Having a healthy emotional life allows us to use and benefit from our resources and talents, and use inspired emotions to condition our minds (and Heart) in a healthy way—" . . . 'Vedana' is also known as 'citta-sankhara' [mind/Heart conditioner.]" Spirituality comes naturally to most people because it is in large measure connected to the love given by and received from parents, siblings, peers and other loved ones (significant others). We have natural animal instincts that guide us to engage in these kinds of meaningful relationships, to be connected to our families and tribes. Even the most ruthless and corrupt dictators are prone to engage in nepotism, they have a false sense of entitlement, thus favoring their family members with positions and opportunities. This comes from their sense of connection to family, their need for emotional and spiritual nourishment, notwithstanding their other faults. When we go one step further and actively meditate to eliminate suffering, we are developing what is a natural extension of our human nature, but with the intention of sharing our merit and success with society.

There are various schools of thought as to how much effort or interest we ought to have in the experience of jhana, because of the potential hindrance mentioned which leads to a failure or lack of interest ". . . in developing discernment."[75] This is a different kind of warning than the previous discussion of the cajoling nature of the factors of happiness. We need to be wary of superstitions and "visions" that can concoct and create emotions to manipulate our thinking. This seems like a case of taking our spiritual search too seriously in the wrong direction. There needs to be a balance and development of wisdom-in-action associated with the possible emotional states of the mind. Much of this may be learned from others in a Sangha who have already had experiences that we might wish to avoid, and thus we accept the refuge and advice they offer. How do we recognize one path from the other? Those who encourage us to do as they do, notwithstanding, can be seen as suspect. Those who encourage us to find our own path, to develop discernment, and teach us the tools, can be respected and followed.

When we realize the Three Characteristics as described above we still have to be wary: "If we grasp at things and

---

[75]   "For example, when we enter concentration, the mind may gather and rest for a long or a short time, but when we withdraw, we're still attached to that concentration and not at all interested in developing discernment. We may feel that the concentration will turn into the paths, fruitions, or nibbana; or else we are addicted to the concentration and want the mind to stay gathered that way for long periods of time or forever. Sometimes, after the mind gathers into its resting place, it then withdraws a bit, going out to know the various things that make contact, becoming attached and engrossed with its visions. Sometimes it may float out of the body to travel to the Brahma worlds, heaven, hell, or the world of the hungry shades, without a thought for what's right or wrong, as we become engrossed in our visions and abilities, taking them as our amazing paths, fruitions, and nibbana, and those of the religion as well. When this happens, then even if someone skilled and experienced in this area comes to warn us, we won't be willing to listen at all. All of these things are termed wrong concentration that we don't realize to be wrong." (Boowa, 1996)

cling to things, the result is bound to be suffering."[76] This kind of wisdom and direct knowledge is fundamental to obtaining Sukha-jhana. We come to recognize the causes of suffering, how this suffering is overcome (ceases) and the causes of our own existence. We eventually realize that every aspect of our personage, our language and educated minds, our habits, our frames of reference, our well-developed talents—all owe themselves to the culture and society that surrounds us. This should keep us humble and appreciative. This purification—*recognition*—is accomplished along with the development of our Hearts as well. We know when the light bulb in our room is on, and how to turn it off and on again. This kind of simple mechanical understanding comes from experience and the simple learning we have for a long time taken for granted. There are many spiritual attributes that we all possess that fit into this same category of knowledge, so we are most likely well equipped with significant discernment when we put our minds to resolving issues that confront our lives. When we Take Refuge in our Sangha we share our concerns and solutions.

Think of a time when there was obvious and repeated suffering in your life . . . I remember many such incidents and repeated events in my teenage years. I suffered when I began to sweat in my armpits, initially not having been told about deodorant. Then I began to experiment with different brands, and suffered until I found the one which made me comfortable.

---

[76] ". . . that all things are impermanent we mean that all things change perpetually, there being no entity or self that remains unchanged for even an instant. That all things are unsatisfactory means that all things [and choices we make] have inherent in themselves the property of conducing to suffering and torment. They are inherently [or eventually] unlikable, not satisfying and disenchanting. That they are not selves [not mine or me; not part of our buddha-nature] is to say that in nothing whatsoever is there any entity which we might have a right to regard as its 'self' (myself) or to call 'its own' (mine.) If we grasp at things and cling to things, the result is bound to be suffering." (Buddhadasa, 2005, pg. 33)

The more I worried about sweating the more I sweated. I would have rather unpleasant wet stains under my arms, and it took me more or less a year of what I considered suffering before I got a handle on that and became less self-conscious of my natural perspiration. There should be a manual somewhere that teenagers can read to acquaint themselves with all these issues of entering puberty and how to handle the changes in their bodies and social lives. Talk about changes and impermanence, that period from adolescence to adulthood is just one change after the other. However, it is also proof that this suffering can come to an end.

What are the lessons we draw from all those confusing and often emotional experiences of growing up. Certainly the activity of meditation can lead us, like a teacher/ monk holding our hand, through this history of growing older (aging). In hindsight we have this whole encyclopedia of memories of social experiences, some pleasant some troublesome. We can try to put it into words as follows, and examine the second state of piti-jhana more closely: "a momentary joy like a flash of intermittent lightning." When have we had that experience in our ordinary lives? What is the corresponding peace of mind that followed that? This could give us a clue and identify the Sukha-jhana that can perhaps follow and reward our effort, and we practice and learn to see clearly.[77] As we develop our wisdom from studying these emotions carefully, there is a parallel development of our potential to experience a peaceful state of mind.

The simple, direct teaching of a famous thudong (wandering forest) monk popular in the Western world, Ajahn Chah

---

[77] "The Buddha taught us to train ourselves, to contemplate, to meditate. 'Meditation' means undoing these problems in line with the way they are. These are the issues: the issues of birth, aging, illness, and death. These are really common, ordinary things. This is why he has us contemplate them continually. . . When you see [clearly,] you can gradually undo these problems. Although you may still have some clinging, if you have the discernment to see that these things are normal you'll be able to relieve suffering. . ." (Buddhadasa)

asks: "What can you do not to be worried about birth, aging, illness, and death?"[78] The good news is that even suffering is impermanent unless we are one of those people who have as a psychological nature to perpetually feel sorry for ourselves, and cling and repeat those activities that lead to suffering. These basic teachings of overcoming suffering by gaining direct knowledge are found in every Buddhist tradition.

I haven't given much consideration to each of the mentioned sources of suffering: "birth, aging, illness, and death"—because I have previously thought, well that is just a general listing, an idiom or cliché. Perhaps there is more to it than meets the eye, however, as I just described in the example from my teenage years. That is certainly a story of suffering relating to aging. How about birth? I don't have a memory of or know suffering from my actual birth, so I have always considered the generalities of suffering associated with just living when I think of that. We might consider ourselves to suffer for not being born into wealth or a prestigious, noble family. But The Buddha was, and suffered from that until he escaped. Perhaps it would be better to think of the "rebirth" concept in this context, something that can happen every day repeatedly as we seriously and mistakenly engage our egos in the issues of our lives. Furthermore, the suffering from illness seems straight forward enough, we either have pain, take medications or we don't. There are many people who are reminded of suffering every minute of the day because of the

---

[78] "The basic principles of the Buddha's teaching aren't much: just suffering arising and suffering passing away. That's why these things are called noble truths. If you don't know these things, you suffer. If you argue from pride and opinions, there's no end to it. To get the mind to relieve its suffering and be at ease [tranquility,] you have to contemplate what's happened in the past, what's in the present, what's going to be in the future. What can you do not to be worried about birth, aging, illness, and death? There will be some worries, but if you can learn to understand them for what they are, suffering will gradually lessen, because you don't hug it to your chest." (Ajahn Chah, 2007, pg. 46)

illnesses or physical constraints that subdue them. I take my life, being relatively free of illness and congenital defects for granted, but combining that consideration with aging, perhaps I should be cautious, wary and prepare myself more carefully, now that I am on the threshold of old age. In an indirect way, that is what I am doing by developing this book of teachings (I will no doubt review it repeatedly in the future). Which brings me to death; what suffering do I recognize associated with dying? I have experienced the sadness associated with the natural death of loved ones, but even on that score I have been only lightly afflicted compared to many other people. I feel my instinct for survival well enough, but largely because of my Buddhist training I no longer have an intellectual fear of death. I have never seriously experienced a challenge to my survival instinct, however, like being a prisoner of war who is tortured by water-boarding. So, I intend to make these considerations the objects of my vipassana until I get some serious insights about these frequently mentioned topics.

Elsewhere we have studied the taxonomy of the hindrances that prevent and interfere with the frequency of our meditation; we must be way beyond those now, or are we? One or more of them can reoccur when we are least expecting, or we can lapse into the desire for sensual pleasure, for example, because this is a natural instinct and comes into our minds when we least expect it. This doesn't need to interfere with our practice or desire to continue meditation, and as long as we do meditate regularly, we are victorious over those potential hindrances. Thus when we have " . . . internal confidence and unification of mind . . ." we can expect to experience a spiral or cycle of increasing, significant joy.[79] This comes with direct

---

[79] "The second jhana also has a deeper level of concentration. You do not have to watch out for hindrances. The first jhana is still close to the hindrances and to all material experiences. The second jhana is still close to vitakka and vicara, but remote from hindrances. 'With the subsiding of applied thought and sustained thought one enters and dwells in the second jhana, which has internal confidence and unification of mind. . . and is filled with rapture and bliss born of

Irv Jacob

knowledge, and having these teachings repeated in each new context is valuable. And then we proceed to encourage and motivate others to mix some of the practical, actual experiences from their lives with the theoretical possibilities from Buddhist texts.

Preceding this second state of Sukha-jhana there is a certain amount of intellectual development required, that is we study and review, we need to know more-or-less what to expect. We need to have, or know how to—put aside the torments that might confront our daily lives. This is not a complex or abstract notion nor an esoteric knowledge, but an experiential understanding like learning how to tie our shoes. We leave our cares with our shoes outside the sala or wat. In our meditation we should not expect to feel an ecstatic swoon or trance state, peace and quiet ought to be a welcome contrast to whatever happened earlier in the day or yesterday. We should expect perhaps to replay emotions and physical reactions we have had associated with pleasant and dreadful experiences alike. This reliving is what helps us get rid of defilements and suffering, and makes our meditation a personal experience instead of a theoretical exercise. That is what it means, at least in part, to return home, "experience the absence of attachment", to go back to a peaceful and relaxing place in our minds where direct knowledge lives.[80] Losing attachment is a reasonably advanced stage of religious development as we proceed with our Buddhist practice. As we learn the 10,000 parts of Buddhism, we see that there is a lot we can do in our

concentration'... When thought drops away, you experience your entire body and mind filled with joy and happiness. This joy continuously replenishes itself with more and more joy." (Gunaratana, pg. 144)

[80] "Thus, we realize the voidness or nonexistence of attachment through the quenching, disappearing, and ending of attachment. We experience the absence of attachment in many of the aspects [or our lives] while we breathe in and breathe out. Or more simply, we drink, taste, and savor the flavor of Nibbana. Nirodha and Nibbana are synonyms; we can use them interchangeably. Thus, to contemplate the quenching of attachment is to contemplate Nibbana." (Buddhadasa, 1988, pg. 90)

life that is under our control. Nibbana (nirvana), however, is not something we can plan for or cause, it will just happen, not unlike the Sukha-jhana under consideration in the last chapter and beyond. The end of suffering, or ceasing is something over which we have control, and need to expend continuous effort to achieve it. We can focus on "quenching of attachment", we can prepare ourselves according to the teachings, and then we may have our reward.

Even though this *recognition* of Sukha-jhana may follow what seems like a flash of insight, it has happened and you gain from it. When we do experience " . . . bliss, clarity, and non-conceptuality" we may not even know it at first, and other times it will come as a resounding, obvious tranquility.[81] We have to trust that if others can describe these experiences and achievements, then we can come to know and recognize all these in our own practice. This explanation and the following definitions come from the Tibetan tradition.

We described bliss in the very first chapter, and it is easy to confuse all the adjectives that describe the pleasures we can gain from meditation. I can find this place, this feeling where "everything is made of love"[82] when I am walking or hiking in a forest or wilderness area. I like to practice with something as simple as an itch, rather than scratch it, I just watch it until it goes away and it often does, not always; and sometimes I just have to scratch, but either way I get some pleasure, a little bit of bliss. I have difficulty having this same emotion when walking through a subway or crowded and busy public transportation area, although it has happened.

---

[81] "Wonderful experiences can occur when you rest your mind in meditation [in or out of jhana.] Sometimes it takes a while for these experiences to occur; sometimes they happen the very first time you sit down to practice. The most common of these experiences are bliss, clarity, and non-conceptuality." (Mingyur)

[82] "Bliss. . . is a feeling of undiluted happiness, comfort, and lightness in both the mind and the body. As this experience grows stronger, it seems as if everything you see is made of love. Even experiences of physical pain become very light and hardly noticeable at all." (Mingyur)

We learn to differentiate between the various stages of contentment the more we experience and recognize with clarity more details of our lives. When we experience life as an art form, and study all the natural elements, this is how we get some certainty about the meaning of our lives. Before I began this active Buddhist practice, I was doing that kind of self-study, and immersing myself in nature, writing poetry, and listening to birds, etc. I still do that, and love watching birds come to our feeders, but now I have a different frame of reference, and I believe it is more skillful to be watching nature from the point of view of a Buddhist practitioner. I have a sense of seeing through clearly, and I understand in a broader context my place in this nature.[83] And we wash them clean ("disturbing thoughts") while we guard a point where our breath passes unencumbered, only barely noticeable, when we meditate profoundly.

When we compare commentators from different Buddhist traditions, we get translations that are equivalent but they use different terms. When we try to imagine: " . . . an experience of pure consciousness as infinite as space . . ."[84] we may have difficulty doing that. It seems like an oxymoron to explain and think that we have experienced non-conceptuality. It is perhaps like seeing the wind, and we have to have a visual aide to do that. We have to rely on poetry or perhaps mathematics. It is no mean feat to recognize that our mind and Heart is who we

[83] "**Clarity** is a sense of being able to see into the nature of things as though all reality were a landscape lit up on a brilliantly sunny day without clouds. Everything appears distinct and everything makes sense. Even disturbing thoughts and emotions have their place in this brilliant landscape." (Mingyur)

[84] "**Non-conceptuality** [jhana] is an experience of the total openness of your mind. Your awareness is direct and unclouded by conceptual distinctions such as 'I' or 'other,' subjects and objects, or any other form of limitation. It's an experience of pure consciousness as infinite as space without beginning, middle, or end. It's like becoming awake within a dream and recognizing that everything experienced in the dream isn't separate from the mind of the dreamer." (Mingyur)

are, and that in Buddhism we are living as protagonists of a terrific drama, living in a poem.

There is a further analysis that comes from Mingyur's Tibetan tradition. He alludes to a sense of disorientation, like losing one's balance, feeling distraction.[85] In a certain way we are shifting between Piti and Sukha but with no deliberate effort, just a dance, a well-practiced and elegant waltz between these two psychic partners at its best, a falling forward without grace and catching oneself just in time, at worst. I feel a comparable feeling especially when I am in a dark area, and without visual cues I can be very disoriented and close to falling. I have a cane now, but seldom use it just out of stubbornness.

As I read about ancient societies and their habits, lifestyles and cultures, I recognize how very different and meager their physical circumstances were. For example, I just bought a new water heater for my apartment in Bangkok, not so expensive, but what a luxury—never even conceived by people in the time of the Buddha. Of course he lived mostly in a tropical zone where cool water was refreshing and useful more-so than any notion of hot water. Simple pleasures would have entertained people, so the minds operating in those times were the same as ours, even though only a few were taught to read and write. Many were educated in rhetoric, memorization of stories, and elocution in their own native tongues. The training they received would have developed their minds much the way we are taught in schools, notwithstanding our modern curricula. But considering our vast accumulation of knowledge, and that our society has lived through and past the Age of Enlightenment, perhaps we don't have so far to go as we think to gain enlightenment. This is an encouraging thought. Or is the enlightenment we seek in Buddhism about

---

[85] "Some people, furthermore, feel a sense of **disorientation**, as though their familiar world of thoughts, emotions, and sensations has tilted slightly—which may be pleasant or unpleasant . . . When distractions of this sort occur, just make them a part of your practice. Join your awareness to the distraction." (Mingyur, pp. 209-210)

spiritual knowledge rather than the scientific and philosophical knowledge?

The activities of their minds, for people who lived during the time of the Buddha, would have been substantially the same as ours when they related socially to their Sangha, friends and families. There are many lessons that we need to recognize from the ancient teachings that are relevant for today. One is the simplicity and efficacy of direct awareness, although this comes after we discard a lot of other superfluous psychological baggage. "If merely treated to 'bare attention,' negative influences will pass away."[86] This is the same for us today as it was 2,500 years ago, except today we tend to over intellectualize and make meditation harder than it needs to be. How remarkable that Buddha and the culture at that time achieved such wisdom and clarity, considering the status of social development in other corners of the world which still lived in primitive circumstances. And when we achieve this "passing away", it is possible and desirable to protect these results at the end of the meditation session, and this is how we grow and change our lives.

This is like a trade secret, or "mistier" as it is known in romance languages. Perhaps the best kept secret of Buddhism, that the pains, destructive emotions and challenges of our lives can just disappear when we hold them at the "guarding

---

[86] "The Buddha found what he was looking for by means of vipashyana [insight meditation] . . . a meditation session [requires] a workable degree of mental **calm and concentration** in preparation for vipashyana . . . the mind is opened and awareness is directed to all that enters its sphere. Often at first a great deal of hitherto submerged psychological material arises into consciousness. This is a very positive process; the darkness is becoming [clear to the light of] conscious. Old fears and phobias, traumas and repressions can now be hospitably entertained in full awareness. The meditator is neutral towards them, neither rejecting nor repressing—nor, on the other hand, identifying and hence becoming carried away by them. If merely treated to 'bare attention,' negative influences will pass away. This is a very real and effective form of psychotherapy." (Buddhadasa)

point" and just watch them with direct awareness, 'bare attention'. Consider these terms synonyms for *recognition* and direct knowledge. This is the key lesson of cessation of suffering, and the most important technique to be taken from this seventh step of Anapanasati which gives the process of recognition—as part of the twelve steps of the turning of the wheel—a mythical significance.

This is what we can expect to achieve by no particular effort once we both recognize the stages of our mind development and also move into Sukha-jhana. This is not stoicism or repressing feelings, in fact the opposite. It is having and holding feelings, but not being conquered by the consequences of emotionalism, nor by " . . . all the crises in this world."[87] This is the same phenomenon today as it was 2,500 years ago. This reference to the resonance of emotions leading to war is a rather dire warning that seems to exceed the relevance of meditation practice for our own little world or Sangha. But think of the conflict that is raging somewhere around the world as you read this (as I write this it is the rebellion in Syria and the government repression). Will there always be a cauldron of killing and terrorism somewhere? When we recognize that this is based on the intense emotions that build up and resonate into conflict, we are better equipped to make informed decisions as voters.

It is perhaps a simple formula to suggest that the mere recognition of the problem is a key to the cessation of suffering, and I resisted this idea when I was first confronted with it.

---

[87] "Once we can regulate the feelings, we will be able to keep our life on the correct path. When we are foolish about the vedana, [emotions] we become slaves to materialism. This happens when we indulge in material pleasures, that is, the flavors of feelings. All the crises in this world have their origin in people not understanding the vedana, giving in to the vedana, being enamored with the vedana. The feelings entice [cajole] us to act in ways that lead to disagreements, quarrels, conflicts, [the opposite of compassion] and eventually, war . . . because people act unwisely through the deceptions of vedana." (Buddhadasa, 1988, pp. 67-68)

It seemed like there needed to be some kind of penance, contrition, confession or forgiveness as is the case in many other religions. But that is not the case. We don't even need to place a value judgment on the emotion or circumstance; we just watch it until the air leaks out, so to speak. If we can't solve all the issues surrounding suffering, and it is not desirable to remove ourselves from all the people in our lives who give us grief, for example, there is this simple technique. We can deal in this manner by having 'bare awareness' with any one or more of the conditions, complications, determinants (of the conditioned, co-arising factors) and attachments that have caused our suffering once we see them for what they are. We can know that this Insight is attainable based on the testimony of experienced meditators and from our own experience. That direct knowledge will give us confidence in our ability to make everything get right, and this has huge implications for our lives. Even with a formula, there is much work to do, however.

At the beginning of this chapter I asked the question: "Does it simply boil down to watching the breath and mindfulness at a guarding point in meditation?" In an important way it does because our emotions can change from one moment to the next. If suffering can be overcome through our own human, mental activity, simply by removing any one aspect of any particular suffering, then we can make huge progress just from meditation. "What's the laughter, why the joy,\ When the world is ever burning?\ Plunged into darkness,\ Won't you look for a lamp?" (Dhammapada, vs. 146) If the work we do in meditation changes our behaviors, then we are following the lamp of Buddhism and that's where the rest of the story is told. When Buddhism gets absorbed and we make changes, we do so without suffering. We practice the spiritual art of controlling piti and sukha so that they benefit our lives.

This is not a trick, no Brahman sacrifice, i.e. killing goats, is required; it is just watching the reality of our emotions that is otherwise not always made clear. Attaining and perfecting dispassion is perhaps an advanced state, eliminating one prior determining factor, which may not even be a direct cause, is often easier. Cessation of suffering may be potentially a process that can proceed on many levels, so we learn to break the problem into its component parts and find the one or two that are most easily changed or solvable. As many as there are issues from which we suffer, there are many more solutions and only one promise of cessation that applies uniformly to all. This is like the Unified Theory of physics applied to human social conduct.

We can be too impatient to obtain the state of *Nirvana*, however. Nirvana means freedom from all worries, troubles, complexes, fabrications and ideas, and "all" is a very big word for anyone's life. Nirvana is said to be not comprehensible for those who have not attained it. The knowledge and wisdom required grow more slowly than our life experiences.[88] But we do gain perspective; we can imagine what it would be like to be on the other side of the river, when we can clearly see that the terrain is much like that which we are experiencing where we stand. This limitation of distance is not a cause of suffering however, it is just a realistic challenge and we can think of overcoming it as an inspiring goal! And nirodha, which we can imagine and create, is one of the big keys to our success. We may still wear the wrinkles of our efforts, however.

In review: The cessation of suffering can be attained through *nirodha*. Nirodha means the unmaking of sensual craving and conceptual attachment. These are generalities of course and how do the details actually manifest in our own lives? The third noble truth expresses the ideal also that suffering can be ended by attaining dispassion and direct knowledge. Or does that just mask the problem in many cases? But certainly there is more to it than just recognition and dispassion as well, there has to be effort. Curiously, it is easier than we might think, because, as suggested earlier, if we remember that only one of the twelve theoretical causes or determining (conditioning) factors of suffering has to be dissolved, then we can see how it

---

88   "A person of little knowledge\ Grows old as a plough-ox grows old.\ His flesh increases:\ His wisdom does not increase." (Dhammapada, vs. 152)

might be possible to recognize skillful solutions even for some very serious issues in our lives. Nirodha extinguishes all forms of clinging and attachment, because we lose the craving and we just don't go back there.

Chapter Eight

Recognition of the Path

Key Words:

Eight-fold Path, meta-cognition, emptiness, wisdom/panna, Existentialism, adinava/unhealthy, assada/attractive, pliable, barter, infinity.

Why Should I Meditate?

Meditation is where the supra-mundane resides, and I call this the poetic side of Buddhism. We can benefit from the "supra-mundane" aspect of recognition as a kind of alchemy for our characters. In meditation we take advantage of the fact that suffering and the **concocted,** conditioned causes of suffering, are very destructible and have no essence. We can gain a feeling of **equanimity** toward the highest joy and all the lesser and minor ones too. When we move into the third Piti-jhana ". . . a flood of joy . . . breaks like waves on the beach." In meditation we recognize that life just is, thusness, and we get to make (and/or accept) our own superior meaning. We recognize the Sukha-jhana as the supra-mundane, the unseen tidal movement that energizes our lives. Meditation on an object involves discipline, and is the key to changing our perceptions; thus to the way we act. We barter leading a virtuous life for the tranquility that we can achieve during meditation. By this time, because of our meditation, we have a pliable and useful Heart to control every worthy aspect of our lives. In mediation we rest like a pebble settled [weightlessly] on the riverbed, that is when we begin to find our rest, our peace. We recognize that craving, ignorance, delusions will disappear gradually through appropriate meditation. We develop an optimistic vision of a brighter future without being in a frustrating cycle of depression or dependency. In skillful meditation we utilize feelings as the mind-conditioner—we feel enthusiasm for life, energetic, and optimistic; these are positive conditioned mental states.

Recognizing where we stand along the marvelous and noble Eight-fold Path, is a rather complex task, one that should be taken seriously at least once a year like Lent for a Catholic. I will name and review each of these eight steps later in this chapter but first I want to identify and recognize the categories or analysis that has grown up over the years. I don't intend to make a thorough study of this for each possible tradition of Buddhism, because there are differences and various styles of analysis, but I have picked a framework that seems reasonably well accepted and one which I find useful. There are three common groupings: *precepts (conduct), concentration (attentiveness), and wisdom (understanding)*; each of the elements of the Eight-fold Path fits into one of these groupings. This also describes the content areas, or areas of concern and the scope of the Eight-fold Path. In other discussions we have been concerned about the Five Precepts (or eight or ten) as the most common grouping of ethical guidelines and the Eight-fold Path is associated with that only tangentially as far as I can tell. It is comparable to the operating system of Buddhist morality; if we use a PC or an Apple, we don't concern ourselves with the operating system, we just go about using all the applications and programs however we choose on the framework of the operating system. So there is a little bit of Right Effort, for example, that gets involved in everything we do, in one way or another.

We cannot blatantly violate the Five Precepts and expect to have a flowering of our meditative skills.

That is the kind of discussion we need to have with ourselves during this once a year or so survey; are we on the right track? We benefit when we follow the example of the Buddha by recognizing the efficacy of the Eight-fold Path. "Vision arose, insight arose, discernment arose, knowledge arose, illumination arose within me with regard to things never heard before: 'This is the noble truth of the *way of practice* leading to the cessation of stress'. . ." (Appendix II) Furthermore there is the discussion in many texts about mundane and supra-mundane (transcendent, esoteric or abstract); with the mundane being the practical every day arrangements we make, our direct knowledge, and how these are influenced by (or affect) the teachings of the Eight-fold Path. Then, and this is where the religion of Buddhism gets involved; there is the abstract nature of each of these eight steps, and we need to evaluate our lives as to how these ponderables (as opposed to practical items) are shaping up. "Things that are wrong and bad for you\ Are easy to do;\ What is both good for you and right\ Is most difficult to do."[89] This is a commentary about the level of difficulty associated with following the Eight-fold Path and the level of commitment and devotion (Taking Refuge) that is involved, so it is a word of caution to remember to meditate for one's own benefit for sure.

---

[89]   "You should not neglect your own benefit\ For another's benefit, great though it be.\ Understanding your own benefit,\ You should pursue your own benefit." (Dhammapada, vs. 163, 166)

Impermanence is ironically a constant throughout this discussion; it can perhaps be best described as the personality of infinity. It is reasonably easy to recognize how our lives are constantly changing in so many ways on the practical side of things. But on the abstract or supra-mundane level, what changes? Talk about infinity can be confusing, or worse, we can be convinced that we actually understand something that is nonsensical, " . . . what is left is infinite awareness."[90] If that makes sense to you so much the better, "Bully for you!" as they say. This exercise in the use of infinities was described by the 19th century mathematician Cantor when he developed his original techniques for manipulating different infinities. That is not something we need to concern ourselves about during meditation, unless we happen to be compulsively drawn into those theories. Most likely that will be a serious distraction. Contemplating one infinity will be more than sufficient for purposes of seeking and surpassing the third state of Piti-jhana, and we probably shouldn't waste much time on that either. But this is the neighborhood where the supra-mundane resides, and I prefer to call this the poetic side of Buddhism, because that's the way I understand it best. But for many people, that is what draws them to Buddhism after they have tried yoga, spiritualism or other "New Age" teachings. Monks devote their lives to creating "merit" that they then share with others as fast as they can, and somewhere in this understanding is the melding of the supra-mundane with the practicality of each practitioner's life.

This "awareness of awareness" is like being mindful of being mindful, which seems like—if you were walking you would trip on your own feet. How many times can you reflect on reflecting? How many times can you step on your dance partner's foot before they ask to sit down, thank you very much? Seeing our image reflect in two opposing mirrors is a useful

---

[90] "Awareness of infinite space requires infinite awareness [or visualization.] The thought of infinite space drops away and what is left is infinite awareness without an object. You dwell in boundless consciousness, pure awareness of awareness." (Gunaratana, pg. 108)

object lesson. We can recognize "mindfulness" as of course one of the cardinal steps on the Eight-fold Path (grouped in the category of concentration), and this is often associated with carefulness, Insight, awareness, wisdom method, introspection, vipassana, and meta-cognition. Frequently this skill is said to be the primary distinguishing factor between humans and apes or dogs, etc. (I like to think that we have a lot more going for us than any of the lower species, although I have always felt an affinity with whales.)

The idea that we can meditate, and should, on the changing and temporary nature (impermanence) of our thoughts and identities was accepted by educated people long before the Buddha came along. "The ego . . . was ephemeral, because it was subject to time. Not our real self . . . in an intense act of cognition, we would achieve moksha ("liberation") . . . In the course of his meditation, he [Samkhya movement] learned to concentrate on the buddhi to the exclusion of all else in the hope of catching a glimpse of the purusha [higher self.]" (Armstrong, pg. 193) The "buddhi" as an ideal of the enlightened bodhisattva, is likely the precursor to the tradition of using "bud—dho" as a mantra to coincide with breathing in and out. The Buddha would later repudiate the existence of *purusha*, which is one of his most serious departures from the intellectual/spiritual tradition from which he derives so much of his Dharma.

Siddhartha is often credited with having been an adept student of the yoga meditation teachers he encountered before his enlightenment, so it is no wonder that this concept of "impermanence" is the first of the three characteristics of the world (along with dukkha and anatta). This feature of all the world and our natures is also what gives us the hope of eliminating suffering, because not only are pleasant experiences impermanent, we learn to recognize that suffering and the **concocted,** conditioned causes of suffering, the complications we create for ourselves, are also very destructible and have no essence, such as what we might otherwise associate with a mountain, a fragrant jasmine rice or a bend in the road. So suffering will disappear (and we recognize that it can even be prevented) given the right encouragement, there is no inevitability, no "it's god's will", or physicality to it, no essence. There should be no-one to say: "You can't do that." Even the most apparently inconsequential and unassuming student can progress to be a stellar Buddhist leader if they are given the proper encouragement. Buddhism is "open-handed" and available to all. "Even the gods envy\ The mindful Fully Awakened Ones,\ Who are wise, intent on meditation,\ Delighting in the calm of non-attachment." (Dhammapada, vs. 181)

Even though Right Mindfulness is often listed as the last of the Eight-fold Path elements, it is usually taught as the priority for meditation retreats and is taught by lama, yogi and Hindu teachers as well as Buddhist monks. Getting to know all about the other seven elements is just as essential for *recognizing* and developing purification in our lives. These are just as essential to Dharma ideology (the operating system) and thus fundamental aspects of Buddhism. Right View (understanding)—Right Thought—Right Speech—Right Action—Right Livelihood—Right Effort—Right Concentration—are the rest of the lineup and must be thoroughly understood with direct knowledge, each in their own right (pun intended). How do we go about recognizing all of these? How do we adequately evaluate these in terms of both mundane and supra-mundane considerations? Answers to these questions are the frequent subject matter for Dharma Talks (the equivalent of Sunday School lessons). Elsewhere in *Buddhist Sutras: Lesson Book,* I have collected a chapter of information dedicated to each of these with numerous quotes and applications, so that might be a good place to start, and these are not specifically discussed here except as they come up in reference to other subjects. Consider this to be a first step, *recognizing* the scope and menu is the first aspect of having wisdom. "Panna (wisdom as it blooms) realizes the true nature (characteristics, qualities, conditions) of all things."[91]

---

[91] " . . .We make the citta-sankhara, the Vedana (feelings), calm and peaceful . . . either by samadhi—a higher level of concentration; or

This is the big picture (as discussed in chapter two), part of the work we need to do, and a thorough-going contemplation, a progress report, about once a year should suffice. We might recognize this as the meat and potatoes of Buddhism (except for the meat part).

In this eighth step of Anapanasati we work specifically on 'calming the mind-conditioner' during our breathing which is of course a further refinement of calming our emotions. This is a rather poetic presentation dealing with step eight once we recognize piti and sukha as tools, and we practice incorporating Sukha-jhana into our lives in an increasingly more complex way by protecting the insights we receive. Recall that we had a rather extensive discussion about the breath as a conditioner of the body in chapter three, and how this was important for our understanding of our inter-connectivity to humanity, and in an esoteric way to the subtle forces (chakras) that influence our bodies (real or imagined, i.e. psychosomatic) and our physical health. Well, the mind-conditioner plays an equally important and parallel role for our minds by influencing how we think. Just as we feel enthusiasm for life and for studying the Dharma, for example, or optimism that we can prevent and eliminate suffering, and discipline so we can pursue and persist in our practice; these are conditioned states of the mind that make our meditation practice skillful (Right Effort). Our emotions are responsible for these states of mind and this leads to a direct confrontation with the way we experience suffering. These are like spices in a good curry, all of which are integrated and essential.

This mental conditioning happens whether we want it to or not, so it can be negative or positive, we choose. We deliberately seek positive conditioning when we acquiesce (because it does not happen by making an effort, just by the opposite,

---

by the wisdom—panna- method. We aim at the one pinnacled mind [single-mindedness] that has sati or Nibbana as its object. Panna (wisdom as it blooms) realizes the true nature (characteristics, qualities, conditions) of all things—we understand how piti arises and what will cause it to cease." (Buddhadasa)

relaxing and being receptive) to move beyond Piti-jhana of the third state, " . . . a flood of joy . . . breaks like the waves of the ocean on the beach." As you move beyond this rhythmic contentment, someone looking at you might see you sway in your sitting, half-lotus posture, or in your chair. "You gain a feeling of equanimity toward even the highest joy."[92] This is where we make contact with the abstract, supra-mundane aspect of Buddhism and leave behind for a minute all the other minutiae of dharma ideology. Equanimity also means forgiveness of anyone who has transgressed against us. If we were violated by theft or abuse we throbbed with pain (piti), and the opposite of that is to throb with forgiveness. Perhaps we can recognize this as the Hollandaise sauce that adorns our lives? As long as we cannot forgive we are stuck in the suffering of the offense that created our problematic emotions. "Whoever has done an evil deed\ But covers it with a virtuous one\ Illuminates this world\ Like the moon freed from a cloud." (Dhammapada, vs. 173)

To recognize that life just is, thusness, and we must make (or accept) our own superior meaning, is perhaps a disturbing concept for many people. When you hear the preaching of the pusillanimous politicians pandering to their presumptive constituents about their religious convictions, you wonder how a serious adult could possibly accept and retain such nonsense beliefs. But of course most people do one way or another, they depend on fallacies of logic such as: "What other explanation could there be?" In fact they expect politicians to have religious convictions, atheists generally make unpopular candidates. These beliefs determine how we explain our reality as a duality, beyond just seeing our existence as a given.

---

[92] "Your mind turns toward bliss and one-pointedness in a way that is more delicate, refined, and stable. . . You gain a feeling of **equanimity** toward even the highest joy. It is just more material substance really. It is subtle, but it is still tying you to the hectic world of thought and the senses. You let it go and the joy fades away by itself." (Gunaratana, pg. 106)

"Being and non-being are notions created by you . . ."[93] Reality can only be—being, it is a kind of logical tautology. How do we make sense out of this? Think of infinity as about *being* only. This is another way to acknowledge *emptiness, because there is only being!* So this perspective is not easy to grasp, but when it is, it is just felt like the tidal flow (Sukha); much more subtle than the breaking and frantic waves (Piti). If Piti-jhana is the breaking waves of emotions, then we can learn to recognize the Sukha-jhana as the supra-mundane, the unseen, gentle but known tidal movement of our sub-conscious.

Close your eyes and follow the discussion included here coming from the Tibetan tradition, and use this opportunity as part of an objective self-evaluation. Choose a single object like the sky with no clouds for your focus initially. "Practicing like this 'one drip at a time' . . . We're actually resting the mind in its natural clarity . . ." We might see a soft light when our eyes are closed with our peripheral vision.[94] We look at

---

93   "Reality cannot be described in terms of being and non-being. Being and non-being are notions created by you, exactly like the notions of birth and death, coming and going. If your beloved one can no longer be seen, it does not mean that from being s/he has become non-being. If you realize this truth about your beloved, you will suffer much less, and if you realize this truth about yourself, you will transcend your fear of dying, of non-being." (Hanh, pg. 295)

94   "Objectless shinay meditation doesn't mean just letting your mind wander aimlessly among fantasies, memories, or daydreams. There's still some presence of mind [the connection to your Heart] that may be loosely described as a center of awareness . . . you're still aware, still present to what's happening in the here and now. When we meditate in this objectless state, we're actually resting the mind in its natural clarity, entirely indifferent to the passage of thoughts and emotions. This natural clarity—which is beyond any dualistic grasping of subject and object—is always present for us in the same way that space is always present [as a dim consciousness during dreams.] Objectless meditation is like accepting whatever clouds and mist might obscure the sky while recognizing that the sky itself remains unchanged even when it is obscured . . . [your] Buddha nature is always open and clear

and find our Heart's center, perhaps like feeling a warm glow in our abdomen. As passive as this approach to meditation seems, we recognize how equanimity relates to our lives, and it is what concentrates our focus so we can proceed to do Insight meditation centered on an object. From this Insight we gain direct knowledge that is a foundational element to Purification as we eliminate the craving and clinging in our lives. This focus involves discipline, another element of a well-conditioned mind, and is the key to changing the way we perceive sensory information; thus by extension (because we usually act on what we know, feel and see, etc.) to the way we act. This leads in a cycle like the thrust and pull of a pump and is comparable to alternating the steps on the Eight-fold Path of Mindfulness and Concentration.

There is an additional explanation that can help us recognize the distinction between the emotional states of Piti and Sukha and how these affect us. Using direct knowledge, knowing "what is"—"The wisdom method [Insight] we contemplate the assada and adinava of Piti."[95] In this case

---

even when thoughts and emotions obscure it. Though it may seem very ordinary, all the qualities of clarity, emptiness, and compassion are contained within that state . . . All you need to do is rest within the awareness of your mind . . . The most effective process is to rest the mind for very short periods many times a day. Otherwise, you run the risk of growing bored or becoming disappointed with your progress and eventually give up trying altogether . . . Practicing like this 'one drip at a time', you'll find yourself [in samadhi concentration] gradually becoming free of the mental and emotional limitations that are the source of fatigue, disappointment, anger, and despair, and discover within yourself an unlimited source of clarity, wisdom, diligence, peace, and compassion." (Mingyur, pp. 139-141)

[95] "Through the wisdom method we contemplate the assada and adinava of Piti. Asada is an element's attractive quality, its charm that deliciously tempts the Heart. Piti has an enchanting flavor [as we have already noticed.] Adinava is an element's unhealthy consequences [think of the 108 defilements]. The adinava of Piti is the fact that it excites and disturbs, that it drives away tranquility [Sukha] and is the

we are getting directly to the emotions that relate to craving, greed, envy, ambition and desires. This is what it means to develop and utilize fortitude and strength of character. Putting together the desires with the consequences is the best way to prevent further suffering, and we can burn off past suffering by exposing its roots and, as we have learned, often by eliminating just one determining factor. Just as when we bake bread, the chemistry changes, the dough rises and becomes a nourishing loaf, a thing of beauty.

As we move wholesale into our pure Hearts through the contact with the one infinity where our lives are inevitably in the center, we contemplate this natural state in a reflective manner as we glide into: "The [third] jhana is pure focus upon no-thing-ness."[96] Imagine this central point between two continuous lines extending to past and future infinities and this is how we perceive this literal "nothingness". So it is possible to see that this is the very opposite of any kind of ecstatic, energizing, tantric or other yogic excitement. We rely on our clarity and understanding of anatta (causes) for any information we need about the cosmos that surrounds us rather than the confusion and duplicity of the many religious scriptures or the perfidious words of pedantic politicians and preachers. Our words that necessarily come from our ordinary language have difficulty distinguishing between the subtle levels of jhana, but the emotion that causes throbbing tears seems to give a useful clue. Instead of observing the breath, we can observe

---

foe of vipassana. Once we realize this, piti dissolves [like turning on a light to expose a thief.] This is how to drive off Piti with the panna technique . . . At this point, the mind is able to regulate the feelings. It has developed the kind of mastery and self-control where the feelings no longer have the power to drag us this way or that." (Buddhadasa, 1988, pp. 65-67)

[96] "This next jhana [third] is often called the 'base of nothingness.' The infinite awareness of the previous jhana has no object. It is empty, vacant, and void. [We] turn our awareness toward this emptiness. The [third] jhana is pure focus upon no-thing-ness. Our awareness dwells on the absence of any object." (Gunaratana, pg. 108)

the slow, more subtle beat of our hearts or a faster beat during emotional excitement, and examine the analogy between these. "Emptiness" for Buddhists never means worthless or nonsense, but open to expressions of awe. Not having an absolute meaning given by a god, scripture or erstwhile prophet, for example, is no more difficult to accept than the familiar use of a simple pronoun (i.e. she or whom). This is neither a defect of Buddhism, nor a source of pain or suffering once we have experienced the Sukha-jhana of this third state. The intellectual battles of Existentialism become trivial and we recognize these as so many useless mind games.

Looking back over what we have studied we recognize that dealing with our emotions as one of the four foundations of meditation has huge ramifications for our lives. It is not just the frosting on the cake, but the emotional flavor and sweetness of the cake " . . . because of the great power and importance of the Vedana."[97] We at least know how to develop the mind's ability to be independent of feeling and to have control and awareness of the Vedana with our mindfulness in the same way we can move from Piti-jhana of the third state, to Sukha-jhana. As previously stated, emotions are the source of the tensions and human quarreling in society, and certainly many different emotional outbursts interfere with the normal progress of habitations of families. But once we develop in our practice "Then the mind glides into the third jhana, where a more refined state of happiness is dominant."[98]

---

[97] "It is clearly important that we take advantage of this ability to control the feelings for the rest of our lives. This tetrad [5-8] has been included in the practice of anapanasati because of the great power and importance of the Vedana." (Buddhadasa, 1988, pg. 68)

[98] ". . .When the mind loses interest in the first jhana and is ready to drop it completely, you don't have to make any volitional effort to move on to the second jhana. It just happens. It happens in the same sequential order for everyone [today as it was 2,500 years ago.] When the preparatory state is well established, what comes next will simply happen—naturally. That is the nature of Dhamma. . . After attaining the second jhana many times, you find it not giving you that same

Once we develop this capacity we become the peace makers in our family circles and beyond. We learn to recognize the Right Effort that it takes to make this Right View fruitful for a wholesome and rewarding meditation practice that changes our lives. This is no more challenging than tuning into public television for Nova or Discovery and enjoying the knowledge gained, rather than watching some sitcom and vicariously experiencing an imitation of life.

We have gained some serious purity based on our ability to critically *recognize* and then analyze the challenges in our lives. By this time we are ready to move forward, because along the way the behaviors we pattern in our lives match our facility with meditation. We cannot be engaging in serious violations of the Five Precepts, for example, and still expect to have this kind of flowering of our meditative skills. As previously suggested, I call this the **barter** that we have to consummate, to trade a well disciplined and virtuous life for the tranquility that we can achieve during meditation. I have not noticed the use of this terminology or wording in other commentaries, but the concept is there when we talk about gaining merit, and the macho slogan: "walking the walk". This is the journey of the Heart, and an effective way to gain direct knowledge, not unlike going back and forth in our walking meditation. "We can put the citta [Heart] into any state that is appropriate or desirable."[99] This is when we have a pliable and useful Heart to control every worthy aspect of our lives, and we are no longer creating suffering for our future. We will still find some suffering that is residual, i.e. growing old with its inevitable consequences, but we can work on that, one issue (or determinant) at a time.

---

joy and happiness born of concentration that you experienced at the beginning of the second jhana. Joy becomes stale. . . Then the mind glides into the third jhana, where a more refined state of happiness is dominant." (Gunaratana, pg. 148)

[99] "Once we fully know the various mental states and conditions, both positive and negative, then we can put the citta into any state that is appropriate or desirable." (Buddhadasa, 1988, pg. 74)

I like this image taught by a famous Yoga teacher, to which I alluded earlier, and this is as close as I wish to come to yoga exercise for now. "Resting like a pebble . . . You begin to find your own rest, your own peace."[100] This is a very useful metaphor, this leads to Right Thought (Intention) and I believe this is a skillful poetic image. We have achieved most of these gains by simply learning to observe and watch, as we studied in the last chapter by developing "bare awareness". "Health is the best possession,\ Contentment the greatest wealth;\ Trust is what makes the truest kin;\ Nibbana is the greatest happiness."[101] This all goes with peace of mind.

Following the Eight-fold Path to the cessation of suffering based on clear *recognition* is no simple task, and I know this because I keep learning more about it as I progress not only in developing this book, but in my own meditation practice. But curiously enough, it is a path that can be easily taught to children. In fact it is probably more difficult for many adults to *recognize* the benefits after they have developed all their preconceived ideas and the complications in their lives. "If you apply yourself to distraction\ And not to concentration,\ If you

---

[100] "The great Zen Buddhist Thich Nhat Hanh says . . . keep a half-smile on your face. Breathe slowly and deeply, following each breath, becoming one with each breath. Then let go of everything. Imagine yourself as a pebble that has been thrown into a river. The pebble sinks through the water effortlessly; detached from everything, it falls by the shortest distance possible, finally sinking to the bottom, the point of perfect rest. You are like a pebble that has let itself fall into the river, letting go of everything. At the center of your being is your breath. You don't need to know the length of time it takes to reach the point of complete rest on the bed of fine sand beneath the water. But when you feel yourself resting like a pebble that has settled [weightlessly] on the riverbed, that is the point when you begin to find your own rest, your own peace. In that peace you are no longer pushed or pulled by anything." (Forstater, pg. 83)

[101] "Savouring the taste of solitude\ And the taste of calm\ You become free of fear and free of evil,\ Savouring the taste of joy in the Dhamma." (Dhammapada, vs. 204, 205)

abandon the goal—clinging to what's dear—\ You'll envy the one who applies himself to the goal." (Dhammapada, vs. 209) So we all need to be ready to help others along the Path to reach their goals, rather than hinder them in any way from achieving peace.

It is not enough to just know that there is a path to the end of suffering—it is a gradual path of self-improvement that requires work, which is summarized in one word, nirodha, and is described by the details of the Eight-fold Path. We can't do it all at once, it would be a rather large pill, more like a bolas. It is the middle way between the two extremes of excessive self-indulgence (hedonism) and excessive self-mortification (asceticism); and it leads to the end of the cycle of rebirth (i.e. repeating bad habits) and ego gratification in this lifetime. This is a saving grace for our practical daily lives. No longer do we need to merely "wander on the wheel of becoming" in a frustrating cycle of depression or dependency. Once we *recognize* the end to craving, ignorance, delusions, and all the associated ill effects, these will disappear gradually from our Hearts. This is indeed the supra-mundane aspect of "recognition", a kind of alchemy for our characters.

That may seem like an optimistic vision of a brighter future as we progress along the path, and it is, but there is an element of realism, of having experienced direct knowledge, knowing that thousands of others have preceded us and succeeded. *Recognition* is also an intellectual achievement at this point, because certainly we will have a lot of good ideas but we won't be able to implement all of these as fast as we can dig them up. We can add patience to that list of attributes that goes along with mental conditioning, and when we make notes in our journals about how our lives are blooming, in a year or even less we will certainly see that we have made progress if we persist. (Add persistence to the list while we are at it.)

Chapter Nine

Encouraging the Heart

Key Words:

Encouragement, self-discipline, Practice, Mingyur, citta, psychology, mind development, Object, "origination", absorption, rapture, raga, dosa, moha, Full Moon, mental capacity, "simultaneous mind", attachment, Zen, liberation

Why Should I Meditate?

Meditation is studied and supported by correlating changes in the mind based on neuro-science and psychology. *Mind development* has a special meaning in meditation and these benefits are worthwhile motivating factors. "When the mind [Heart] is unsurpassed, [s/he] discerns that the mind [Heart] is unsurpassed." etc. (Satipatthana) We learn about the phenomena of "origination & passing away". For Insight meditation there is no substantial, self-existing self [no—atta] as the point of observation during meditation. We can accept the world of the Buddha (i.e. suchness, cause and effect), this is Taking Refuge in the Dharma (the triple-gem). Experiencing tranquility can be thought of as the moment of liberation, and we can share and protect this after the fact. We share encouragement with our Sangha when we grasp and protect wisdom. In meditation we gain "Liberation"—*empty of attachment,* not grasping or clinging, we feel Nirodha. It is a realistic goal of meditation to know our minds, then improve. Developing our Hearts to stabilize our lives as well as eliminate suffering may be the most beneficial gain from meditation.

When I first began to study meditation seriously, I thought one primary objective was to develop the mind in order to have more self-control, or self-discipline. This was based on a literal reading of some of the commentaries I encountered. However, that wasn't my interest because I have always been able to control myself; be the designated driver in a party group, for example. In fact I was rather overly disciplined at times, having succeeded as an officer in the Air Force until my retirement from the Reserves, I always had the discipline to be at the right place at the right time, and to avoid drugs, and didn't enjoy being around people who repeatedly failed at this. I was annoyed by people who were not punctual to a fault like I was, and they were often annoyed with me, so thus I didn't have very many friends. That latter part hasn't changed much, but I am much less judgmental now than in the past. In fact I make it a practice to find ways to compliment people, especially students, my wife and grandchildren, repeatedly and often, irrespective of their habits. This simply reduces their and my suffering. But I still regard myself as a loner, perhaps an introvert, even withdrawn, and not upset at spending 95% of my life alone, perhaps that helps me be a better student of Dharma.

Of course following a skillful study of the Dharma is not about me, is it? Nor anyone else in particular, except it is about each of us collectively. In fact if the student of Dharma from the very beginning doesn't relate the teachings and knowledge s/he gains beyond himself/herself as s/he proceeds, and becomes caught up in generalizations, theory building, taxonomies of knowledge, and such; then a vital part of the Practice will be missing. We gain some self-awakening as an intermediate step to obtaining full-awakening.

If we think that Buddhism is just a good idea, we won't have these experiences in meditation.

When I began studying I noticed that each of the secondary texts had bits and pieces of information, none were complete or comprehensive. Some of the most important teachings, such as "purification", and the concept of Nirodha, are very difficult to discover, although now that I know where to look the puzzle is solved. But there are still some puzzles in my mind, not as many as at first, but I have questions and I am only gradually finding the answers as I continue to study. I try to make sure that I am studying as much as I meditate, not that it really matters to balance such things, but I have this idea as a theory about Practice.

I used to force myself to go to church on Sundays (Unitarian) just because I enjoyed so much not going, I was concerned about my tendency to become somewhat of a hermit. This was another act of self-discipline because although I usually enjoyed having gone, seldom did I enjoy the prospect of moving in the direction of going. I helped develop a Buddhist study group for the very purpose of being more social, especially more involved with like-minded people in a rather loosely formed Sangha. (Those are the people who helped me try out the *Buddhist Sutras: Lesson Book.*) I received a lot of positive encouragement and feedback, and felt welcome notwithstanding my own social reticence. "The one who's endowed with good character and insight,\ Who's firm in the Dhamma, a truth-speaker,\ Who does his own work—Folk will hold him dear." (Dhammapada, vs. 217) This is the promise available to everyone who joins a compassionate Sangha.

So if I didn't need to meditate to develop self-discipline, what other possible reasons are there, I wondered? First we take guidance and encouragement from the Buddha as we work to gain a full-awakening relating to the kind of suffering we experience. "Vision arose, insight arose, discernment arose, knowledge arose, illumination arose within me with regard to things never heard before: 'This noble truth of [suffering] *stress is to be* comprehended'." (Appendix II) Now I would answer that the primary reason is to eliminate suffering from my life, and of course that involves realizing that suffering "is to be comprehended," in this way we are meant to be happier. Much of this we have to learn from other people, watching drama, reading classic novels and other socialization and enculturation. As general as this concept is, my "awakening" has not resulted in my being more of a social animal.

The monk and author Rinpoche Yongey Mingyur from the Tibetan tradition, is no doubt a lot more disciplined and social than I am. He offers a lot of good techniques that are specific, useful, and even pragmatic. In his popular book, *The Joy of Living*, he discussed the psychological science that has been correlated to support the usefulness of meditation. I took this as encouragement and this kept me going and strengthened my interest because I was one of those also who, when first confronted with Buddhism, thought that I wasn't really a victim of suffering. I think now it was the case of not seeing the forest because I was and had been seriously bogged down among the trees of suffering for all sorts of reasons. It takes a while to get a perspective, to collect a full-awakening, to understand enough to feel how important it is to practice.

Other people in my study group have expressed this, initially what amounts to an illusion of not suffering. Fortunately for them it has taken only a few weeks of study to begin to see the diverse kinds of suffering in their lives, for me working alone, it took somewhat longer. Then I came across the teaching of the Venerable Acayiya Maha Boowa Nanasampanno, a "forest monk" of northeastern Thailand. He among others teaches that meditation is largely about developing the Heart—as a functioning allegory—that is closely associated with character, compassion, empathy, spirituality and other desirable attributes. I guess it was an insight for me, to his credit, to accept his encouraging teachings as being most significant for my meditation practice. His entire collection of lectures and books is available free for downloading off the internet. No kidding! What seems like the most important teaching of all is available entirely free (aside from the obvious cost of ink and paper if printed.)

Another practice that I have questioned is that regarding the importance of the Lunar Cycle, and the tradition of observing celebrations and rituals on the occurrence of Full Moon. Most Buddhists feel a special religious significance to the days of the Full Moon, in part because it is thought that the most important events in the life of The Buddha occurred on that day. According to tradition, The Buddha was born during Full Moon, his "renunciation", his Enlightenment, the delivery of the first sermon, the passing away and other important events during his life occurred on Full Moon days. This "hagiography" developed in the oral tradition, and it is probably not to be taken as historical fact. This can be thought of as the work of biographers and authors perceived to be uncritical or "reverential" to The Buddha's life tradition. Thus, most active Buddhists make a special effort to develop their spiritual practice on these days, including fasting, praying and group Sangha meditation retreats. Many people find this kind of ritual encouraging and even enjoyable.

Of course these observances preceded the development of Buddha's teachings; in Hindu and yoga practice there are many traditions relating religious activity to the cycles of Moon. It may be the case that there are traditions associated with Moon in every culture around the world, it is an obvious and approachable poetic image for everyone.[102] Buddhism is just one more tradition that enjoys special teachings that

---

[102] "Ancient belief in India says that the moon is the controller of the water, and circulating through the universe, sustaining all living creatures, is the counterpart on earth of the liquor heaven, 'amrta' the drink of the gods. Dew and rain become vegetable sap, sap becomes the milk of cow, and the milk is then converted into blood. Amrta water, sap, milk and blood, represent but different states of the one elixir. The vessel or cup of this immortal fluid is the moon." (Thera)

incorporate the activity and cycles of Moon into religious traditions.[103]

Many of these traditions have found their way into and are preserved in our ordinary Western culture. The word 'lunatic' is obviously derived from the word 'lunar' and suggests a connection between sanity and cycles of Moon. Low-tides and high-tides are a direct result of the overpowering influence of Moon, and by extension many traditions infer that analogous changes can occur in human bodies, as well as in animals and plants. There is a lot of archeological evidence that agriculturalists as well astrologers and mystics have associated optimum planting and cultivation timing with Full Moon cycles. How much of this would stand up to scientific investigations is questionable, but there is a certain romantic attraction to ordering one's life to these cycles, especially if other choices are equal or arbitrary. Even if we don't believe that there is any occult or esoteric significance, and even if we think that Moon in fact stimulates changes in our bodies, modifying metabolism, electrical charges, pH of fluids and blood, so what? All this tradition seems innocent enough and a good excuse to reorient our lives, look at the calendar for ritual days and make our practice more effective.

---

[103] Vesak or Visakah Puja ("Buddha Day") Traditionally, Buddha's Birthday is known as Vesak or Visakah Puja (Buddha's Birthday Celebrations). Vesak is the major Buddhist festival of the year as it celebrates the birth, enlightenment and death of the Buddha on the one day, the first full moon day in May, except in a leap year when the festival is held in June. This celebration is called Vesak, the name of the month in the Indian calendar.

Asalha Puja Day ("Dhamma Day") means to pay homage to the Buddha on the full moon day of the 8th lunar month (approximately July). It commemorates the Buddha's first teaching: the turning of the wheel of the Dhamma (Dhammacakkappavattana Sutta) to the five ascetics at the Deer Park (Sarnath) near Benares city, India. Where Kondanna, the senior ascetic attained the first level of enlightenment (the Sotapanna level of mind purity). http://www.buddhanet.net/festival.htm

I have subsequently discovered a few more reasons to meditate and to work on *mind (citta) development*, because this term has taken on a whole new meaning than what I originally imagined. When I discuss meditation with fellow practitioners now, I relish the idea of suggesting and encouraging these people to see this larger picture, and I pass along this and other worthwhile motivating factors.

The collections of reasons for meditation at the beginning of each chapter are one example of how we can take a simple act of recognizing and extend that into a full-awareness of the intended teachings, and hopefully extend that into self-awakening and then eventually to full-awakening. Collecting and organizing are higher order skills (than just recognizing or remembering) involving a more rigorous and challenging level of cognitive demand, but also more rewarding. As I read and study these in retrospect, what seemed a useful idea at the time, now seems like an inspired achievement.

However, since this study has in every step up to now been concerned in one way or another with the mind, it seems redundant to now focus again and strictly on the mind as one of the Four Foundations of Meditation, indeed as the very object for meditation, but that is where both teachings, Anapanasati and Satipatthana, take us. My understanding has evolved the more I use and contemplate these guided meditations, and this suggests that I will continue to benefit from *activity* along with intellectual inquiry, and this by itself is a very encouraging discovery. To the extent that this translation of *citta* as mind is strictly correct, this can be seen as a skillful direction, but to the extent that it can also be interpreted more aesthetically as **Heart**, then there is a good deal more that can be hoped for and taken from the Dharma teachings relating to "citta" development—Heart development. And that is precisely the interpretation I would like to describe and share by emphasizing this different translation.

In this next exercise the first step is a pre-test: "List as many characteristics or aspects of your mind that you have experienced or know about?" Do this on a separate sheet of paper (no peeking) before you turn the page. I repeat here and supplement the steps that are taught in the Satipatthana meditation, beginning with the searching question: "How does a monk remain focused on the mind?"[104] It is this passionate and compassionate side of our minds that makes up a truly important aspect of what we come to know as Heart. We are being told by this ancient tradition to look "wholeheartedly" beyond the simple thinking function and see the emotive and passionate side of our minds.

Perhaps this very first question of Satipatthana was signaling; otherwise why ask the question if it is just another sequence of mindfulness training. There was more which ought to be taken into consideration, i.e. the Heart, than what we understand as simply mind, as our basic thinking and memory functions. Continuing:

"When the mind [Heart] is without passion, he discerns that the mind [Heart] is without passion.
When the mind [Heart] has aversion, he discerns that the mind [Heart] has aversion.
When the mind [Heart] is without aversion, he discerns that the mind [Heart] is without aversion.
When the mind [Heart] has delusion, he discerns that the mind [Heart] has delusion.
When the mind [Heart] is without delusion, he discerns that the mind [Heart] is without delusion.
When the mind [Heart] is constricted, he discerns that the mind [Heart] is constricted.
When the mind [Heart] is scattered, he discerns that the mind [Heart] is scattered.
When the mind [Heart] is enlarged, he discerns that the mind [Heart] is enlarged.
When the mind [Heart] is not enlarged, he discerns that the mind [Heart] is not enlarged.

---

[104] "And how does a monk remain focused on the mind [think of this as Heart] in & of itself? There is the case where a monk, when the mind [Heart] has passion, discerns that the mind [Heart] has passion." (Satipatthana)

137

When the mind [Heart] is surpassed, he discerns that the mind [Heart] is surpassed.

When the mind [Heart] is unsurpassed, he discerns that the mind [Heart] is unsurpassed.

When the mind [Heart] is concentrated, he discerns that the mind [Heart] is concentrated.

When the mind [Heart] is not concentrated, he discerns that the mind [Heart] is not concentrated.

When the mind [Heart] is released, he discerns that the mind [Heart] is released. [unbinding?]

When the mind [Heart] is not released, he discerns that the mind [Heart] is not released. [The discussion of unbinding will come later.]

In this way he remains focused internally on the mind [Heart] in & of itself, or externally on the mind [Heart] in & of itself, or both internally & externally on the mind [Heart] in & of itself.

Or on the phenomenon of passing away [elimination of craving and attachments] with regard to the mind [Heart,] or on the phenomenon of origination & passing away with regard to the mind [Heart.]

Or his mindfulness that 'There is a mind [Heart]' is maintained to the extent of knowledge & remembrance. And he remains independent, unsustained by (not clinging to) anything in the world. [This refers to the previous discussion of recognition and direct knowledge.]

This is how a monk remains focused on the mind [Heart] in & of itself." (Satipatthana)

Obviously we are using our mental capacity and activity to follow these instructions, but the directions and questioning is being posed because there is more to see, and it only makes sense that the Buddha would have intended that something other than the instrument being used was that which was under consideration; the Heart is the obvious candidate. My understanding of what goes into making the Heart in the best Buddhist interpretation consists of parts of our "feeling (compassion), memory, thought and consciousness." (Boowa)

Certainly these are elements of the mind; in fact it makes me wonder, what else is there?

Are these terms synonymous? Of course this is a rather broad definition of the Heart too, not really a definition just an indication. This activity of analysis points out the difference between "recognizing" and "full-awakening". In our Western culture we have a vague, romantic idea of what our differentiated Hearts are: as a unique functioning part of our minds. And clearly this allegory has wide popularity and general, understandable significance in ordinary usage in Western culture, i.e. during Valentine's Day. It is distinguishable from what we know broadly to be our minds in all those Freudian and Jungian ways, and in the simple, ordinary way that if you say, someone has a kind-Heart, others will likely understand.

I believe that analyzing and interpreting this passage of the sutta in this way makes it a more meaningful exercise, not the only possible exercise (another is related to the pretest—how many aspects did you list?). And when we recall the definition of the Heart, apply it also to Tibetan teachings, we notice a differentiation as well between the mind and "the term simultaneous mind . . ."[105] Again, this recognition happens in our mind by necessity, but the use of the terminology *"simultaneous mind"*, is a way to distinguish and explain the

---

[105] "Understanding the nature of the mind in Mahamudra is conveyed by the term simultaneous mind [Heart.] The term signifies that the mind's awareness and its manifest events literally 'arise together' in each moment of experience. Another way to say this is that the mind's awareness and the events of ordinary consciousness form an inseparable pair [like the image in a mirror, I believe this is an attempt to describe the Heart] and that the perception of duality is erroneous. Direct realization of the mind's non-duality [no Soul] is an essential prerequisite to awakening the mind . . . The observational perspective during Mahamudra meditation is not the ordinary sense of self. Ordinary special insight meditation on emptiness helps determine that there is no substantial, self-existing self [anatta] that can serve as the point of observation during meditation [contrary to what is taught in yoga.]" (Brown, pp. 13-14)

existence of the Heart. When seen in this way with the words rearranged, it is hopefully easier to get to this understanding, even though I have never heard any questions about this concept. Perhaps I can just leave any further justification and analysis for the reader to parse out of the text as part of their practice.

Thus when we review the first four steps of Anapanasati we see that the work we are engaged in deliberately or incidentally, is to encourage each other and ourselves to develop and then utilize our Hearts as a vessel to hold all the attributes we endeavor to develop in the course of practicing the Buddhist "technology". We test it and try it out by using our breathing as a background activity or tool, then move on to developing piti, sukha, tranquility, equanimity, etc., as enlargements of our Hearts. "We should build up the so-called 'uggaha-nimitta' or conceptualized image . . ."[106] I explain this concept of the Heart as an allegory, more than a metaphor or simile. This is like orchestrating and arranging, then explaining the parts and movements of a symphony, then playing it; and the total work is the development of the Heart as a conceptual part of our minds. This is not unlike growing and nurturing vegetables or flowering plants, as our recognition expands into full-awakening. We will find that just as when we attend a movie with a catchy tune and we leave singing it to ourselves, the work we do as described to develop our Hearts will create this kind of harmonious, melodic, development of our characters. We don't just see and hear the content,

---

[106] "Actually there are four stages altogether: 1) to follow or to run after (the breathing) 2) and to observe, 3) to build a 'nimitta' [object or image] 4) and finally to contemplate on the absorption (Jhana). . . after having followed and observed the breathing, we should build up the so-called 'uggaha-nimitta' or conceptualized image, and then contemplate and concentrate on the 'Jhana' or absorption. 'Vitakka' (or thought [recognition] conception), 'vicara' (or discursive [self-awakening] thinking), 'piti' (or joy) and 'sukha' (or happiness) and 'ekaggata' (mental concentration that reaches the top point) will be evolved." (Buddhadasa, 2008, pp. 88-89)

but we absorb an essential emotional aspect of the movie. This delightful attitude is useful and positive for our lives; a characteristic we can carry with us wherever we go and it effects whatever we do.

We use our breathing as a ritual to condition our emotions, eliminate clinging, craving—attachments . . . There is no "atta" that bestows a sacred obligation, we are free (even obligated) to explore and develop our inspired choices.

We can encourage others, we can "bring the horse to water", but we can't make our friends drink the water, nor can we prepare the horse to be ready, we can only prepare ourselves and try to understand the importance of drinking the water on a regular basis. "You learn how to direct and sustain your attention . . . these skills [are the] 'factors of absorption'."[107] We can learn the mechanics of meditation, but miss or dismiss the essence, which is to eliminate and prevent suffering, and the development of our Hearts. As we develop and expand this capability in ourselves and share it, we answer the riddle of how do we help other people become happy. We have to prepare for an enlightened level of understanding by developing compassion and *purification* in our lives, beyond

---

[107] "When concentration and mindfulness are combined, the power of attention is transformed into a spotlight that illuminates a particular experience in the same way that a theater spotlight holds steady on a single actor until it's time to focus the audience's attention elsewhere. You learn how to direct and sustain your attention on a single experience rather than letting the mind jump from one thought or feeling to another as it usually does. In Pali, the ability to direct attention is called vitakka [recognition,] and the ability to sustain it is called vicara [full-awakening.] The Buddha referred to these skills as 'factors of absorption'." (McLeod (Moffitt), pg. 42) (compare to #106)

the beginning level of recognition. We have to sincerely accept that the world is as taught by the Buddha (i.e. suchness, cause and effect, the Law of Karma); this is Taking Refuge in the Dharma (the triple-gem) with the Heart, not just with our minds. If we just believe or think that Buddhism is a good idea, we probably won't realize the most significant, life changing experiences. But when all these conditions are met, this is how we can remain focused on the Heart, to paraphrase and interpret the Satipatthana Sutta.

By way of further explanation of possible stages of meditation, consider the next and we can say highest level of absorption. "The fourth jhana penetrates the five aggregates . . . at a nearly subatomic level."[108] Are we splitting hairs in the sense that we are looking for wisdom and meaning when the important thing is just to have the experience; or perhaps we are here just for a moment inside the Heart, not unlike being in a half-dream state? Like being conscious between sleeping and waking? To succeed at this level we are using our imaging and visualization skills, not our creative or inventive skills. We are working at the level of non-fiction, not fiction, not just making it up as we go.

Clearly our minds are rather complex activity centers made up of only barely differentiable elements, these elements have different sources or regions physically in the brain, and likewise these are functionally different and temporally separate. The mind can operate on more than one level at a time, but our mindfulness or attentiveness can operate only on two levels, not three or five at once. When we move beyond Piti-jhana at this state "of 'floating' joy literally lifting the body . . . raising it above the ground" (Gunaratana) and

---

[108] "In the fourth jhana, nonverbal, non-conceptual realization begins to take place on a regular basis. . . Endowed with this powerful concentration, the fourth jhana penetrates the five aggregates and sees their impermanence, unsatisfactoriness, and selflessness at a nearly subatomic level. This is not inferential or theoretical knowledge. It is nonverbal, non-conceptual, and experiential, a direct seeing of the intrinsic nature of the aggregates." (Gunaratana, pp. 153-154)

try to experience Sukha-jhana at this fourth state we cannot. It is a state of tranquility, sometimes called rapture, or a level of absorption that just comes on its own, it is defeated by our effort to try, because that is functionally doing more than two mental tasks at once, so the effort is ineffectual. You can't will it into happening at the same time as you are mindful of its existence because it relates to the single pointed samadhi meditation associated with Right Concentration. You probably don't really learn anything there either (except to deepen your devotion or motivation), since it is not a state where there is any significant mental or intellectual insight activity, since it is at "nearly a subatomic level", it is a visceral feeling, almost a notion but yet we can have continuous vision, as we will discuss in chapter sixteen. This explanation of the limits of our minds functioning just came as I was rewriting and editing this text. I had not understood it this way before, although I had accepted it as being useful. This is an example of how we learn by doing, by chewing over and examining the concepts, such as "Heart" closely and repeatedly.

If there were any doubts in one's mind about the efficacy of Buddhism or ritual practice, perhaps this is where these would be erased once and for all, at least in retrospect. Since there is no serious Insight or contemplation going on because there is no discursive activity of the intellectual apparatus of the mind, gains are made at other levels. It is a state of peacefulness beyond mention (although ironically I am trying to describe it), a moment to recharge, it enhances conviction and develops our Hearts, so as much as it might be desirable to explain it or hear more details about it, it is just a happening, not a pedagogical event that can easily be described, only felt, as far as I can see. Perhaps coveting this kind of mental high was what encouraged the Beat Generation to use LSD or Marijuana, etc., to create a synthetic Jhana [Zen.] But I cannot describe that nor their intentions from first-hand knowledge. My young life was and has remained too conservative, mocked by self-discipline and drug free, so maybe I am too naïve to discuss this and I have been deprived; a philistine of the world and wonder of drug use. But if that is the worst complaint that can be leveled at me personally, I will take it.

I can imagine this state, however, like using some kind of CAD computer program to move around and change the perspective of 3D objects in a room. So take this idea as an example because we are well equipped to condition the mind with our emotions, and this is a skill that will have huge implications for our lives. "What is the condition of the mind now? Analytical? Challenging? Questioning? Peaceful? Content?"[109] We observe the Heart at the same time, in the very moment of its existence as we feel peace generated by our mindfulness. This is the purpose of step nine, and we have had a glimpse of what our Heart is like with compassion and selflessness at its core, so we might know what to expect. When we are with others who we need to impress, our presentation is so much about managing our image and emotions; when we are alone, what is the point of expressing an emotion; it is enough to understand and watch these?[110] Nothing much about human nature in this regard has changed in 2,500 years.

In each case so far, in the First and Fifth and now the Ninth step of Anapanasati, the purpose is to examine the status and characteristics of each pertinent element of the Four Foundations of Meditation. (The same function will occur in the Thirteenth.) It is more of a review than an original activity

---

[109] "Our study of the third tetrad of anapanasati [which] is concerned with the citta, the mind-Heart, and is known as cittanupassana (contemplation of citta) . . . Many different states of mind have arisen since the beginning of our practice, even in this short time. We must observe the state of the mind at each step. What arises in the citta? [Again, think of this word as synonymous with Heart.] What is the condition of the mind now? Analytical? Challenging? Questioning? Peaceful? Content? What are the mind's characteristics at this moment?" (Buddhadasa)

[110] "Others' faults are easy to see,\ While your own are hard to see.\ The faults of others\You winnow like chaff;\ You hide your own\ As a cunning gambler hides a bad throw." (Dhammapada, vs. 252)

to begin our study of the mind by ". . . experiencing the different states of mind".[111] There is nothing here about self-control or discipline, which becomes an assumption albeit an important one for some people. And we learn how this contributes to the development and enlargement of our Hearts to full-awakening, and creates our most intimate connection to this active and compassionate Heart. Furthermore, encouraging and expanding the discussion of each of these aspects of our practice takes us to another level of sophistication and toward the development of wisdom.

Recall how we might experience ". . . 'floating' joy literally lifting the body . . . raising it above the ground." This can be thought of as the moment of liberation that we can share after the fact, as an experience we use as encouragement for those with whom we study when we grasp wisdom and protect it. This experienced author suggests: "This is where the factors of enlightenment you have been cultivating all come together."[112] This is an explanation by effect rather than by the

---

[111] "Whenever the mind sees something clinging to it [an ambition or desire], [we can] release that object [by focusing on it and applying liberating breathing.] Here are the four steps [of meditation] that deal with the mind: 9) experiencing the different states of mind, next 10) gladdening the mind, then 11) concentrating the mind and 12) liberating the mind. Through them we successfully complete our study of the mind." (Buddhadasa, 1988, pg. 82)

[112] "A different sort of equanimity develops in the fourth jhana, where consciousness is unified by concentration. In the fourth jhana and beyond, sensory impressions do not arise at all. Your equanimity is not based on any of the six senses. It arises based purely on concentration or one-pointedness of mind, along with mindfulness. There is no room for sensory experience and thus equanimity is smooth and continuous. . . The perfection of equanimity allows all the other factors to unite. This is where the factors of enlightenment you have been cultivating all come together. All the wholesome things you have been doing in your daily life—little by little, here and there—consolidate and produce results in the fourth jhana [as with making merit.] When the fourth jhana is attained, its equanimity is based on this unity of

---

145

details of experience. It takes a certain poetic interpretation to understand this and equate it with the earlier comments of Buddhadasa Bikkhu and Brown as quoted above. But that is another one of those reasons to meditate, to be inside the poem rather than being strictly speaking the author or commentator. Indeed this encourages as well as explains precisely what it is like for a Buddhist to live inside a poem.

Going back to the guarding point (we haven't forgotten about that) after this experience we can contemplate aspects of Dharma with a refined Heart, and apply this to our lives. Imagine the complications that have occurred in your life from craving, lust or from intense desire for owning a home, for example? Those too young for this will have to use other "raga" (intense desires), or other attachments for contemplation "If there is lust, then thoroughly contemplate its presence to distinguish what kind of lust it is . . ."[113] and study that.

We have all been angry or afraid at one time or another. "When the mind is oppressed, irritated, offended, or resentful, it is called dosa."[114] These details are often associated with the experience of physiological depression. I am not a trained

---

mind. . . because your senses are not responding to sensory stimuli." (Gunaratana, pg. 160)

[113] "There are many different characteristics of the mind to contemplate . . . whether the mind has lust (raga) or is free of lust -- sexual, or of money, jewelry, gold, food, housing, and possessions is also called raga . . . lust for love [from others . . .] If there is lust, then thoroughly contemplate its presence to distinguish what kind of lust it is . . . If there is no lust, then contemplate its absence. Breathe in and breathe out while experiencing the actual state of mind in this moment [finding the purity of your Heart.]" (Buddhadasa)

[114] "The next characteristic of mind to contemplate is dosa (anger, hatred, aversion) . . . Any dislike in the mind is dosa; it can even arise from within, without any external object [self-loathing or lack of self-esteem . . .] When the mind is oppressed, irritated, offended, or resentful, it is called dosa. If the citta is free of anger and hatred, then know that state. This is the second characteristic to observe." (Buddhadasa)

psychologist (although I did study educational psychology before and during my preparation to be a teacher) so what I know about depression is mostly hearsay or academic, secondhand fortunately. Whether meditation can mitigate the symptoms of clinical depression or not depends on the person's commitment to practice and if they are amenable to accepting encouragement, otherwise a solo practice will not likely be very curative. Most people who experience serious depression will need to seek professional medical help.

Which of the temptations we experience do we dismiss as being perfectly natural or just part of being human? "The third characteristic to observe is moha (delusion and confusion) . . . a false hope. . . contemplate this state of mind while noticing breathing in . . . out."[115] This is how we go back to work in step Nine, using the momentary experience of Jhana as our tool kit, like a knight with new shining armor. Yet we can get caught up in our ignorance and delusions, so we need to be open and discuss the details of our practice with others in order to avoid the problems associated with moha.

Recapping: A feeling of wanting, grasping is a sense of *raga.*[116]

Dosa does not like, does not want, it is negative, pushing away.

Moha is ignorant; it does not know what is wrong and right, good and evil, running in circles. (If you can recall the Five Hindrances, then review each and notice to what stage of arising or eliminating of each you have obtained.)

---

[115] "The third characteristic to observe is moha (delusion and confusion). Moha is feeling infatuated with something because of not knowing that object as it really is [as with a new acquaintance, a false hope.] Doubt, hope, delusion, expectation—we cannot avoid dwelling on it. When one kind of thought or another ferments in the mind, it is called moha . . . If citta is empty of delusion, then contemplate its absence. Always contemplate this state of mind while noticing breathing in and breathing out." (Buddhadasa)

[116] "There is no fire like passion,\ No grip like hate,\ No net like delusion,\ No river like craving." (Dhammapada, vs. 251)

Considering these categories and stages of thinking is an active and useful activity for meditation, as is the following: to contemplate whether our minds are easily distracted, and whether we have a superior or common mind. "We need to know whether the mind is distracted or undistracted . . . Contemplate this pair [superior or common citta]."[117] Listening to peaceful music or sounds like that of the temple gong, and doing walking meditation to circumnavigate the temple three times (clockwise), can prepare the mind to be undistracted prior to meditation. Can the higher, superior citta be thought of as a description of the enlightened Heart? Or is it about being compassionate and generous with alms and dana to our Sangha? This kind of self-knowledge is useful in order to develop a plan for future meditation.

These instructions are too general (to have a superior mind) and need to be fleshed out with personal details, one event and consideration at a time. This is where the list of defilements comes in handy, when we review these one at a time we can follow that list as an agenda, and see how the various possible states of mind influence each detail of the defilements. Further consideration becomes more subtle and difficult to discern for me, perhaps it is like the different state of mind resulting from hearing and appreciating jazz compared to hard rock music. "Another pair of states to consider is whether or not this mind is supreme and unsurpassed . . . where there is nothing better?" Or are there finer things yet to come?[118]

---

[117] "Next, we need to know whether the mind is distracted or undistracted . . . We contemplate the mind's character while breathing in and breathing out. We practice in order to know all types of citta . . . Is the mind sharper than usual, more satisfying than usual, higher than usual? If so, contemplate it. If not, it is a common state of mind. Contemplate this pair [superior or common citta] while breathing in and breathing out." (Buddhadasa)

[118] "Another pair of states to consider is whether or not this mind is supreme and unsurpassed . . . where there is nothing better? If there is this highest mind, contemplate it clearly in order to understand it. Breathe in and breathe out with this kind of awareness." (Buddhadasa)

Can we do the puzzles in the newspaper? Or is that on a different level? Have we achieved final satisfaction about an understanding of "non-returning", like the perspective of an Arahat? That superior mind exists in each of us, but possibly we have not come to accept it or to utilize it consistently.

I have taken several of those non-judgmental, multi-scalar personality tests over the years. I am usually rated high in analytical skills and somewhat lower in empathy and artistic interests. These tests show how likely we are to exhibit problem solving skills, but don't measure any parameter regarding our abilities to benefit from meditation that I know about. I suspect I should cultivate more empathy, however, just how to go about that is not entirely clear. Developing more self-awakening may be a step toward developing empathy, which is related to expanding my Heart as well—in a step-wise progression?

We can encourage each other in our Sangha to develop these talents, and this is the skillful activity of making a social connection with our Heart—truly a blessing to be hoped for. It is accepted in our Western culture to call this kind of camaraderie a function of our "Hearts", just as we might fall in love using our Hearts. Or, are we confounded or bemused by existential angst or befuddled by other questions common to Western Philosophy? We can examine our status during this step; just as we can know if " . . . the mind is concentrated. Is it or is it not in samadhi?"[119] Can you easily focus on one object for a minute or two? That's enough for now. We use counting to ten breath cycles in Zen, but when we can count to 100's, are we that much more prepared? Or is settling into 10 breaths using "Mu" or "Bud—dho" enough?

We finally come to the direct consideration of nirodha, the goal of this book. To what extent is our mind liberated? Are we " . . . *empty of attachment,* not grasping or clinging to

---

[119] "The next pair is whether or not the mind is concentrated. Is it or is it not in samadhi? . . .Know whether the mind is concentrated or not while breathing in and breathing out." (Buddhadasa)

anything, or if it is not yet liberated."[120] When we can know that and be honest with ourselves in meditation, there is nothing to lose. Are we preoccupied with the ups and downs of the stock market, and how this influences our IRA retirement funds? and how can we pay for the new remodeling we want to apply to our house, etc.? What about buying a new or different car? Can we put these cares aside completely for the period of our meditation?[121]

This step nine of Anapanasati explains an important purpose of meditation; to know our minds and the full awareness of the suffering we experience (no self-deceit). This gives us a lot to think about and to share, not the least of which is to have a solid understanding of the benefits and purposes of meditation. How much of that can we obtain on our own, and to what extent do we need to meet with other people to encourage and be encouraged. A little success will give us encouragement and incentive to do more and practice more often, but don't expect too many gains at once, measure progress in terms of months and years rather than in units of days or sittings. Perhaps that is the significance of Full Moon and lunar cycles, periods in the year during which we

---

[120] "The last pair is to see if the mind has been liberated, if it is empty of attachment, not grasping or clinging to anything, or if it is not yet liberated and still clinging to something. Does the mind have attachment or not? . . .Right now, is there anything arresting the mind or is it free? Whatever the case, know it clearly. Breathe in and out with this awareness. . . Make it as distinct as possible . . . By practicing like this, we learn to know ourselves and the kinds of thoughts that are typical for us . . . Our primary aim, however, is to know our mind as completely as possible [and listen to our Hearts.]" (Buddhadasa, 1988, pp. 70-74)

[121] "Not through precepts and observances alone,\ Nor yet by much learning,\ Or attainment of concentration,\ Or dwelling in seclusion,\ Do I reach the happiness of freedom from desire\ Not experienced by worldly folk;\ Nor has a monk attained confidence\ If he has not achieved the destruction of the defilements." (Dhammapada, vs. 271-2)

can expect to make noticeable, albeit modest progress. This discussion introduces us intimately to the development of our Hearts as another purpose of meditation—to control and stabilize our lives, to the importance of full-awakening along with identifying and eliminating suffering, of course.

Chapter Ten

Encouraging and Anatta

Key words:

Atheist, devas and bramae, mystery, Rational Buddhism, Anatta, abhinna (transcendent knowledge), beliefs v. knowledge, gladdening the mind, defilement (kilesa), extinguish dukkha.

Why Should I Meditate?

Carrying on extended and lucid conversations with ourselves in meditation is a skillful method. We can thoroughly examine the causes of existence; see these as explainable, beautiful, like a symphony. During meditation we can join humanity in reverence to our shared causes of existence, beyond natural selection and propagation of species and feel unity. We can find meaning (as a goal) based on the associations we make with other people in and out of our Sangha. By Taking Refuge in the Sangha, we celebrate one third of Buddhism and Meditation. Meditating—compared to praying—stems from entirely different motivation, internal rather than external to a god or saint, and involves many other considerations. During meditation we can expect to gain inspiration? We are born with the capacity and talent to meditate, we are endowed (by natural causes) with this functional ability as part of our Buddha nature. This is the threshold point, to begin to work skillfully with our minds, and if we are deliberately in control of our thinking, then go for it, let's use it. There are two kinds of joyfulness: defiled joyfulness as with piti, and joyfulness free of defilement (kilesa)—similar to sukha after meditation training. During meditation we are able to delight and gladden the citta (Heart) using skillful techniques. Giving encouragement before and after group meditation is contagious and will come back in positive ways.

I have come to this concept of Anatta naturally, being of a rather materialistic orientation of mind. I am an atheist and have been for some forty-five years, and comfortable with that. So accepting the Buddhist concept (this understanding has come more slowly) of "no-soul" was a natural idea for me, in fact it is a necessary condition of my acceptance of the religion of Buddhism. I know of people who cling to their Western religious belief in an anthropomorphic god/creator who have a difficult time with this aspect of Buddhism. But there are Buddhist traditions which teach and use deities as integral to their Dharma as well. The ancient teachings have become (or were initially) sufficiently ambiguous to be used to inspire both atheists and disciples of gods. So people who don't think the way I do can find solace in these traditions, and I don't try to change anyone's beliefs.

I notice that hard case deists interested in Buddhist concepts seem to gravitate toward some Hindu sect, and there are many more Westerners involved in "secular" yoga (exercises) than in Buddhism. Perhaps more than 90% of the US population is living with one of the ancient belief systems that espouses or rather depends on the existence of a god/creator figure. These can be regarded as primitive belief systems, because in each case they rely on miracles or teachings that defy scientific discoveries and methods to create a rationale for their uniqueness. Any religion that perpetuates the killing of a human/god (human sacrifice) as a redeemer or a savior, and then reenacts that and celebrates a ritual of drinking blood (cannibalism) should be suspect and regarded as a primitive religion unworthy of serious consideration. Such a religion does not likely have as its foundation the truths of human nature.

But of course one function of a religion is to fill the life of the adherent with explanations for those phenomena of nature that otherwise go unexplained by any simple, natural explanation (i.e. the causes and teleology of suffering and the making of merit). The dynamics of US politics proves this sad fact time after time. And more recently I have learned that this concept of anatta is even more complex, and probably ignored by most Buddhists. Achieving a full-awakening to the causes of suffering is what the Buddha did, it is certainly a step to enlightenment when we can abandon these causes, and a step toward peace of mind. "Vision arose, insight arose, discernment arose, knowledge arose, illumination arose within me with regard to things never heard before: 'This noble truth of the *origination [causes of]stress is—that stress is to be* abandoned' (Appendix II) . . . It is generally agreed that there is no creator god, but many Buddhists have reverence and often acceptance for other "nature" gods, devas or Brahmæs in a world of spirits and ghosts. These nature beliefs are perhaps intended to help alleviate the causes of suffering, stress, etc., and are quite prevalent; and more than being a belief, this is just the accepted explanation of how the world is, even for many educated Buddhists. But for the rest of us, we are on our own, responsible for full-awakening to and elimination of the causes of stress.

The best explanation of Anatta connects our lives and existence with a series of materialistic causes, a cosmology more closely aligned with modern chemistry and geology than with any ordinary religious perspective or a creator. I am comfortable with and emphasize this materialistic perspective in "Rational Buddhism" described in *Buddhist Sutras: Lesson Book*; but for many, calling the mysterious phenomena surrounding life on Earth by other names such as devas or spirits, is harmless enough. Not unlike the cause of the sound of a radio that is inexplicable to the untrained, the world functions under the control of physical causes no matter what they are called, whether we know about them or believe in them or not.

I remember being fascinated in my youth by the idea (and believing) that since we could not understand the creation of elemental life, there had to be some kind of deistic intervention or divine cause. Wherever there was a mystery, there was god's hand at work. And gradually as the mysteries disappeared as I studied more, there were fewer and fewer places for the devas and Brahmæs to exist. Now I suspect that it is just a matter of time before science figures out the precise mechanism and origins of life (more than cloning), we already know most of what happens, and why, i.e. evolution, the natural causes. We ought to crack the code reasonably soon. And the laws that control the development of organisms here on Earth are certainly robust and apply throughout Universe, just like the physical laws that make molecules, crystals and describe their properties, etc.

I don't try to convince people away from their beliefs, not in the Western world nor in the Oriental world. People have beliefs because they need them, their beliefs often enable them to thrive in an otherwise complex world that is explainable by only the small percentage of people who have had a sufficient amount of higher education. And what could I do to replace their beliefs? Many "Secular Humanists" have tried to evangelize atheism, ironically, but none have succeeded. Can Buddhism sustain those who find their way out of the nurturing religious dogmas which are taught to most children in the Western culture? How can my extreme rationality possibly assist more than just a few people to function without a traditional belief system? We can encourage people to come to their own understandings, they ought to be encouraged but not convinced, and thus they will have the psychological strength to deal with all the inevitable existential questions that remind us every day that we are essentially alone with no fairy god father or mother to look after us. The causes of our existence are mostly explainable, even though none of us has a full awareness of all of these; likewise the causes of existence for any animal are a matter of natural selection and propagation of species, but that is only the beginning of the story. We are part of that miraculous, often inexplicable and beautiful nature, albeit somewhat less colorful and more self-destructive than most other species. We find meaning in our lives based on the associations we make with other people, our families, offspring and siblings, and encouraging this kind of association is one third of Buddhism when we Take Refuge in the Sangha. No wonder the Buddha emphasized this community of believers as equal to the teachings.

If we are going to have a conversation with someone, it is reasonable and polite that we have attention and continuity in our speaking without unexplainable distractions. This is a demonstration of mindfulness as well as respect to have a coherent, logical and ordinary conversation. How important is mindfulness in our ordinary daily lives? "To be distracted is to allow another mind-moment to draw awareness away from what is intended and toward something else . . ."[122] As simple as this sounds, keeping awareness on an intended objective for even a few minutes without being distracted, is actually an advanced skill. We get away with random thoughts because nobody else cares how confused our minds are to begin with. It takes a calm mind to hold "pure awareness" for a minute or more, but with practice that can be easily doubled. Many people who have spent a good deal of time in a religion, whether Muslim, Jew or Christian, will have had substantial training and experience giving and kneeling in prayers of

---

[122] "According to the Abhidharma [Buddhist psychological] literature, the practitioner learns to observe the mind not as a continual flux but as discrete moments of awareness or mind-moments . . . To be distracted is to allow another mind-moment to draw awareness away from what is intended and toward something else . . . mindfulness as 'continuous imagining—that is, a certain style of holding' . . .Practicing mindfulness entails applying pure awareness to an immediate sense object [phenomenon] without getting lost in thinking about the object, and then holding that awareness moment by moment without distraction . . . (Brown, pg. 140)

one kind or another. All that talent will certainly give a new Buddhist meditator a head start (pun intended) when it comes to focus on their minds and the causes of their lives. It is an entirely different function, meditating, stemming from entirely different motivation, internal rather than external (not praying to a god or saint), and many other differences; but still the tacit knowledge, like tying our shoes, has crossover benefits. (I use the same knot more or less for tying my pants.) When I first started with Zen meditation counting ten breaths without losing count was a challenge, now I seem to be able to just keep counting, for whatever that's worth, and I can recite "bud—dho" at the same time to relax. Like holding your breath underwater, with practice you can extend your times, but it is of little practical use after a minute or so. Whereas carrying on an extended and lucid conversation, utilizing our self-awakening with family members and friends can certainly come in handy in our ordinary lives.

As suggested there are still many Buddhists who hold the existence of Devas and Brahmæs, in a Brahmæs world that surrounds us presumably as a basic truth.[123] How are we to understand this series of claims, literally or in some symbolic way perhaps? This is certainly Dhamma language at its most obscure, and in fact this Burmese monk quoted suggests that if anyone who doesn't accept this literally as truth, even though

---

[123] "According to the exegesis in the first chapter of Sagæthævagga saṃyutta, this statement may be assumed to have been made by a Brahmæ (a celestial being of the Brahmæ world; a noble being) from the fact that his life span was described as having ranged over many worlds. The Pæ'i gæthæ (stanza) may be translated as follows. 'With the same urgency and dispatch as someone whose breast has been impaled with a spear or whose head is on fire would seek immediate relief from the affliction thereof, the Bhikkhu who is mindful of the perils of Samsæræ (round of births; cycle of the continuity of existence) should make haste to rid himself of the defilement's of Kæmaræga (sensual pleasure) through Samatha Jhæna (quietude as a result of abstract meditation)'." (Sayædaw)

they can't perceive the Deva, etc., it is a "manifestation of low intelligence." [124]

I quote this to suggest that Buddhist teachings rely on many different poetic and mythological images, and tolerate these kinds of abstract teachings. After all, it is what happens in one's own mind that is of concern, not how the message and teaching is delivered. Buddhism has always been able to tolerate this kind of diversity; however it would be better form not to try to convince people of one idea or another by some kind of insult to their intelligence.

This Burmese monk continues his argument suggesting that "There are methods through the practice of which such experience and knowledge can be attained." Knowledge of Devas and Brahmæs, that is.[125] What this amounts to is an

---

[124] "Certain people do not believe in the existence of Devas and Brahmæs on the ground that they have not seen them personally. This is because they do not have the ability to perceive and because their level of knowledge and observation is low. They might turn round and say that they do not believe because their high intellect and rationality would not permit acceptance of the existence of Devas and Brahmæs. As a matter of fact. . . Buddha had spoken of Devas and Brahmæs through personal knowledge of their existence and this has been supported by observations of persons endowed with Abhiñña (transcendent knowledge) and by Arahats. Buddha in his omniscience had perceived more abstruse and refined dhamma and expounded them also. Arahats with superior intellects have had personal experience of these Dhammas and had thereby supported Buddha's exposition. If for the reason that they cannot see the Devas and Brahmæs, certain people will not accept their existence, we may conclude that their intelligence is still inadequate" (Sayædaw)

[125] "We accept such facts [from science] although we do not know them through personal experience, because we can use our rational thinking and accept them as plausible. If we aspire for personal experience and knowledge of these facts, there are methods through the practice of which such experience and knowledge can be attained. Jhænas (mystic or abstract meditation; ecstasy; absorption) and Abhiññas achieved by such practice can lead to conviction as a result of personal experience.

epistemological challenge, how do we come to know what we can know—only by experience, experiments, from scientists, or from the inspiration of our meditation experience of jhana (Zen)? Is there any limit to what we could come to believe through meditation if we accepted as fact all or any of the delusions and visions in our meditation practice? Since the time of G. Galileo (then Newton) the necessity of experimentation and repeatable verification was the scientific standard for knowing, but of course that was almost two thousand years after The Buddha. Issues which are not testable can just remain as questions, they would suggest, which was the same message The Buddha described with his famous four questions he would not answer. One of Newton's more obscure statements is to suggest that just because you can't prove a theory is wrong, doesn't make it right (paraphrase). Sayædaw suggests that there are "methods [that] exist by practicing" whereby we can come to know the truth about any odd question we might have, or does this apply to a specific kind of issue? This is of course the foundation stone of believing for him and for many Buddhists, as well as for other religious people.

How do we fact check our creative minds? If we can be convinced of the existence of Devas etc., can we be just as convinced of the existence of a creator god and his/her spirit children that live inside each human? Thus we would not accept the teaching of anatta, or at the very least we would have a much different interpretation of what the Buddha meant when he promoted that as essentially one/third of the Buddhist Dharma (along with aniccam and dukkham). When we have our own beliefs do we make a concerted effort to encourage others to believe these as well? Where do we draw the line? Buddhism has this kind of internal contradiction from the oral record that has been passed on for 2,500 years. Many societies have augmented Buddhism by adding preexisting nature teachings and practices. We tend to think that the

---

It is therefore irrational to adopt the attitude of non-acceptance of a fact just because one has no personal knowledge of it while methods exist by practicing which such knowledge is attainable." (Sayædaw)

ancient monks and Arahats who inhabited such modern communities as Sukothai, had the same rational views as we have today, when certainly their cosmology was based on Devas etc. and celestial worlds, hierarchies, hells, as well as other superstitions.[126] Is it okay because they didn't know any better? Then how do we rationalize so many similar beliefs still thriving in the world today?

It is nice to know that we are actually born with the capacity and talent to meditate (some people have it more than others), that way we are endowed with this functional ability to gain self-awareness, not unlike our Buddha nature, or what is often referred to as Buddha-hood. If we have facility with controlling our thoughts, perhaps that is a measure of the capacity of our Buddhahood and an indication of our likelihood to gain full-awakening. This capacity is pre-installed in our hardware so to speak; we are just practicing to get better in touch with that from a religious and spiritual perspective as a central aspect of our Hearts.

But we are not pre-wired with rational-scientific thinking, we have to learn or be taught this kind of sophisticated analysis. Common sense and intuition are not very useful scientific tools. Intuition is just what it becomes, often an emotional inspiration after our lifetime of reading and listening to our teachers and families. These are the threshold points when we actually begin to work skillfully with our minds, and if we are deliberately in control of our thinking activity whenever we want to be, that is part of full-awakening and we are ready to expand are Hearts and move beyond that.

Now after we have studied our minds' characteristics on any given day in step nine, we move on to develop "the mind joyful, delighted, and content."[127] What was our mood when we first sat down? Does this state of contentment have anything

---

[126] "Seeing danger where there is no danger\ And not seeing danger where danger exists,\ From taking up wrong views\ Beings go to a bad destination." (Dhammapada, vs. 317)

[127] "Part two of this [third] tetrad -- [step ten] is delighting the mind [from Dharma] . . . or gladdening the mind to make the mind joyful, delighted,

to do with cosmological truth? Does it come from recognizing the cause of suffering, or must we move to the next level of full-awakening first? Have we deliberately changed our state of mind with long or short breaths? Or by controlling our emotions, which is the mind-conditioner. How can we encourage others to succeed, to find contentment as well, and is that kind of encouragement important? Is this what it means to try to make other people happy? So many cults and gurus get caught up in mind control and preying on vulnerable people. When we leave the world of speculation about Devas etc., we are following the advice and encouragement of the Buddha, by not trying to answer certain questions about—before life and afterlife—that he thought were a waste of time. It is enough to just gladden the mind and be joyful. Having the strength of mind, full-awakening, to be objective and strongly independent is, however, a rare characteristic.

Here is a basic tenet of Buddhism that is often overlooked. "We require the delight that comes from knowing and using Dhamma . . ."[128] This kind of psychic and spiritual nourishment is an essential ingredient in mental health, as was described in chapter five. This higher joyfulness may be, at least in part, what is meant by "devotion." We can think of this as the silent singing of the Heart; not unlike what we can achieve when we are in the moment, in the poem of chanting with our Sangha. We can set aside our rational minds for a few minutes, and just relax in full-awakening, our natural spirituality. We can best share this higher joyfulness by being available to listen to other peoples' problems or comments, like the famous Kuan-yin—Chinese (often feminine) bodhisattva of mercy

---

and content. It is important to be able to control the mind so that it feels satisfied and glad while breathing in and out . . ." (Buddhadasa)

[128] "We do not have to endure a sorrowful mind because we can control it . . . [but we do not seek the satisfaction] rooted in materialism and sensuality . . . We require the delight that comes from knowing and using Dhamma . . . Thus, there are two kinds of joyfulness: defiled joyfulness [temporary as with piti] and joyfulness free of defilement (kilesa) (similar to sukha)." (Buddhadasa)

and compassion. Can we learn to listen like the same icon in Theravada—Avalokiteshvara? This buddha, or compassionate bodhisattva is described as existing in the Land of Bliss, as standing by the side of Amida to welcome the deceased to the afterlife. She encourages many people to lead an ethical life just by listening to their problems, as an inspired example of "direct awareness". Aside from being the source of many beautiful images, she is a popular object of devotion, a model for friendship and counseling, a worthy example and a beautiful metaphor.

The logical extension of this perfect compassion is to say encouraging and complimentary statements to our Sangha members before we enter the sala to share our sitting. We should choose our companions wisely, compliment them, then rely on their wisdom.[129] That is a useful way to encourage everyone, to cause positive feelings when each member is doing the same, to use the gladdening we naturally feel to relax and open our Hearts. We continue to expand this gladdening in our meditation with our in and out breathing.[130] Sharing sacred and special moments with Sangha members also creates this kind of joyfulness. We can become the cause of the determining happiness and camaraderie that surrounds our social culture (as opposed to being a cause of suffering). This is the first step to sharing loving-kindness, metta, with the larger, impossible to known community of the world, etc.

---

[129] "Take delight in awareness:\ Guard your own minds.\ Lift yourselves out of the bad road\ Like the tusker sunk in the mud.\\ If you find a skillful companion\ Who walks with you, well behaved and wise,\ You should walk with him[/her,] joyful and mindful, Overcoming all dangers." (Dhammapada, vs. 327-8)

[130] "Joyfulness comes from the feeling of being successful, [from the feeling of being loved or appreciated,] of having correctly and successfully completed an activity. An easy way to delight the mind is to return to practicing steps one, two, and three again. Go back to the beginning and practice each step successfully. Then there will be contentment and joyfulness with each completed step. This kind of gladness is associated with Dhamma." (Buddhadasa)

I had the experience of attending a dedication ceremony at a foundry where Buddha icons were to be caste from brass on this day. The molds were stacked, top side down, preheated, grouped together, 14 of them (same in the next batch). Next to that was a kiln/furnace where inside a large vat was used to melt the brass and the workmen put the brass ingots into the vat through the stout chimney of the short furnace. The participants had prepared food and offerings, and one table featured five of those rather tall, green, hand-folded banana tree palm decorations with flowers and buds fastened artfully all around. I was told the four shorter ones placed at each corner of the table were to invite the spirits from the four corners of the compass, and the tall central, green folded creation, was to attract them to join the ceremony and leave their positive forces in the icons being produced. The 50 or so laypeople seeking merit and 11 monks acted out this drama faithfully, incorporating what amounts to a nature religion into the Buddhist practice. For these people this was an essential and joyful practice in each detail, to follow the rules of nature, to create a numinous character to the icons which would be distributed to wats around the countryside. (The second batch didn't get the same attention because the group adjourned for lunch on the other side of the building.)

I was welcomed by people in the group because I was a guest of Pa (my daughter-in-law's father). There were plenty of smiles and cordial greetings from friends meeting friends (I thought that positive spirit alone would bless the icons) as the women prepared a lunch for the monks, and the rest of us mingled and smiled to prepare for the ceremony. I was given a piece of brass foil upon which I could write the names of my dearly departed (two of my brothers had recently died, Joe and David, and Dani Adams, a church friend who passed recently). This went into the vat to be part of the icons forever. Those who read this chapter can think of themselves as likewise a participant in a spiritual ceremony, even though they are reading by themselves in a comfortable chair in their own home and we are years apart. As we read, we may feel delight from being relieved of a good deal of suffering, from being part of this cheerful community, by having achieved success in our meditation practice, or just by having completed a worthwhile project, or at least now we see the light at the end of the tunnel? How often do we count our blessings? To have found and accepted Buddhism is to be blessed.[131] We are surprisingly alike with respect to our needs and wants, and even thoughts, and certainly interconnected by way of our desires, as were the 50 people who convened for the icon ceremony. The same causes which created our own bodies and minds, acted in only slightly different circumstances to create each member of our Sangha. If we share 99% of our DNA with apes, then we certainly share more than that with any person with whom we might get acquainted.

Giving encouragement to others is contagious and is likely to come back onto ourselves. If we are alone in the world, being alone together is more than just a consolation at times; it is a basic human need. This is a simple example of cause and effect, when we foster good relations, we might see immediate returns for ourselves, and whether we feel we need that or not. In the opposite way, when we make a public spectacle of or ridicule by insulting taunts, such as has been prevalent in the cartoon images of Mohammad and derision of Islam; then no wonder there are negative reactions, hatred, and in the extreme, violent recriminations against soldiers and US embassies. These reactions are understandable, although there are plenty of other economic and religious reasons to explain their anger, so the violent reaction are no less despicable. Certainly we promote free speech as a political right, but we must also respect what is sacred in each person; their sense of devotion, their right to privacy and the pursuit of happiness, and respect their civilized religious dedication no matter how much we might disagree (as long as they do no harm).

---

[131] " . . .We are the most fortunate of human beings, one who has found Dhamma and is able to eliminate dukkha." (Buddhadasa, 1988, pp. 74-76)

These ceremonies, such as my day at the brass-works, are useful if they foster in each participant a larger sense of compassion and a community spirit that can support joy and sharing. What is the harm of filling the air with a myth or interesting allegory to help us understand the significance of Buddhist teachings? If our lives and minds change to become more reverent and calm, that is a good thing. We study about the causes of suffering,[132] but if we give half as much time to concern ourselves with the causes of joy, and encourage practices that build on this for each of us, we will gain the merit of that positive attitude.[133]

When we take a sincere interest in others, we know about their families and remember the details of their lives that they have shared and refer to that in respectful conversations, then we are surely benefiting ourselves indirectly. And when we share our successes and failures with members of our Sangha, we make ourselves vulnerable and "emotionally available" when we promote full-awakening, thus we live each day to avoid creating suffering for tomorrow.

---

[132] "When we are certain that we can extinguish dukkha [our faith is serene,] or when we have gained the best that humans can possibly achieve, then it is normal for us to be joyful and content. We study the Dhamma to understand what will eradicate suffering, to realize our maximum human potential. Then we are content. We are able to delight and gladden the citta using this skillful technique." (Buddhadasa, 1988, pg. 76)

[133] "But for those in whom mindfulness of body\ Is ever rightly undertaken,\ Who do not practise what should not be done,\Who persevere in what should be done,\Who are mindful and wise,\ The defilements go to rest." (Dhammapada, vs. 293)

Chapter Eleven

Encouraging Cessation of Suffering

Key Words:

Stress, Dalai Lama, retreat, sharing merit, parisuddho (purity), mental effluents, 'ekaggata-citta' / concentration, kilesa.

Why Should I Meditate?

In meditation we face stress (unease) squarely to reduce it, and work for liberation, then share merit with all those other suffering, stressed out people? When you begin meditation the mind gathers to rest—no matter what the level of concentration—how long it stays there depends on and creates Liberation. When you have investigated [and analyzed] to the point where you feel tired, and the mind wants to rest in its home of concentration, let it rest as much as it wants. When it comes time to put this (stress) all aside and examine the rest of our lives, that is when I go back to my room (home) and meditate by myself. During restful concentration we get flashes—aha moments. To develop Concentrating means to train the mind, to have good qualities and be ready for work. We listen to our Hearts in meditation and become—*steady, pure and prepared.* If meditation were fun, more people would be engrossed in it more of the time, and it would be a better

166

world. When the mind is focused on a singleness of purpose, it can recharge its batteries.

This is the last chapter under the category of having a Pure Mind, so if we don't get it now, have we lost our chance? Buddhism is more forgiving than that "thank heaven". But as we get back to it in this chapter, we use the tools that are taught in the eleventh step of Anapanasati to progress along the path of Purification. How can we encourage and inspire each other in the knowledge that suffering can be diminished, how do we grow out of our cravings and internalize the truth that life, no matter how sour it seems on a given day, can get better?[134] This was the promise and admonition of the Buddha for whom a "Vision arose, insight arose, discernment arose, knowledge arose, illumination arose within me with regard to things never heard before: 'This noble truth of the *cessation of stress is to be* directly experienced' . . ." (Appendix II) We can achieve this full-awakening and eliminate suffering, we just have to know how to go about it and make the necessary effort.

We have done a lot of work in the first four chapters of this section to "recognize" and deal with any problems we might have; we have begun to understand how important it is to "encourage" others and ourselves to live a happy and positive life, work for full-awakening and move along the path to enlightenment. Next we need to encourage our family members and friends to live together in harmony and to be forgiving and tolerant of differences, emphasize each other's talents, and facilitate the fulfillment of all our responsibilities (by helping each other accomplish duties to work and family.) But encouragement extends into many facets of our lives like the mycelia of a useful and aggressive fungus, like a useful and flavorful mold in a cheese.

---

[134] "Those who are subject to craving\Crawl around like a trapped hare.\ Bound by fetters and bonds, for a long time\ They undergo suffering again and again.\\ So a monk should put away craving\ If he desires his own freedom from passion." (Dhammapada, vs. 342-3)

So in meditation we are busy doing something, it's just something else than what we are doing to make a living or communicate with friends.

In my sleep and often in relaxed moments of quiet when I am not working or absorbed in some reading, or watching a movie, I look back on various aspects of my life when I was young, I suppose everyone does this. I had my first paying job when I was eight years old, then I went with my mother, sister and brother to the strawberry field to pick. My mother went mostly to encourage and help the others earn some extra money for clothing (I was too young to stay at home alone), she worked hard too, even though it was difficult and demanding work especially for a large, overweight woman. My brother, David, got promoted to being a "straw boss" because he was big and strong (six years older than me), and my sister Wilma found some friends and worked hard with them. I don't remember how long we worked together in the strawberry patch, probably not much more than a week. I remember eating a lot of strawberries too, some people grew to despise them because of that, I grew to love that tart, fresh, juicy-sweet flavor. Later in my teen years I looked forward to finding work picking beans, cherries, pears and apples.

It was in those days when summer vacations meant that any healthy member of the community could go out and help with the harvest in some way, but those days shortly came to an end as general welfare increased, child labor laws discouraged underage children from working, and workers from other American countries came seasonally to harvest the crops. I learned how to persevere hour after hour when I wanted so badly to just walk off the job, but never did until the scheduled time. I suppose I learned that from my Mother's example and encouragement. I recall when I picked pears, my oldest brother, Joe, took his Saturday and worked with me on his day off, then he gave me the money he earned as a bonus and incentive for the time I had been working during the week. I saved most of that money and used some of that for my college tuition. We never thought working hard, and furthermore, needing to work was in any way associated with long term suffering because of the benefits it provided. The reward for work was usually immediate and it was easy to connect the work with benefits for the whole family, and the cause and effect.

Now-days people think their jobs are the number one source of their suffering and stress. How do we end that suffering? People who have never had the experience of living in poverty or without basic needs, or living hand to mouth, perhaps don't appreciate the job they have as a gift or blessing. They have the luxury of being stressed out, curiously enough. This is what I would call a determinant of stress, the work environment is a place where negative or positive things can happen, and interpersonal relations can cause conflict or fulfillment, where people are pushed into performing exciting challenges or doing work for which they do not feel qualified. Our stress and suffering don't come usually from the surprises in our life, those are abrupt and momentary. Our stress comes from the difficulties we experience in our hum-drum daily grind, which over and over antagonizes us with "the same kind of discomfort and tension".

Do we all need to have had such a dreary experience to know the unfortunate consequences? Or is there a way to short-circuit that process and learn from the experience and advice of others? How do we abandon the undesirable and harmful feeling? how do we gain liberation?[135] What can we learn from reading fictional novels, for example, when the protagonist gets into trouble and comes to a sad or disastrous ending? Can we avoid those social traps that often make up

---

[135] "The word 'liberated' may have two implications: one implies the mind is the one that is doing the liberating [i.e. in meditation,] the other implies that 'all the harmful feelings have simply slipped out of the mind'. . . . When the mind possesses mindfulness and wisdom, it abandons all the undesirable or harmful feelings [cravings] together with the causes of mental defilements."(Buddhadasa, 2008, pg. 249)

the structure of novels and otherwise cause stress in our lives? Can we read history or biographies and benefit from those? Where did John Doe go wrong? What, you've never heard of him? That's because he went astray, couldn't listen to good advice, got stressed out and never amounted to being a useful or famous person. It's one thing to make claims for "liberation, mindfulness and wisdom", but quite another to actually own a significant amount of these characteristics. Sloganeering runs rampant throughout Buddhist teachings, presumably with the understanding that the details will be provided by the full-time monks who are on the ground with the people.

We can spread the word and help our family members and acquaintances enjoy their work and breaks, and benefit from down time to make it function as ***up-with-meditation time***.

How do we fix stressful circumstance for our own lives? Or can we who are not particularly stressed by work, share merit with all those suffering, stressed out people and somehow help them? That is probably the indirect route. The Dalai Lama is on a mission to reduce the suffering in the world. And it is certainly part of the religion of Buddhism to promote that mission as a duty for all of us, even though we cannot expect to have such a universal impact. Removing stress, however, seems such a trivial matter in the face of the global consequences of ecological destruction, it is such an individual matter, but that does not mean we cannot do our part to liberate ourselves, be encouraging and be good listeners. Certainly the causes of stress as well as most other causes of suffering are independent for each of us, yet we have more similarities to other people in our lives than differences. We can hold a rock in our hand, but we cannot hold the mountain. The cessation of suffering is an on-going task, self-awareness then full-awakening is an additive process, thus this is realized not all at once but incrementally, and that is fine. So if we get to work on the rocks we encounter, eventually the mountain will be less daunting. (That's a dandy slogan!)

Here is a simple beginning: When we learn to concentrate properly ourselves, we can do a better job at focusing our energies and then encouraging others, and we might legitimately hope to do something to better the lives of our family members, to encourage Sangha members, but that requires some skill and discernment. "Use your discernment to investigate conditions of nature (sabhava dhamma) both within and without."[136] It is as simple as that. It is during these moments of concentration that we get those flashes, or aha moments, such as early in this writing I was inspired to choose the name for this book "Nirodha"; a concept that seemed to embody the goal of this work. I hadn't set out to accomplish that, it just came as a moment of discernment, I suppose. As temporary and impermanent as this analysis and "resting at home" is as a therapy against stress, so our stress will most

---

[136] "So what is right concentration like, and how should you practice for the sake of rightness? This is where a few differences lie. When you sit in concentration and the mind gathers to rest—no matter what the level of concentration—how long it stays there depends on the particular strength of that level of concentration. . . Once it withdraws, try to train yourself to explore [that] with your discernment. Whatever level of discernment corresponds to that level of concentration, use it to investigate and contemplate the physical properties (dhatu) and khandhas. . . All that is asked is that you investigate for the sake of knowing cause and effect, for the sake of curing or extricating yourself: Just this much is what's right. Use your discernment to investigate conditions of nature (sabhava dhamma) within and without, or else exclusively within or exclusively without. Contemplate them in terms of any one of the three characteristics (ti-lakkhana) until you are experienced and astute, until you can find the openings by which you can extricate yourself step by step. When you have investigated [and analyzed] to the point where you feel tired, and the mind wants to rest in its home of concentration, let it rest as much as it wants . . .This is right concentration. Be aware of the fact that concentration is simply a temporary resting place." (Boowa, 1996)

certainly return. Yet it is absolutely a blessing that we have this capacity for change in our lives to depend on.

I recently walked through the streets near the open air "backpacker" market, Khao San Road Market and surrounding area in Bangkok. The proprietors who work at the stalls selling food had self-respect and were keeping their areas clean, sweeping since I was there early. The relatively better off people, who have the kiosks and stores selling all kinds of stuff, clothing, statues, spoons, sandals, etc., work hard and seem to be engrossed in their work and seem to count themselves lucky for having their little corner on the sidewalk. They don't exhibit any signs of stress, they smile at you and encourage you to buy and then offer discounts. Only when you bargain hard and perhaps offer a price that is the actual lowest possible, probably the true value, do they seem to frown and look forlorn. The restaurant workers seem to be happy enough, although some were looking around, seemingly for something better. The owners of the travel agencies, massage shops and jewelry outlets seemed to be doing alright, so where was there any stress or suffering? Location, location, location, and there were plenty of customers even in the morning when I was there. We can't know what is in the hearts and minds of all these otherwise effective and active people.

The visitors moved by, preoccupied with their journeys, passing for this brief moment in their lives when our paths crossed if only in this cursory way, perhaps never to return but hopefully they leave with pleasant memories to carry from this market, and wherever else they will visit in Thailand? What kind of suffering have they encountered, or what kind of defilement have they indulged in? Perhaps that will result in some suffering? I think that stress is a Western psychological condition, a learned behavior, and of course like everything else, we are probably exporting that around the world too with our grotesque styles and annoying brands. Ha! It seems rather cynical to think that any of these people might be born with or fated to suffer from more stress than others because of some anomaly in their DNA. There is suffering just being a victim of all the visual onslaught of commercialism, the knock-off brands, but of course I could have easily chosen to avoid all that, so I can't blame anyone; and so no suffering. Right? Since I have been to Bangkok nine times now, and this was my first visit to this market, I can hardly call my visit there in any way an experience of inevitable suffering. It wasn't an exceptional joy either, although I will probably come back on my next trip.

I could see that there were a few of the tourists, obviously men who had shaved their heads for their visit to a retreat or some such Buddhist experience, who were engaged in a higher and better purpose than just this commercial experience. There were several stores that sold Buddha icons and other religious paraphernalia, I didn't buy any on this visit, although I have often in the past elsewhere. One good thing about this market is that since they cater to "farang" foreigners, they have sizes that fit larger people like me. I bought a couple of pairs of sandals to fit my size12 feet which I couldn't find before, and a couple of XXXL shirts (equivalent to XL in the USA). So in that way I must have eliminated some suffering of my own by satisfying a want? I didn't think about that at the time, but there is a certain compulsion to buy something, anything even though I don't really need another shirt. So perhaps I was just indulging a craving to have more. It's all a fairly innocent activity, more like a pastime after having shopped at these kind of markets dozens of times. I always have this reflective experience, like being a sociologist and trying to figure out some interesting and theoretical law of humanity, etc. Being in the moment of the experience doesn't seem to be very sensational; it just seems to be an experience that I study as I go. I don't go to the market as I would go to a wat for any sort of uplifting experience, so it is nearly impossible to be disappointed. But as someone who has been trained in Economics, I always enjoy seeing Adam Smith's theories come to life, like watching a movie that I have seen so many times, and I know the words by heart.

When it comes time to put this all aside and examine the rest of my life, I go back to my room and meditate by myself. I move on to " . . . concentrate the mind in samadhi and immediately drive away any unwanted feelings."[137] This Concentration is also an important step of the Eight-fold Path, so I don't take it lightly. I have been blessed with a reasonably good attention span, and read, write or concentrate for hours on end doing such things. But when it comes time to sit in meditation and just try to stabilize my mind, and presumably do nothing; that has always been a little more troublesome for me. I found that when I went on my first Buddhist, silent retreat, I had to focus the first two days on adjusting to having so many days in a row that I would not do anything physical, paint a wall, or repair plumbing etc. So rather than have to adjust to being active, I had to adjust to being still and doing nothing hour after hour, concentrating only on my thoughts and it was not so easy to do! It was a good relief for me when I found out that I had a job to do, as did everyone, so at least once a day I could be slightly productive. (I volunteered to consolidate the paper from the toilets and burned it along with any trash in the cans, etc.) I didn't have as much trouble with the not talking part as I did with the frequent periods of sitting and meditating at first.

Of course that is not the entire story is it? "In step eleven, concentrating the mind means to train the mind so that it has good qualities and is ready for work."[138] If we can do this,

---

[137] "Step eleven [of Anapanasati] is to concentrate the mind (smadaham cittam). This step is not difficult because we have been practicing with concentration from the beginning, especially in step four (calming the body-conditioner) and during step eight (calming the mind-conditioner). If we could do it before, then we can do it now. So we concentrate the mind in samadhi and immediately drive away any unwanted feelings." (Buddhadasa)

[138] "Most people misunderstand, thinking that if the mind is in samadhi, we must sit absolutely still—stiff and unable to move. Or they think that in samadhi we should experience no sensations whatsoever. This is wrong understanding. . . .Here in step eleven, concentrating the mind means to train the mind so that it has good qualities and is ready for work. It is prepared to perform its duties as needed. If the mind has correct samadhi, we will observe in the mind three distinct qualities.

then we know that the Five Hindrances, if not conquered, are at least put aside for the period of our skillful meditation. Meditation is not intended as a period of inactivity or leisure, it is just a different kind of work, and the job is to reduce our suffering and share that freedom with others.[139]

When we are diligent, our efforts are not being defeated by lingering emotions relating to stress or other sad memories. Recall that this is the third part of conditioning our minds (as described in chapter nine) which is another way of saying developing our Hearts. If we are not experiencing some nagging guilt, that would be unusual also. We all carry a little (some a lot) of baggage with us from previous relationships or failed experiences. Is it possible to gain self-awakening and then lose it? How much can we hand off and share with others? And if possible, how is it best to make that happen? We can give each other a little encouragement and a lot of forgiveness when it comes to issues such as guilt. This guilt will dim our minds.

Again we can see the value of the Precept against intoxication. In Bangkok it is against the law to sell beer or alcohol between 4:00 and 6:00 so drivers will make it home safely. Apparently this practice has reduced accidents. How could we have this clear and active mind to drive, let alone to meditate, if we were half drunk?[140] Meditation is not about being in a stupor. When we are wholly sober, we learn to listen to our Hearts—*steady, pure and prepared.* So in meditation we

---

1) The quality of mind that is firm, steady, undistracted, and focused on a single object is called samahito (stability, collectedness)." (Buddhadasa)

[139] "Those who are attached to passion follow a stream\They have made for themselves, as a spider follows its web.\ But, cutting even this, the wise go on, without longing,\ Leaving all suffering behind." (Dhammapada, vs. 347)

[140] "That mind is clear and pure, not disturbed by anything, un-obscured by defilement, parisuddho (purity). . . A citta is fit and supremely prepared to perform the duties of the mind, kammaniyo (activeness, readiness)." (Buddhadasa, 1988, pp. 76-77)

are actually busy doing something, again it's just something else than what we are doing to make a living or communicate with friends. It's time we use for ourselves—and in that sense it ought to be thought of as the most valuable time of all. Each opportunity we get, we ought to encourage others to take this essential time for themselves, to be at peace. This was one of the marketing justifications for attending the silent retreat, but there is a nugget of truth in that the time we spend on self-awakening is time improved.

If we want to be at peace, achieve Concentration "samadhi", or hold an object at our guarding point with firmness (sati) as the breath moves by, the proper method is, once we have chosen our object, set it aside and focus on the clues or signs that led us to that object—in this way: This is a hint or guide from a successful monk, how to accomplish Concentration, so if we want to concentrate well, we look for its tracks, whether that is the calm breath, the slow heartbeat, or the "bud—dho" mantra taught in Thailand. These and other rituals are functionally devices, "tracks" that help us achieve our main goal of eliminating suffering. The ancient promise is: the reward for samadhi is to overcome temptations and be at peace.[141]

Earlier we studied our mind to see what its status was. To successfully navigate this effort of Concentration and to stabilize our minds, we look again to see what is happening. We use our breath in and out to create the focus of mindfulness. But " . . . just as when you follow the tracks of an ox: You're not after the tracks of the ox. You follow its tracks because you want to reach the ox."[142] So we take care of these preliminaries

---

[141] "But the one who delights in calming his thoughts—\Who, ever mindful, contemplates the foul [not the fair] \ He will finish it.\ He will cut Mara's [temptations] bond." (Dhammapada, vs. 350)

[142] "The same holds true if you focus on keeping the breath in mind. Whether the breath is heavy or refined, simply be aware of it as it normally is. Don't set up any expectations. Don't force the breath to be like this or that. Keep your awareness with the breath, because in meditating by taking the breath as your preoccupation, you're not

well as we begin each meditation session, before we can expect to benefit from Concentration. Then we focus the mind into a state of strength and skillful one-pointedness.[143] Then we can benefit from Insight when we take the mind on a broad ranging search for ways to end suffering; while to begin with, we had concentration which was intended to focus the mind on "a single point" to develop perspicuity. (I like that word.) We go back and forth in a rhythm of awakening, encouraging ourselves to become happier and liberated.

I have noticed how young students when I am substitute teaching, often report that they are bored with school, or a certain activity they perhaps don't enjoy, like study-hall. I think now how important boredom is, it is the calming of the mind, and it is a signal that we ought to in fact be meditating at that moment. For the last several years, sleepless nights, moments of waiting for a bus or boredom, are blessings for my meditation practice. I use them like someone just gave me a piece of apple pie, and I always over-indulge on that. We can spread the word and encourage others to have this kind of modest eagerness about their silent moments. In this way we

---

after the breath. The breath is simply something for the mind to hold to so that you can reach the real thing, just as when you follow the tracks of an ox: You're not after the tracks of the ox. You follow its tracks because you want to reach the ox. Here you're keeping track of the breath so as to reach the real thing: awareness [the result of mindfulness.] If you were to start out just by holding on to awareness, you wouldn't get any results, just as you wouldn't be sure of finding the ox if you simply went around looking for it. But if you follow its tracks, you're going to find it for sure." (Boowa, 1996.)

[143] "This kind of mind is most firm or stable because it has gathered all the strength it needs [presumably.] Normally the mind is a blur like the light of a dim lamp. It is not strong, but if all the rays are being gathered to one point, it becomes strong like a curved lens which gathers sunlight at one point whose reflection is able to set fire to, say, a piece of paper. In the same way, the mind is being 'gathered' to a single point and it thus becomes strong and stable. This is the quality of a mind that has 'samadhi' in it." (Buddhadasa, 2008, pg. 233)

help our family members and acquaintances enjoy their work, or certainly their work breaks, and benefit from their down time to make it function as *up-with-meditation-time*. This kind of encouragement should always be given with compassion and perhaps with a little humor to lighten the burden even more. (The "ox track" instruction is a good example of that.)

Here is a poem I wrote while waiting in a coffee shop, just to pass the time, because I think that writing in this genre of "stream of consciousness" can be a version of meditation: examining our thoughts and putting them on paper to see, and who knows, maybe something useful will be recorded incidentally in the next sentence.

Slower than watching an apple ripen.
This napkin had such an innocent and naïve beginning
But today it plays a much more sophisticated role as scroll
to receive and record forever the most sacred thoughts
of a most sacred Buddhist monk. Not my thoughts,
except that these ideas happen to come also
      through my mind to this paper
but the inspired and wise thoughts of a monk, or perhaps many
or perhaps every monk one time or another,
      who has had the same thought
Which relates to the simplicity and satisfying character of
      elements of nature—both man-made and natural—
      that surround me now in this moment
Because We have all recognized that these elements
      are changing ever so gradually,
their causes for existence are well known, not mysterious
even though concealed by their surfaces so
      they give only momentary satisfaction
which We gratefully acknowledge and acquiesce
to surrender in advance to the inevitability of decay
      transition, replacement and obsolescence.
This will happen, but knowing this in advance
makes the change in an important way trivial,
And mitigates against what might otherwise be

a cause of stress or suffering.
Live happily monk(s) and followers
who see this peacefulness in nature.
I.J. Hall, Bangkok, Coffeol,
Siam Tower, March 20, 2012

It is clear to see from the examples I have given in this chapter, different stages of the mind where I and others were prepared to do what was necessary—not like the school kids who couldn't function in study-hall without some outside stimulation. These examples of working people show how the mind is when it is ready to function. "It gives rise to a happiness which can be used for the practice of an ever higher Dhamma . . ."[144] Encouraging others to Concentrate is made easier when I can point to immediate and beneficial consequences. If meditation were found to be fun, more people would be engrossed in it more of the time, and it would be a better world we live in.

It is no secret by now how to go about stabilizing the mind. We use the practice found in step four of Anapanasati, control the body by controlling the breathing until we hardly notice any movement of the abdomen or exchange of air, and this will lead to a stable mind. Further we studied the mind-conditioning by moving past any sense of active piti or even relaxed sukha. But it is not all to be fun and games. "An 'ekaggata-citta' (a one-pointed mind) has 'nibbana' as its mind-object (arom) [rather than any subject matter.] . . . 'samadhi' refers to the mind that strives towards the calmness and coolness of life."[145]

---

[144] "If [the mind] were ready, there would be fun in the [activity.] So even the practice to attain the path (magga), the fruition (phala) and 'nibbana' needs this kind of active mind which is stable and full of 'samadhi'. . . It gives rise to a happiness which can be used for the practice of an ever higher Dhamma. . . this is also the cause for one's mental and spiritual progress." (Buddhadasa, 2008, pp. 237-238)

[145] "Citta-sankhara which is 'piti' and 'sukha', is a double-edged sword. If 'piti' cannot be controlled, there will be distraction. When 'piti' promotes joy, and delightfulness as well as 'sukha' or happiness

179

This latter is the mind with Concentration that fulfills the goal of that step of the Eight-fold Path. The best plan in general is to encourage others and allow ourselves to alternate during meditation with 'samadhi' and 'vipassana' or wisdom meditation to overcome suffering, and erase defilements. When the mind is focused on this singleness of purpose it can recharge its batteries, so to speak, and very carefully accomplish its purpose to subsequently extinguish defilements and perhaps one or more causes of suffering. Part of continuing our goal toward achieving purification is to encourage other people to find this level of Concentration for themselves. Does all this seem unnecessarily complicated? We follow the breath as if we were following the tracks of an ox, and eventually and inevitably we will find our goal, nirvana.

Each time we meditate we ought to be concerned with dedicating at least a portion of our sacred effort toward eliminating suffering, once recognized. We could perhaps carry a collection of ideas with us as with a sack of pebbles, and by turn identify each one at a time, gradually working on the whole sackful of suffering we identified. (Or wear a mala with 108 beads?) One way to do this is to go back to the basics, use the techniques we have discussed and practiced (that's why it's called practice), and work to improve our lives. We can easily use the method of Direct Awareness, and from that we get release. "With release, there is the knowledge . . ."

---

become the distracting factors, nothing can be done. The mind becomes immersed and deluded in the fun and tastiness of things. [Many people stop there.] It goes wild. Therefore 'piti' and 'sukha' need to be controlled or restrained so that calmness prevails. With the mind stabilized, things can be done. Failing to control 'piti' and 'sukha' means providing them the chance to become 'kilesa' or mental defilement that will take charge of the mind. There will be no clearness and no good quality and stability of the mind. . . An 'ekaggata-citta' (a one-pointed mind) has 'nibbana' as its mind-object (arom) [rather than any subject matter.] . . .'samadhi' refers to the mind that strives towards the calmness and coolness of life." (Buddhadasa, 2008, pp. 239-241)

that we have achieved something important for our lives.[146] Again we are first ready for work by gaining Concentration, if just for a few minutes; then we look for the cessation of suffering, one time-honored goal of meditation; of course there are other goals. When we encourage other people to achieve their goals, we pave the way for our own success and the spontaneous achievement of Nirvana. "There is nothing further for this world." That means we are ready to live in peacefulness, this is not about ending our lives. And when we "get it" in this way, sit down and write a poem that we can read in the future and share with others, thus we share our fully-awakened Heart. "Riches destroy the fool,\ But not the one who seeks the other shore.\ Through craving for riches, the fool\ Destroys himself as he does others." (Dhammapada, vs. 355) The benefits of birth and inheritance notwithstanding, we all need to learn to balance our lives according to the middle way.

---

[146] "Just as if there were a pool of water in a mountain glen—clear, limpid, and unsullied—where a man with good eyes standing on the bank could see shells, gravel, and pebbles, and also shoals of fish swimming about and resting, and it would occur to him, 'This pool of water is clear, limpid, and unsullied. Here are these shells, gravel, and pebbles, and also these shoals of fish swimming about and resting;' so too, the monk discerns as it actually is, that 'This is stress. . . This is the origin of stress. . . This is the stopping of stress. . . This is the way leading to the stopping of stress. . . These are mental effluents. . . This is the origin of mental effluents. . . This is the stopping of mental effluents. . . This is the way leading to the stopping of mental effluents.' His heart, thus knowing, thus seeing, is released from the effluent of sensuality, released from the effluent of becoming, and released from the effluent of unawareness. With release, there is the knowledge, 'Released.' He discerns that, 'Birth is no more, the holy life is fulfilled, the task done. There is nothing further for this world'—Samaññaphala Sutta, Digha Nikaya." (Boowa, 1996)

PART III
Enlightened Mind

Chapter Twelve

Encouraging Along the Path

Key Words:

Insight, creative meditation, nirvana, Enlightenment, complications, stability, preparation, discernment, clinging, effluents, spontaneity, khandhas, Ajahn Mun

Why Should I Meditate?

If we have problems we cannot answer, in meditation and Concentration, the answers will often come. Stability is internal and when developed in meditation practice, it will help us in our daily lives. In Buddhist meditation we develop mindfulness and discernment to overcome an erratic mind. In meditation we can gain balance between, *purity, steadiness and preparation.* We use walking meditation to develop 'Uninterrupted mindfulness of everything' as we watch karma as it happens and learn to disrupt complications. The more you investigate in meditation, the more skillful you get, the more astute your discernment. Meditation should be enjoyable and rewarding, not a hardship, or we will cease doing it. When we have inspiration and protect that, we compare it to everything else we know or have studied, and later we analyze it to test its validity.

Somewhere in the previous chapters there was a mention that Nirvana has no causes, it is the un-conditioned aspect of dharma. This is perhaps what is also intended by the Christian concept of salvation by grace that comes to each person, even to sinners, whether they do anything to earn it or not. I think there are some important differences, but the concept that Nirvana has no cause, suggests that it leaves no tracks, such as the ox we followed in the last chapter. So how do you find it? What is the difference between being enlightened and finding nirvana? If you can't follow its signs to a point of discovery, how is it possible to ever benefit from this much-hallowed goal? In this and the next few chapters the reader will find answers to these questions, perhaps not all the answers but some.[147]

Most likely we have had a taste of Nirvana from time to time, and I think I'm there when I eat a slice of perfect apple pie. Obviously that is just a sensual pleasure, one that I will lose when I accomplish Nirodha, or will I? When I eat this pie I know in advance that it will be a temporary pleasure, impermanent. I will never be entirely satisfied, and eating the pie is not part of my identity in any way, not even a significant cause of my existence. It is not defilement as long as I come by the pie honestly, and I am always more than willing to share a piece with anyone who happens to be around. If I go to a potluck social dinner, I often bring a freshly baked apple pie, and even when there are so many other deserts that we cannot possibly eat all of them, the apple pie is often all gone. That kind of sharing gives me a simple pleasure too, which has to be, if not part of nirvana, at least a step in the right direction. But I can see that my pleasure is a conditioned response, and in fact it is a good example of what that means.

---

[147] "The monk who dwells in loving kindness,\ Confident in the Buddha's teaching,\ Attains the peaceful state,\ The blissful stilling of conditioned things.\\ Monk, bail out this boat!\ Once bailed, it will go lightly for you.\ Cutting off both passion and hatred,\ You will go to nibbana." (Dhammapada, vs. 368-9)

At some time in the past I learned to like and take pleasure in eating and sharing apple pie, So?!

There are many such details of our lives that are just our own reality and have no particular significance for our spiritual development if we don't attach to them, or create some kind of fetish around the object. I think I'm pretty relaxed and casual about apple pie. Once I get used to other achievements I generally minimize their importance as well, perhaps that is a kind of modesty, a way of not attaching to these activities. Then there are those aspects of life that relate to the Eight-fold Path, and become integral to our practice. These are factors that we use when we are fully-awakened to change our lives every day; that is how we go about relieving suffering the same way the Buddha did. "Vision arose, insight arose, discernment arose, knowledge arose, illumination arose within me with regard to things never heard before: 'This noble truth of the *way of practice* leading to the cessation of stress *is to be developed'* . . . ." (Appendix II) We also have to rely on the encouragement of others (and vice-versa) to obtain what "is to be", full-awakening.

Awakening as with fulfilling the steps of the Eight-fold Path, "is to be developed"; it is at once a curriculum that we work on to make incremental progress, and a taxonomy of the Dharma that is most urgent. But since Nirvana has no causes, how can we expect to work on that? Look back over your life and see when you felt safe, when you felt relaxed, when you engaged in helping other people first. Perhaps there were moments there when you could taste Nirvana, but it faded. What was the reason you did not sustain all that high level contentment? This brings us to the next teaching; consider "these three qualities—steady [firmness], pure and prepared [activeness]—are interdependent . . ." We are taught to develop all three of these attributes of character in order to thrive in our chosen Buddhist tradition.[148] Is the problem

---

[148] "In the Twelfth step we realize that if there are any problems in life that we cannot answer, then we can concentrate the mind [with direct awareness] and the answers will automatically come . . . Some

here that we have set up a stack of Dominoes, and when one falls it knocks down the rest? In fact we have been working progressively on purification, "purity", in each of the last few chapters, and in the middle of our progress, of course we don't have that level of ethical or understanding of religious behavior completely. We know that purity is interconnected with *stability—and preparation,* which is the one thing we have direct control over by studying outside of meditation. Preparation is study and practice, so that is what we have to keep doing. Stability is internal and one of the features of our mind that we develop as a talent or aptitude in our meditation practice and this is certainly a trait that, once developed, will help us in our professional work and in every aspect of daily lives, but it is also a work in progress for most of us.

In public school every student is encouraged to work hard, learn the whole lesson and do their homework; some students thrive, others get behind and lose out on the benefit of a great start to their lives. In Buddhism, we have the concept of re-birth, each day we can seize the initiative and take steps to change our futures in a positive way, what will motivate us to do that? But even if we make a new start we may be behind the curve, but we should not despair. "Keep [the mind] clear and clean. It will be in a healthy condition." An ordered mind? Which is that, prepared, stable or pure?[149] How much of that character

---

teachings call this insight or creative meditation. We can observe that these three qualities—steady, pure and prepared—are interdependent; they are interconnected in a single unity. There cannot be purity of mind without stability of mind. If there is no purity, there is also no stability. And there must be stability and purity for there to be activeness. The three work together as the three factors of the concentrated mind." (Buddhadasa, 1999, pp. 77-78)

[149] "It is like when we are working. We have the drawers of the table drawn out and everything is spread on the table. Upon having finished the work, we [put] keep everything back into the drawers and the table is clean and cleared of all things. Do the same with the mind—keep it clear and clean. It will be in a healthy condition. Everybody should have such a mind, a mind that is made to be at ease, cool, progressive

can we control on purpose, how much is pre-determined by our DNA, nurturing or instincts? How do we accept the encouragement of others to achieve these virtues? Or should we seek some combination of all three characteristics?

The more you investigate your body and your life, until you understand clearly, the more thoroughly you benefit from the affairs of feelings, mind, thought-formations, and cognizance, because these things are whetstones for sharpening discernment step by step.

When I first read this coaching, I thought this was a really nice analogy or story, but I wondered: How does it apply to my life? When would I apply this mental "at ease . . . clear and clean" mind? If my life is full of complications that interfere with my taking the next step, or taking a step I think I ought to have taken 15 years ago, but for so many reasons I couldn't, and now I am in a rut: "what should I do?" (In this case I am thinking of my study of Buddhism.) First we have to get the mind steady to make a rebirth possible and successful, just like those elementary students who are getting their first experience of trying to accomplish something, and they don't necessarily see why it is so important. Or can we find a different solution? If we are dissatisfied with our job because . . . what can we do? What change can we actually accomplish in the context of our complicated lives? Food for thought.

Is this preparation also an impossible task? Does enlightenment mean that we need to have or develop an encyclopedic mind? Part of the answer comes from understanding that each of these—steady, pure and prepared—are not discrete items, such as a Domino. They are incremental, if we have half of what we might eventually achieve, we can still operate, like a car with a smaller than

---

and happy in the present as well as in the future." (Buddhadasa, 2008, pg. 263)

average engine, we have difficulty with the hills but we can climb them. And because they are interconnected—if we have more steadiness, and less purity for the time-being—then that can make up for at least part of the deficit. And if we have only occasional activeness, thus lack steadiness, that will be a limiting factor, but can this be compensated in part by exceptional preparation? At least this is my operating theory: "answers will automatically come." So I don't necessarily concern myself with also trying to keep a perfect balance, I just work on each sequentially the best I can; I notice (or accept feedback from others) when one aspect is particularly weak and tackle that for a while. This is the tone of the encouragement and advice I give others as well: don't get caught up trying to maintain a perfect balance, likewise don't work on just one aspect of meditation to the exclusion of the others, but look for a leveling in a more or less casual, sequential, and none compulsive way. Meditation should be enjoyable, and our life can reflect this joy; not some kind of hardship, physical or psychological torture, or we will cease doing it.

But we should have a plan and a method to proceed (Anapanasati and Satipatthana), and that is what we get in this next teaching. We "realize the benefits and advantages of non-attachment [nirodha] . . ." at first a kind of intellectual achievement, then we work toward that as a goal of full-awakening.[150] This kind of liberation from clinging, using

---

[150] "Step twelve . . . is liberating the mind (vimocayam-cittam). Liberating the mind means not letting the mind become attached to anything [living in our Heart's desires.] We make the mind let go of anything it is grasping . . . Liberating the mind from all attachments has two aspects: the mind can let go of all these things, or we can take these things away from the mind. The results are the same. Then we observe if there is anything to which the citta continues to cling. If so, we try to release those things from the mind . . .[and purify our Hearts.] Scrutinize the dangerous and painful consequences that all attachment (when we cling to something as 'I' or 'mine') inevitably brings. Then examine and realize the benefits and advantages of non-attachment [nirodha.] What kind of happiness is present [with

this single aspect of our lives as an objective, is actually, as described earlier, an effective way to eliminate suffering, thus we make progress in self-awakening. Our progress along the Eight-fold Path is incremental, it is to be cultivated; we remove the obstacles to our meditation practice one at a time. We don't take on the whole problem at once, but we look for the determinants and conditioned elements, find one or a few that we can eliminate, and the suffering will disappear once and for all. Tradition teaches us that clinging can be found as an element in the majority of suffering, thus it is often the subject of Dharma talks or enters as a detail of the talk, so we can liberate that by conscious effort right at hand—in our minds. We don't have to get help from anyone, or rely on the opinions of others; we can just do it through our vipassana practice using all or any of the techniques we have learned. Again, this is what it means to take refuge: valuing the advice of the ancients and finding a way (having a method) to accept that into our lives on a practical basis.

What we are doing in this fourth part of the third tetrad, step twelve of Anapanasati, is to condition the Content of Consciousness (our memories and inherited instincts, etc.) In step four using our breath we conditioned our feelings, in step eight using our feelings we conditioned our minds, and now in step twelve we use our minds (and mental formations), and the specific effort to liberate our minds, to condition our consciousness (and perhaps our "super-ego") and mental continuum.

As if to echo this teaching, the great forest monk, Boowa (Bua), describes two key points to improving and making more effective (skillful) our meditation practice, and gratefully these are two attributes that we have been developing all along . . ."If mindfulness and discernment are interrupted, you should know that all the efforts of your practice have

non-attachment?] . . .Examine both sides of the coin . . . Observe this every time you breathe in and out." (Buddhadasa)

been interrupted in the same instant." (Boowa, 1996)[151] We know something about mindfulness by now; we have practiced it frequently and utilized its helpful features in our meditation. 'Uninterrupted mindfulness of everything` is often accomplished during walking meditation, when we realize that we can watch karma as it happens (in the same way we watch segments of our stepping) and disrupt that which would create complications for our futures. But "discernment", how is that developed? Is that the same as wisdom, or more basically, the ability (receptivity in our character) to take good advice?[152] How is having discernment related to being fully-awakened? When we have a result or inspiration during meditation, we protect that and remember it, we compare it to everything else we know or have studied, we analyze it to test its validity; those steps, I believe, are important aspects of the process of discernment. We learned earlier that elimination of stress in our lives was based on this quality of a liberated mind. *Liberation* comes as an achievement of applying the best discernment we can put together both from our own effort, from our preparation and from the encouragement of our teachers and Sangha members. So perhaps we know what to do, we just have to keep doing it.

There is a reason why I have delayed expanding on this concept of discernment until this twelfth step. It comes as the culmination of our activity of learning about, knowing and

---

[151] "The most important points, no matter when I teach you—and they are teachings that lie close to my heart—are mindfulness and discernment. These qualities are very important. If you lack mindfulness and discernment, the results of your practice will be erratic. The progress of your efforts will be interrupted and uneven. The techniques of your intelligence for curing defilement will be lacking, and the results—peace and ease—will be sporadic. If mindfulness and discernment are interrupted, you should know that all the efforts of your practice have been interrupted in the same instant."

[152] "There's no meditation in one without wisdom,\ Or wisdom in one who doesn't meditate.\ The one in whom are both meditation and wisdom\ Is close to nibbana." (Dhammapada, vs. 372)

preparing our minds. We have now the frame of reference necessary to appreciate how discernment is an essential characteristic of our thinking, but it was otherwise a vain hope, a rhetorical flourish. It is a bland statement to admonish anyone to "exercise enlightened discernment" until they can actually understand what the heck that would mean in their lives. At the simplest level, discernment is recognizing the differences between otherwise similar concerns, like appraising diamonds, there are important criteria for quality grades. It's much more complex than sizing eggs or noticing shapes; you have to also look inside to see the clarity, color, imperfections etc. So it is in our lives with discernment.

We can discuss these "results and inspirations" with other members of our Sangha, and let them encourage us and share and apply their discernment as well. We can compare conclusions as we might compare craft-work at a community fair. The first, mindfulness and all the activity we have studied about developing and expanding Insight, is what leads to discernment gradually. These are "the crucial tools for eliminating all defilements and mental effluents (asava)."[153] This is a good definition of what liberating the mind means. Boowa always seems to emphasize the development of the Heart and—'to make them clear' to the Heart—as well as to make insight (mindfulness) meditation useful (or skillful), then employing discernment (wisdom) to the results. It sounds like a simple formula, but of course this is an art not a science. I am trying to frame this discussion in the most simple, practical terms possible, with the intention of showing how it all fits together, and that it is actually achievable.

---

[153] ". . .I have never seen any qualities superior to mindfulness and discernment in being able to unravel things within or without so as to make them clear to the heart. For this reason, I teach you these two qualities so that you'll know: To put them in terms of wood, they're the heartwood or the tap root of the tree. In terms of the Dhamma, they're the root, the crucial tools for eliminating all defilements and mental effluents (asava), from the blatant to the most extremely refined levels, once and for all." (Boowa, 1996)

It's time to use a little discernment and take stock of where we are in our progress. We are " . . . practicing various ways of controlling the mind."[154] Even if we know from our preparation what that is about, we can't necessarily do that consistently, steadily. "Or he remains focused on the phenomenon of origination with regard to the mind, on the phenomenon of passing away with regard to the mind . . ." (Satipatthana) This is a shorthand reference to what is the whole caloric element of Dharma, just as sugar, fat, protein and carbohydrates are the nutritional factors that create essential energy, and too much can be stored as fatty tissue creating overweight, heart disease, diabetes, etc. So these "phenomena of origination" is a technical name for the causes of merit as well as the causes of suffering. This is what we do before we work on liberation—so every day we are at choice and we examine the causes of suffering that arise and threaten our tranquility. For some traditions Right Thought is named Right Intention, and as many people know, our intentions dictate our actions and the serious changes in our lives. When we develop our intentions along the lines of purity, then we will be ready to make the best possible decisions when we are confronted with choices.

We just voted and we have vote by mail, so doing that was a very explicit process of making choices among candidates and approving ballot measures or not. It's not possible to know how our vote might create suffering or joy for our future, but one thing is for sure, voting is likely a way to make merit, it feels good. Soon we will look at and realize other aspects of

---

[154] "Recall that the first tetrad (steps one—four) concerned the breath and the body. The second tetrad dealt with those feelings that result from the calming of body-conditioners, the breathing. We studied the mind's feelings although not yet the mind (citta—the Heart) itself at that point. We studied the mind-conditioner and learned about the conditioning of the citta. Then we learned to control the citta-sankhara, the mind-conditioners. The third tetrad we [are studying] the citta and practicing various ways of controlling the mind." (Buddhadasa)

Dharma, but before we do, we have a further discussion about discernment, as we examine these ancient teachings.[155]

How do we test our discernment? It is an intermediate or simultaneous goal—along with learning and implementing the details of our training about purification—to develop wisdom or what may also be called discernment. How do we use our new talents? How best can we encourage other people to follow us along the Path, or just how can we share our insights? We have to not only engage our entire frame of reference and our best judgment when we set out to employ discernment, we have to be willing to accept encouragement and enlightened advice from other experienced teachers. This recognition of the importance of Taking Refuge, as the equivalent of being willing to take good advice, came to me as an insight of discernment, for example. Since that recognition, I have been not only more comfortable with Taking Refuge, but eager to do it at appropriate times.

If we have patience we gradually expand our discernment by our deliberate Right Effort. We learn in our preparation about "the factors that conceal the mind."[156] Then we take

---

[155] "So this is how the wise monk\ Can make a beginning here:\ Guarding of the senses, contentment,\ Restraint in the monastic rule.\ Find friends who are good for you,\ Of pure livelihood, unwearied." (Dhammapada, vs. 375)

[156] "The more you investigate the body until you understand it clearly, the more clearly you will understand the affairs of feelings, mind, and phenomena, or feelings, labels, thought-formations, and cognizance, because all these things are whetstones for sharpening discernment step by step. It's the same as when we bail water out of a fish pond: The more water we bail out, the more clearly we'll see the fish. [But is that good for the fish?] Or as when clearing a forest: The more vegetation we cut away, the more space we'll see. [But what are the ecological tradeoffs in terms of wildlife habitat and erosion?] The things I've just mentioned are the factors that conceal the mind so that we can't clearly see the mental currents that flow out from the heart to its various preoccupations. When you use discernment to contemplate in this way, the currents of the heart will become plain. You'll see

195

steps to counteract the consequences of this concealment, like an antidote. Does developing discernment mean we will lose our spontaneity? Does it mean we give up a significant portion of our possessions and our life style? Or does it help us answer the most important questions associated with our relationships with others, like getting a clear view of the bigger picture? A necessary step toward purification—and encouragement—is what Boowa is trying to do for us in his teaching. Full-awakening "is to be cultivated", but the details of " . . . the currents of the heart" are left open to our own inspiration. Even so, his is an optimistic prediction and assumes a serious effort on our part.

There are trade-offs and responsibilities to understand as Boowa completes his analogy about draining the pond. As we learn the details and techniques of meditation, we are to learn the art and the finesse of success. "Focus instead on how expert and agile you can make your mind at investigating."[157] Consider liberation: the result of applying discernment, but when we work it backwards, we see that we had to work on reducing the factor of clinging, and we had to be aware of the

---

the rippling of the mind clearly every moment it occurs—and the heart itself will become plain, because mindfulness is strong and discernment quick." (Boowa)

[157] "As soon as the mind ripples, mindfulness and discernment—which are there in the same place—we'll be able to keep track of it and resolve it in time. But be aware that in investigating the five khandhas or the four frames of reference (satipatthana), we aren't trying to take hold of these things as our paths, fruitions, and nibbana. We're trying to strip them away so as to see exactly what is the nature of the fish—namely, the heart containing all sorts of defilements. The more you investigate. . . You needn't count how many times you do it in a day. Focus instead on how expert and agile you can make your mind at investigating. The more you investigate—and the more skillful you get at investigating [cultivating self-awakening creates merit]—the more the astuteness of your discernment, which is sharp and flashing as it deals with you yourself and with conditions of nature in general, will develop until it has no limit." (Boowa, 1996)

relationship between purity, steadiness and preparation. So when we do the analysis, we truly notice that these teachings and encouragements are interrelated and interconnected. For Boowa I suspect, to preach about discernment is to suggest that we should all be like his teacher, Ajahn Man (Mun). But it took both of them many years of meditating in caves and in the forests of northeastern Thailand to achieve their most polished development and understanding of Buddha's teachings, then they gratefully interpreted that and passed it on to the rest of us so our Refuge would be more enlightened.

Once we can take each step of the Eight-fold Path and make sense of that, know how much Right Effort is for example, then we can feel we have developed a useful discernment. When " . . . the mind is under our power and within our control, we put this mind to work."[158] That is what we set out to do along our path of purification when we begin to make the essential *realizations* that improve our lives. It is always useful to recall that we can "condition" positive outcomes "make merit" instead of conditioning negative suffering.[159] It is no accident to use the term "conditioning" more often associated with the arising of suffering, but when we apply a positive effort we create peace, happiness and joy. We don't have to accept encouragement or remember all these details, no, we do not need an encyclopedic mind, but having the ability and humility to read and review from time to time, and take good advice from others (Refuge), doesn't hurt.

---

[158] ". . .this well-trained mind has been brought under control; in the fourth tetrad we use it to study Dhamma, the truth of nature . . . Once the mind is under our power and within our control, we put this mind to work. Please observe how the four tetrads [the sixteen steps] are interconnected: first, the kaya-sankhara; second, the citta-sankhara; third the citta itself [samadhi;] and finally Dhamma, which comes next, the facts (saccadhamma) of nature (Dhamma-jati)." (Buddhadasa, 1988, pg. 83)

[159] "The monk who's rich in happiness,\ Confident in the Buddha's teaching,\ Attains the peaceful state,\ The blissful stilling of conditioned things." (Dhammapada, vs. 381)

Chapter Thirteen

Realization of Conditioned Arising

Key Words:

mudu (gentle and supple), kammaniyo, instinctual, mental continuum, formations, boon/making merit, defilements, bodhicitta

Why Should I Meditate?

Uninterrupted mindfulness of what occurs in the mental continuum . . . this is protecting the gains from practice. We meditate to observe and change the mechanism (and formations) of our thinking, and this may be the most direct and accessible way of making these changes. We must expect to meditate for the rest of our lives to maintain the gains we make and touch repeatedly the great joy we are beginning to realize. We share after meditation and true happiness will occur when society as a whole improves and develops. The happiness of individuals comes from Buddhist training and is for the realization of the ideal Buddhist realm. When thoughts are purified "no longer obscured by elaborated thought" the awareness-itself and brightness are manifest, this is a victory of realization. Our highest concern is to become interested in the training of the mind to be objective about potentialities. What we work on in meditation has ramifications for many people (perhaps we ought to take it more seriously.) In meditation we gain realization, and share these, thus we expand our impact and positive changes in our lives. We learn about our minds and we can make it *delightful* at any time we wish it to be so.

As we begin to work on the formations of our minds, my first thought is, I will be working with my opinions, beliefs, memories and the skills I acquired as a student and subsequently. As true as this is, these are not the most important formations that are being suggested. For Buddhists "the primary goal is to develop continuous awareness . . ."[160] So we will be working on the psychological factors that help (or distract) our brains operate as a smoothly functioning mind, as well as making reference to our knowledge base and examining our frame of reference (or our complexes). Much of this involves the brain we inherited from our parents and from our species, based on our instincts and DNA. I learned as a pre-service teacher while taking a course in child psychology, that 80% of our mind is pre-wired, inherited, if not from mythical previous lives, the equivalent of that in terms of genetic gifts and aptitudes. But there is a lot to examine among the practical formations that we control each day, such as how do we relate to the ritual aspects of Buddhism? How often do we donate and look for ways to be generous and helpful to our Sangha? In what ways does compassion operate in our lives? How do we answer the calls for help from our family members, community and country?

---

[160] "Contents of consciousness . . . includes the virtuous and non-virtuous mental factors, perceptions, thoughts and emotions . . . Regardless of the type of support used to train mindfulness, the primary goal is to develop continuous awareness without discontinuities or lapses in awareness. From the perspective of mind, the goal is uninterrupted mindfulness of everything as it occurs in the unfolding mental continuum. This is . . . protecting the mental continuum." (Brown, pp. 140-141)

Answering these questions may be the most important reason to meditate, considering there is virtually no other way that we can reach in, so to speak, and observe and change the mechanism of our thinking (and consequently of our suffering). How do we go about changing the inheritance of the Five Khandhas—by observing our minds over and over, and creating new habits? In teaching, the most modern theory has it that there are eight different intelligences that each of us possesses in varying degrees of dominance. "Gardner believes that eight abilities meet these criteria:

- Spatial
- Linguistic
- Logical-mathematical
- Bodily-kinesthetic
- Musical
- Interpersonal
- Intrapersonal
- Naturalistic

He considers that existential and moral intelligence may also be worthy of inclusion." (Gardner) (It is beyond the scope of this book to describe each of these categories of intelligence.) If this latter were true, it would explain how some people take to meditation easier than others, assuming that a more highly developed "existential and moral intelligence" would benefit or pre-dispose someone to be more involved with their Buddha nature, and in what we might call the art of meditation.

The ability to reason and do mathematics is obviously different from one person to the next because of the level of intelligence we possess relating to visualization and abstract thinking. It is possible to develop each human potentiality according to these capacities, and when that occurs we are " . . . engaged and competent and therefore more inclined to serve society in a constructive way."[161] Scientists now have tests to evaluate these intelligences, and when teachers know the propensities of their students, even when they don't make a formal assessment, they can create lessons that key off these various intelligences, observe the results, and make up lessons that take advantage of each student's natural difference. The unstated element here is that having one or more deficiencies in these intelligences is a serious predisposition to social suffering. When we can't do, perform or learn like other people around us, we will suffer. When we remember that half the people in our communities have below average intelligence, we can begin to understand a huge source of potential suffering.

We can do the same kind of assessment for ourselves by observing the facts of our lives with discernment, once we read about and study the details of this technology. That leaves the flexible 20% of our minds to function based on "free will", the discretionary part that gets hung up in defilements, concoctions, complexes, karma and conditioned arising or it doesn't. Thus there are many people simply incapable of making intelligent, well informed choices. We have to understand our strengths and weaknesses in order to make progress in Buddhism. When we realize how suffering operates in our lives, and how to prevent it, we will experience "unbinding" as the Buddha taught: "Vision arose, insight arose, discernment arose, knowledge arose, illumination arose within me with regard to things never heard before: 'This noble truth

---

[161] "Gardner defines an intelligence as 'biopsychological potential to process information that can be activated in a cultural setting to solve problems or create products that are of value in a culture' . . .there are more ways to do this than just through logical and linguistic intelligence . . .the purpose of schooling 'should be to develop [all the] intelligences and to help people reach vocational and avocational goals that are appropriate to their particular spectrum of intelligences. People who are helped to do so. . . feel more engaged and competent and therefore more inclined to serve society in a constructive way'." (Gardner, 1999)

of stress *has been comprehended* . . ." (Appendix II) In step thirteen of Anapanasati, we try to make sure that our " . . . mind is mudu (gentle and supple) . . ." and we can think of this as the texture of our Hearts.[162] As you practice through the first twelve steps of Anapanasati Bhavana, notice that each is impermanent, but since we know that in advance, we are prepared for it, it does not cause (or condition) any suffering. We might think of our ability to meditate as an aspect of our Intrapersonal intelligence, however since the level of difficulty is minimal, nearly everyone has the capacity to use their minds in productive ways using meditation techniques, if they have the patience and just a little training.

Notice which aspect of your mind you are using at any given time, the acquired propensities or the fundamental, inherited portion? Can you tell the difference, or does it all seem like a single unit? Is our acquired knowledge and personality easier to change than the instinctual part, such as sex drive, response to hunger, response to fear or anger? Of course this is a complicated story, unique for each of us, but ironically by that fact alone we are all endowed comparably. There is no duality between them and us. Yet our goal is to realize the elements of suffering in our lives by direct awareness—so we can change these—this is what we get to do once our suffering has been fully recognized. We get to contemplate these details after the mind reaches an energetic level based on Concentration and steadiness. This is perhaps where many of the Buddhist stories come in handy with devas, etc. to represent different aspects of our inherited nature and expose these to the scrutiny of animated story telling.

---

[162] "The mind has [by now] a great deal of kammaniyo, readiness or activeness, from the practice of concentrating the mind . . . the mind is mudu (gentle and supple) . . . [this is the texture of our Hearts] we return to the beginning step. First, we contemplate just the breath until we see that it is impermanent. We observe that the breath changes and becomes long. Its long duration is impermanent, always changing, getting longer or shorter. Its shortness is impermanent as well . . . The breath's effect on the body is also impermanent." (Buddhadasa)

As we progress and repeat Anapanasati, we will realize a serious focus and attempt to get into the most intense aspect of Buddhist meditation, jhana as described in step five and beyond. This is like taking a break from the above analysis and contemplation and relaxing into a peaceful period of calm and tranquility. Is this an intellectual achievement or just opposite? There is very little contact with the intelligences and vipassana is inactive.[163] What do we have to do to reach this level of absorption? Certainly a single focus, *ekaggata*—Means "to have a single peak, focus, or apex." Single minded. Is this capacity part of our Buddha-nature, thus hardwired into our consciousness, like the constant beating of our hearts, an autonomous function? Or is this an acquired skill?

When you think of these diverse intelligences, and the sub-conscious, the ego, the emotional experiences, the neurotransmitters, and all the details of our minds—what a complex species we are! And yet that is the central field of play for meditation and the rest of our conscious existence, and we are experts at contemplating and utilizing this elaborate mechanism, whether we realize this or not. We can achieve unbinding, free of clinging, craving and other attachments, but this is probably more difficult for people of the highest intelligence. In any case, we need to have respect and reverence for those few people who have exceptional development of their knowledge of Dharma.[164]

This complex mind leads us through our lives and evaluates seemingly an infinite magnitude of information each day, and

---

[163] "This scheme is that of the four Absorptions (jhana), a graduated series of increasingly deep meditative states. In the first Absorption the meditator becomes oblivious to everything around him, though still capable of both casual and concerted thought, and his attention dwells unbrokenly on the object of meditation. In this state he enjoys both bodily comfort and the more refined mental pleasure attendant on such relaxed concentration . . ." (Buddhadasa)

[164] "The one from whom you can learn the Dhamma\ Taught by the Fully Awakened One\ You should honour with reverence\ As a Brahmin honours the sacrificial fire." (Dhammapada, vs. 392)

we make decisions and choices that have implications and influence our future and interpersonal relations on a continuous basis. There is a whole region of our lives that concerns our behaviors, habits and proclivities, sadness and joy, and this is where we engage ethical considerations and moral directives (i.e. precepts) and inspirations. Certainly we all have pleasant, wholesome and long term pleasures that seem immune from suffering, if this is true so much the better. But if these positive experiences end and we suffer from that, are we prepared for this kind of disappointment? Or change? How strongly do we try to control our lives and the lives of others around us? Who suffers from this?

To prevent and avoid suffering we need to take a serious look at the list of "defilements" which is attached at the end of this chapter. I began a serious consideration of this list by choosing one item: Quarrelsome. I initially thought, that doesn't really apply to me—of course that opinion was a serious indication that it actually does. And once I got into a detailed examination of the "formation" of quarrelsomeness I found plenty to fit my own life; times when, even though I thought I was entirely justified, I had been contentious, defensive and argumentative. Being justified is actually beside the point. So this was an introspective activity of using this defilement as an "object of meditation", and in doing so I opened a window into my own life that was enlightening. To really change my behavior, what will I have to do, what kind of psychological training will I have to undergo? What persuasion, incentive or motivation will make me become less quarrelsome? If I have an experience of "absorption" relating to specific events in my life associated with being quarrelsome, will that help desensitize me, to make me the opposite? What is the opposite of being quarrelsome, being compliant, disinterested or disengaged? For now each time I find myself ready to contend in a discussion, I think twice and often find a different way to present my own point of view, or instead look for elements of agreement. It is not my nature to be uninvolved in a serious discussion, no matter how little I am trained in the topic, but I can practice a level of participation that more closely resembles the receptive student, rather than the opinionated, narcissistic debater.

After step Four of Anapanasati we found that we could use our breathing as a ritual, and condition our emotions and eliminate clinging, craving and attachments based on the fact that these mental formations are not permanent.[165] Since there is no "atta" that bestows a sacred obligation on us, we are free to explore and develop according to our own inspired choices. We have the Precepts and other guidance, and beyond that we need to anticipate consequences as a basis of our ethical choices.

As a teacher I have noticed the experience of physical symptoms of anger, when the hair on my neck stiffens, and I get hot and probably turn a little red. I have learned to watch and recognize these symptoms and not respond directly in words, and in less than a minute the emotions subside and change, and I choose skillful responses and solutions. Gratefully this is an example of the impermanence of Piti and the onset of Sukha. There would be no benefit if I were to act out anger in a rash way, no healthy release, since the emotion can naturally subside on its own. The natural impermanence of emotions worked to my advantage in these circumstances, and I believe this is an element of wisdom, certainly it is part of being magnanimous and having equanimity, which are taught universally in Buddhist traditions.

Are we left brain dominant or right brain? Artistic or pragmatic? This is a whole different consideration, and this too can change. Do these "formations" one way or the other, influence how we respond to difficult emotional situations? Does this influence whether we can realize unbinding? Related to Quarrelsomeness, are the personality features

---

[165] "Eventually, the feelings of piti and sukha arise. Watch them one by one. See impermanence in each . . . The calming of these feelings is impermanent as well . . . Next, we watch the citta itself [mind/heart;] it, too, is impermanent. [etc.] . . .Even the liberating of the mind is only a temporary liberation here and thus is also impermanent." (Buddhadasa)

we exhibit responding to the emotions of—Anger, violent temper, Rage—and perhaps others detrimental for our lives and relationships? Or can we sublimate the piti-energy that is naturally associated with these emotional states? When we separate these formations and see how they live in our lives, or not, then we are doing some important work. Often we need a friend or counselor to show us the way to help us recognize these personality traits as mental formations. This explains why we must expect to engage in meditation for the rest of our lives to maintain the gains we make and touch repeatedly the great joy we are beginning to realize?

Does it matter if we believe in devas or spirits or not, as we consider the contents of our consciousness? What are the formations that relate to our spiritual life? What influence would this transcendental, other worldly formation have on our ability to control our desired outcome, *to reduce suffering*? What reactions and perceptions change when this consciousness changes? How does that affect the way we meditate or our expectations from meditation? The details of our lives are all potentially objects for our meditation, and we see when we put our simple goal into this broader context, when we realize the scope and details of our suffering, of our mental capacities and many possible formations—that it is not so unreasonable to expect to achieve this kind of happy, uncomplicated, satisfying life.

Sooner rather than later we have to take the slogans and teachings of the Buddha and all the commentaries, and work these over for ourselves, test them, try them out. I have tried here to suggest a few mental formations that might not be obvious to most people. And going a step further, does our reaching a "deep meditative state" help society improve and develop? Certainly we want to be happier, or to sustain the happiness we have achieved after all of our work up to this point, but can we transfer any of that to others? As we have already described, after each significant period of meditation we share merit in ways that we have learned to do so. But how can we presume to be capable of *realizing* and participating in the Bodhisattva ideal " . . . the realization of the ideal Buddhist realm."[166] The Bodhicitta ideal that we can learn about in the book *Bodhicitta: Higher Truth* is perhaps a less ambitious prospect and more within our reach. We are not just an individual after all or an independent self as much as we might think we are. We can plainly see by now that we share all these mental formations, and when we think, we must realize that somebody else has already had some or all of the ideas that chase through our minds, whether by chance or by whim, or directed by our best contemplation and discernment. When we realize that what we work on in meditation may have ramifications for many people, perhaps we can take it more seriously. If we come to some important realizations and then share these (as I have tried to do in this book) we are expanding our impact and cementing any positive changes in our lives. Is that why we go to the trouble of sharing merit, so in reality the benefits and gains we make will stay in our own lives and become new mental formations for ourselves? There is more to unbinding than this.

Buddhism, just like everything else we touch or see, changes with the times, and we are all instruments of that change. Step by step, how do we get to that ideal realm and realize some spiritual gains? First we acknowledge and recognize the impact of our suffering, take advice (refuge/ encouragement) from other Sangha members—the Dharma and The Buddha—and then eliminate that suffering! We solidify those gains by protecting and sharing these with all those who surround us as we realize unbinding. We all have the intellectual capacity to do this at some level, and many of us have the capacity to create children's stories to help those who are new to the larger world. We must help each new

---

[166] "[Samadhi] concentration, prompts awareness of the need to strive for the perfecting of one's own personality and of all society. If society as a whole improves and develops, the happiness of the individual will be guaranteed. If society is happy, the individual and all of his fellows will be happy. This is the meaning of true happiness and of the realization of the ideal Buddhist realm. Buddhist training is for the sake of realizing such a realm." (Mizuno, pg. 96)

generation develop healthy mental formations, so perhaps their lives will be more enlightened and free of suffering than our own.

What we have been doing for several chapters now is training our minds to operate based on all the important principles developed over a period of 2,500 years. Many people come to Buddhism to gain merit or "make merit" or "boon" by giving gifts or by showing respect to monks. But what is the extension of that merit? In a world of cause and effect, what consequence do we expect from this kind of "boon"? Good luck? Or consider the merit of meditating regularly in the solitude of our own homes, and then declaring that whatever merit we make we share with our teachers, our loved ones, the whole world? This is the way the Dalai Lama does it. He says never to make merit for our self, but give it away as fast as we can. We can and should make more merit tomorrow in the same way. So when we meditate to train our minds, we do make merit in both a spiritual way and inescapably in practical ways by creating a better tool to use. "Training of the mind . . . is the highest concern of us human beings."[167] This is about developing self-possession rather than clinging to the idea that we can pave the way to a rosy future by just performing public acts of charitable giving. We have to reach deep into our ethical lives and improve them.

When we began this chapter perhaps we had a different idea of what it meant to learn to " . . . operate as a smoothly functioning mind." There is more to it than what meets the eye,

---

[167] "Therefore may you all become interested in this matter of the training of the mind which is the highest concern of us human beings? The success of everything depends on the mind. When you become well-acquainted with the facts about the mind, may you all be able to do what you ought to do. May you know every kind of mind and be able to exert control over it, and make it be delightful at any time you wish it to be so. . . Make it suitable for performing its duty at any time you like and set it free from things which ought not to be found in it, driving them away in the manner befitting them." (Buddhadasa, 2008, pp. 269-271)

but it is not so complex or conceptually challenging that we can't all easily get started and make significant gains whenever we set our minds to it (pun intended). I am influenced by my recent visit to Thailand when I participated in and watched on TV these spectacles of monks lined up seated to receive gifts. They have bland expressions on their faces realizing that what they are doing is symbolically more important for the giver, hopefully. I have this vision that they take the gifts and turn them over to their Sangha helpers, and they in turn shuffle the items out the back door, whatever isn't needed, and put it in the temple store and resell it to the next group of spiritual tourists or supplicants who come to "make merit."

Now here is an interesting clue to our success in developing our minds; we can accept the gifts of teaching and tradition that we encounter, take what we can use, save the rest as cash and use it in the future to make whatever improvements or satisfy whatever needs we may have. There is no scheme or deception on the part of the monks, just a *realization* that the significance of their ritual is to help laypeople work on improving their "thought-formations and cognizance . . ." It will be the same unbinding for each of us. This is my hope that we will all achieve some realization of the consequences of our defilements: "Nothing else has the power to reach into the heart so as to bind it . . ."[168] Thus we see the possibility and path to unbinding. There being so many possible defilements to work on, we all need to have a bank of merit and energy to continue with this important work. I hope that we can find the essence of our practice, to relieve suffering. Remember also that there are millions of other Buddhists out there intently

---

[168] "You'll eventually have the knowledge and ability to realize that the conditions of nature you have been investigating in stages—beginning with sights, sounds, smells, tastes, and tactile sensations throughout the cosmos, and turning inward to your own body, feelings, labels, thought-formations, and cognizance—are not defilements, cravings, or mental effluents in any way. The heart alone is what has defilements, cravings, and mental effluents with which it binds itself. Nothing else has the power to reach into the heart so as to bind it. . ." (Boowa)

transferring merit to us, to help us improve our lives! This is not a trivial point, and it may seem disconnected or indirect. But if it's in the heart, a craving for chocolate for example, we can acknowledge it and make the necessary changes, as we have learned to expand and enrich our hearts in earlier chapters. If we need to change the way we regard egos and our personal identity, we do that in our Hearts and it is possible without changing the way we use normal language to refer to ourselves casually. Perhaps this is a koan to put these several ideas together to see how we blend them, like peanuts and chocolate?

There is no essential essence to the Heart; it can be its own worst enemy, or our savior using the capacities that we create. Everything we need to make progress in our lives is right here; ready at hand, a cushion or a comfortable chair for meditation, a foot path for walking, a pleasant space for standing, or a cozy bed for lying in meditation. "All conditions of nature in general are like useful tools."[169] These kinds of metaphors and teaching analogies are useful to prompt us to think deeper, to realize the truth that surrounds us, to apply and extend our understanding and discernment to the

---

[169] "Aside from the heart that is ignorant about itself—searching for shackles for its neck and setting the fires of delusion to burn itself to no purpose—there are no traces of enemies to the heart anywhere at all. We can compare this to a knife, which is a tool made to benefit intelligent people, but which a foolish person grabs hold of to kill himself and then accuses the knife of being his enemy. What precedent is there for making such a charge? All conditions of nature in general are like useful tools, but a stupid person grabs hold of them to bind himself and then claims that the conditions of nature throughout the world [the 80%] have put their heads together to abuse him. Who can decide such a case?—for the plaintiff has already killed himself. If we decide that the instrument of death loses the case to the dead plaintiff, what sort of vindication is the plaintiff going to gain to give him any satisfaction? The heart that's deluded about itself and about its own affairs is in the same sort of predicament." (Boowa, 1996)

particularities of our own lives, as well as to the generalities of the members of our community.

"Nothing lasts forever" and usually that is good news. We see this in the simple way we relate to the circumstances of our lives, and how these change as we proceed with our meditation practice. "We have to see how or what things we like and feel or realize what value they hold for us, then only will we be able to see their impermanent nature in particular."[170] We learned about this as we engaged in the ritual of breathing during meditation. We can also give ourselves a lot of credit by how unbinding has been realized and incorporated into our personality. We go back to the beginning to connect the whole as we learn about the significance of our Buddhist training, and gain a full understanding of the impact of the temporary nature of the details of our lives. Eventually we realize that those simple techniques we began with, end up having serious and subtle, beneficial effects.

When emotional objects (piti) are stabilized, this permits the development of bliss (sukha). When thoughts are simplified "no longer obscured by elaborated thought" the awareness-itself and brightness are manifest, this is a victory of realization. These details give useful hints to the meditator who is the person relaxed in concentration, trying in some small way to improve his/her community. And this explicitness gives us confidence that our meditation practice can be advanced. Each step of the way, we must choose, "Yes, I want to take

---

[170] "Contemplate on long breathing and discern in it the impermanent nature of long breath. Do the same with short breathing and notice its impermanent nature. Also observe the impermanent nature of the concoction that breathing makes in both bodies—the body of breath and the physical body; then see the impermanent nature of the effort made in trying to control the breathing. . . Both 'piti' and 'sukha' concocts and manipulates the mind. The concoction itself is impermanent. . . We have to see how or what things we like and feel or realize what value they hold for us, then only will we be able to see their impermanent nature in particular." (Buddhadasa, 2008, pp. 283-287)

the next step." We have three more steps of *realization* to examine that we can learn from.

I: Quarrelsomeness

A: Inclined to quarrel or disagree
B: It is common in studies of interpersonal characteristics to examine personality variables as static predictors. Yet in recent years it has also become possible to examine personality and related interpersonal processes as they unfold over time in association with event specific cues. The present article reviews research that (1) identifies behaviors that reflect the occurrence of hostile-irritable-quarrelsome traits in daily life, (2) demonstrates both the stability and within-person variability of these behaviors over time, (3) documents event-level interpersonal cues that are systematically associated with within-person variation in quarrelsome behavior, and (4) describes how dispositional level agreeableness and irritability moderate the associations of event-level cues with quarrelsome behavior. The influence of the neurotransmitter serotonin on quarrelsome behavior is also considered. The studies indicate that quarrelsome individuals have reduced affective reactivity to engaging in quarrelsome behavior, increased behavioral reactivity to perceptions of quarrelsomeness in others, and greater responsiveness to change in serotonin levels. (Wikipedia)
C: Argumentative; belligerent; contentious; given to quarreling. What comes to us from the Buddhist tradition is a highly innovative and unique teaching both for India and for the entire world; even unique today. " . . . In the Buddhist and Jain texts which reveal the Buddha's immediate environment a multitude of contending voices speak, as though in a tumultuous market-place of philosophical opinions and ascetic practices. There were indeed public debating halls where ascetics of all stamps gathered to dispute. The public lecture or sermon, directed to disciples but also to

potential supporters, was a common institution . . . Buddha was later to inveigh against those who were 'clever, subtle, experienced in controversy, hairsplitters who writhe like worms in argument' . . . There were different schools of skeptics, philosophers doubtful of the possibility of effective knowledge in this or that matter, and their existence was perhaps the surest sign of the heat and sophistication of the intellectual climate." (Carrithers, 1983, pp. 25-26) This is an example of the intrinsic nature of being quarrelsome and how it has been manifest for centuries. This would also argue against the claim that Buddhism could not have been original and is just warmed over and reformed Brahmanism.

D: —easily irritated or provoked to contest; irascible; choleric

Consider how each of these defilements influences your life! And thus you make significant strides toward "unbinding" when these are no longer part of your habit of living.

discord
Disrespect
excessive
disrespectfulness
Anger
violent temper
Rage
Hurt
Abuse
cruelty
violence
shamelessness
lying
hypocrisy
callousness
deceit
Eagerness for power
Rapacity

vindictiveness
censoriousness
wrath
dominance
prejudice
Intolerance
arrogance
inattentiveness
tyranny
Oppression
unyielding
hatred
Sarcasm
negativity
unkindness
capriciousness
contempt
Hostility

ridicule
deception
stubbornness
intransigence
grudge
cursing
Aggression
derision
Egoism
ambition
Calculation
Obstinacy
Impudence
Sadism
mercilessness
sexual lust
malignancy
Insatiability
Obsession
seducement
Humiliation
manipulation
Haughtiness
conceitedness
irresponsibility
high-handedness
effrontery
Falseness
imposture
know-it-all
lack of comprehension
ignorance
presumption
delusion
prodigality
baseness
dogmatism
dipsomania

lecherousness
debasement
voluptuousness
pretense
Furtiveness
Envy
jealousy
vanity
enviousness
faithlessness
imperiousness
insidiousness
Garrulity
Unruliness
Ingratitude
stinginess
ostentatiousness
pessimism
dissatisfaction
indifference
self-hatred
Torment
obstinacy
hardheartedness
greed for money
gambling
Greed
blasphemy
gluttony
masochism
self-denial
desire for fame

Chapter Fourteen

Realizing the Causes of Suffering

Key Words:

Suffering, emotional blackmail, fading away, sankhara, even minded, raga/attachment, viraga/dissolving, fruition

Why Should I Meditate?

In our meditation practice, to get at the causes of suffering, we have to be specific and personal. When we do that, we equip ourselves with wisdom and maturity to prevent future suffering. Our meditation works when attachment is lessening, when we are even-minded toward sankhara [conditioning] and to life experience. When we reach non-reflective samadhi the mind becomes clear and serene. In meditation direct awareness is the first "secret" to eliminating suffering; we recognize causes of stress and suffering and watch these. We can realize absolute awareness in which the mind is pervaded by true knowledge and understanding. Can I pause before each decision to meditate and identify whether or not there are imbedded the causes of some future suffering? Our meditation is as profound as our deepest knowledge, the inner truth. As our erotic love for attachments begins to fade, anger toward past and present objects of our displeasure dissolves into peace of mind. When our meditation succeeds we no longer fear a collapse of our lives. As we meditate, Dharma makes sense in ways we have not noticed before. In meditation we experience not overconfidence, but unbinding and expand our learned devotion. Before meditation we Take Refuge—in the Buddha, the Dharma and the Sangha—so this refuge returns to us as reward, enhancing stability and peace.

In this chapter we come fully to grips with the necessity to practice in order to Realize that we suffer, perhaps needlessly. "Vision arose, insight arose, discernment arose, knowledge arose, illumination arose within me with regard to things never heard before: 'This noble truth of the origination [causes of suffering] of stress—stress has been abandoned'." (Appendix II) Understanding this unbinding and how that prevents suffering, involves several levels such as the mental formations described in the last chapter; environmental circumstances that surround us, some of which we have chosen; and the social conditions that confront us every day. So, this is not just understanding the causes of suffering in broad generalities, but knowing and explaining how it operates in our lives every time "binding" rears its ugly head. In this chapter we discover and explain the true causes of suffering, thus we are given the keys to overcoming suffering; it can happen. How do we overcome the institutional causes of suffering from prejudice against races, new-comers, poor people, genders or ugly (fat, short or handicapped) people? We may feel that we don't accept any of these biases, but this is an intellectual choice quite apart from the emotional trauma or "chip on the shoulder" that is carried by those who are the victims of this kind of abuse. But what can each of us, or any one of us do to reduce the impact or eliminate these issues in society? We have to be aware of these issues and understand as the first "binding", assuming that we are not caught in the emotional grip of one or the other kind of prejudice, then it is easy to be aware of how and why we suffer.

When I first heard a brief and confusing explanation that "all life is suffering", I was in my early twenties and unprepared to accept this thesis. I accepted the teaching that overcoming obstacles and thriving was a beautiful aesthetic and redeeming feature of life. I believed that I was someone who could succeed and therefore, everyone should feel the same sort of confidence and hope. That kind of confidence, I have subsequently learned, comes from having been given sufficient intelligence at birth capable of problem solving and adapting, or as suggested before, only half the population is above average, so fewer than half of all people in general cope successfully with the vagaries of life without traumatic suffering. Although I suspect intelligent people suffer just as much, perhaps in different ways.

I could see that there were plenty of pleasurable moments in my life, and the religion in which I was engaged taught about inspiration, hope, charity and the victory of happiness as a reward for making sacrifices and living a righteous life. I accepted the concept that I could be inspired and my life could be enriched by appreciation of art, culture, and intimate relationships; so why wasn't everyone else eligible for the rewards from that same kind of vacant hope. In an important way I was in denial about suffering, so obviously I was unconcerned about its determinants and causes. And thus I did not have the discernment or experienced judgment to make correct decisions to avoid the development of suffering for the future. Since my suffering was not fully recognized, it did not abandon or prevent the arising of additional suffering. But that is true for most young people, as I see it now. The mistakes and misjudgments I made are characteristic of so many youth, and I made my share.

There is a logical irony in suggesting "all life is suffering", because of the cynical implication that no matter what we do, we will end up regretting it or suffering from it. If there is no reality of happiness and contentment to look toward, what's the point? That suggests that not only do we need to recognize the importance of realizing the causes of suffering, we also need to distinguish between what can be changed and what need not be changed. The teachings of Dharma equip us with wisdom and maturity to do this and prevent future suffering, eventually, and this is simpler than it seems. If we are flooded with the negative or likewise over-optimistic thinking, we will not find the key to overcoming suffering. So as a quarrelsome youth, I thought this idea of emphasizing suffering was a form of emotional blackmail, a way to prey on otherwise capable people, to get them to acknowledge their suffering, then as a solution, accept a religion that promoted faith, belief and un-scientific solutions. This was like putting a band-aid on a cut without cleaning or administering antibiotic.

The people I knew well saw the explanation of the cosmos according to their religious teachings as reality, so they were not being fraudulent or clever. None of us were "free from desires and discontent in regard to the world . . ." (Analayo, pg. 67) . . . this is unbinding. So we were all in the same boat, and thus it was the accepted normal. We all believed because "what other explanation could there be", and "you can't prove it wrong" so it must be right. These fallacies of logic stacked up one on top of the other until the whole intellectual construction was a solace and a reality for a lot of people I was raised with, and for them still today, i.e. Mitt Romney. Most of the people whom I was close to in my youth, and most of my family are still involved in that religion, and they would deny that life is just about suffering, or that the very fact-of-life is the source of most of our suffering since they think life is a gift from god (and saying otherwise is essentially blasphemy). Now after having many years of experience and observing suffering in the lives of not only all of those people but everyone I have known, I can see the validity in this Buddhist teaching. But this is not intended as a slogan or the essence of Buddhism, it is intended as acknowledging the problem in order to take the necessary and clearly defined steps to realize the causes of suffering, to abandon the arising of suffering, and to systematically eliminate this suffering.

So the First Noble Truth is not strictly speaking a pessimistic or fatalistic statement, even though it is a negative observation, it is an affirmative teaching for our lives. I misunderstood this as a youth, but I realize now that it is simply pointing to the problem so we can more easily find a solution. By its very simplicity it is profound. If you don't recognize or realize what the problem is, how can you hope to identify its causes? And the promise of Buddhism is that suffering has causes that can be recognized and eliminated. Much of the ancient teachings in Buddhism are repetitive generalizations about the reality of suffering and the most significant reasons for that, such as cravings, attachments, clinging, desires and we have discussed others in the course of these chapters. But to get at the causes, do we have to be specific? Or can we work on the general causes of "craving, clinging . . . attachments" and make that a significant part of our personal meditation practice?

It is almost trite to say that we all experience stress from our work place environments, and this may be the single most common kind of suffering as discussed earlier, but what are the causes and consequences of this stress? Are we ourselves moody and difficult to get along with, or is it just our boss who is grouchy and demanding, thus creating stress for us? Do we take this stress home and act out our negative emotions against our family members? How well prepared are we for the job, or have we been promoted up to and above our level of competence (The Peter Principle) and thus constantly confronted with tasks and decisions for which we are unprepared? I have found that when I was functioning at a level well within my capabilities, I thrived, enjoyed work, succeeded and exceeded expectations. Looking back over some forty-five years of various professional experiences I can see where I thrived and where I should have probably chosen a different career path. Hindsight is twenty/twenty they say, but by Taking Refuge in Buddhism we are able to see our future as if through a telescope!

I can see how I ignored much of the stress I confronted, and the stress I experienced was either subtle or overt, but even so there are now consequences from that stress. Recently I was surprised to have needed medical intervention for high blood pressure, and one episode of atrial fibrillation that has been reversed to normal. I can now acknowledge the subtle stress factors that operated on my life both from my work, my genetics and from my family associations. These have finally affected my physical health, no more free ride, as well as my emotional and mental well-being. There were times when I was suffering and wasn't aware of it, and it was quietly taking its toll on my physical systems even though I was otherwise proficient and reasonably successful. So I was likewise oblivious to the causes of this suffering.

I realize now that I am not removed from or immune to the causes of stress and suffering, as much as I have followed strategies for minimizing the effects from any potential suffering. Perhaps the difference is that I can often see it coming, and take a few subtle steps to avoid the suffering. I haven't entirely taken steps to prevent these causes, I have a ways to go, but at least I seem to be more aware of what is happening, and this direct awareness itself is a partial defense. The first "secret" to eliminating suffering is to recognize the causes of stress and suffering, acknowledge these, watch these, and emphasize this bare awareness in meditation. This won't eliminate every source or cause of suffering, but it takes the air out of some of it, the part we control directly, a partial solution. This is the formula if you will, the algorithm of unbinding; to defeat the arising by abandoning one specific cause of each circumstance as we isolate that.

Hindsight may be so much better informed, but no less shrouded in bias than the day to day experiences we encounter and react to. So understanding the assumptions and biases that colored our lives in the past, as well as remembering the details of the circumstances that have shaped our decisions, is what *Realization* is about, as a second step (first: recognize). To achieve this we have to look outside our own nature and education, we have to prepare by studying Dharma, following Satipatthana Sutta, listen to Dharma talks and converse in study groups and retreats with like-minded members of our larger Sangha, otherwise we just keep those biases working their deceit. There is more, however, because when *Realization* is thorough and well grounded, it is usually life changing and consequential; our best intentions and some of the significant causes of our suffering become clear, and our solutions can become operational. We can truly say that arising has been abandoned more and more.

This doesn't have to lead to one mid-life crisis after another, but it might well manifest as a course correction from time to time. For those who suffer from clinical complexes, mental illness, and other pathologies, this kind of Buddhist self-help is certainly insufficient. Professional intervention is now often being incorporated into a more comprehensive program, such as that found in AA or group therapy.

So I have moved from one group of trees to another in the forest of life, but have I really gone to a different more enlightened forest? The stress and the problems I confront are not all new, even though I no longer actively work each day, my retirement is not an entirely new way of life. I try to incorporate Buddhist teachings and abandon the arising of stress, but the changes are subtle and my circumstances still reflect the activities of my past. There is hope, I believe, considering how Buddhism has gradually entered my life and insinuates itself each day more and more as a principal guiding ideology for me. Where will *Realization* lead me? Can I pause before each decision to identify whether or not there are imbedded in that the causes of some future suffering? There is still time in my life for this story to unfold, and indeed part of the goal of compiling this book is to aid the progress of this kind of well-informed course correction, to polish the stone of my own Liberation each time I reread and edit this book.

I recently read an autobiographical book by Pramjuan Pengchan, a philosophy professor who left his work, took early retirement from teaching, and walked from where he lived in Chiang Mai, Thailand, to Ko Sumui on the southern peninsula, a distance of 1,000 kilometers or so (where he was born). I mention this story because the book illustrates how Realization functioned in the life of this former philosopher. His story is probably typical of many other people who have stepped out late in life to find personal understanding, but as such it offers an important perspective. His personal experience is more interesting and extreme than any that has transpired in my vanilla, bland life.

He was an advocate of individual responsibility, perhaps to the point of obsession, for his students and eventually for himself. "It is our duty to individually consider and select carefully the meanings of truth, knowledge, goodness, and beauty . . ."[171] In other words, he is asking his students to evaluate the causes underlying their life choices "meanings of truth . . ." that inspire and inform their decisions, so far so good. But it was his practice as a teacher to expect this kind of maturity and development of insight from his students, and I have this vision of him reading their essays and marking their papers according to how well they achieved the challenge he describes in these words. He refers to this pedagogical directive, and his own failure to have answered it for himself, as the motivation for his grueling trip.

I have seen other examples of this kind of change, for example, when watching an active and pleasure seeking youth settle down into being a productive and dedicated parent for the first time. What a dramatic change can take place based on this new birth experience, and I have seen this be a positive and appropriate change, a maturing and adjusting to an adult life as a parent. I have also seen that when such a positive change does not occur, the habits of a wayward youth can carry over into the parent with disastrous consequences. So if we take these changes, which are reasonably easy to identify, as clues in our own lives, we can better analyze our lives and benefit from our personal history. When we identify how our perspectives about "goodness, and beauty" change, then perhaps we can predict what these changes will cause? That

---

[171] "I desire that all philosophy students be conscious of their role regarding the construction of meanings and values of truth, knowledge, goodness, and beauty. It is our duty to individually consider and select carefully the meanings of truth, knowledge, goodness, and beauty for our own use that is appropriate to us. Whenever the meaning of our life changes, the meanings of the society, the world, and all sentient beings will also change." (Pengchan, pg. 3)

is probably not possible for most people without relying on some dispassionate counselor or wise friend. In an important way it is by degree easier to see the solution in lives of others than in our own, so we must be willing to transfer these lessons to ourselves: "a word to the wise." We can set out in our meditation practice to achieve this result, but only if we have somehow been instructed and motivated to do it, and learned how to be appropriately mindful.

And in a different way Pengchan's struggle and failure to adjust "to be conscious of [his] role . . ." was the motivating cause for the odyssey of walking, unaided (he got help each day along the way) such a significant distance. "I have arrived at a junction where truth and falsehood are inseparable . . ."[172] He was probably a depressed person, and apparently very confused—by his own admission—but we also have to give him credit for such a lucid and clear explanation of the arising of the causes of suffering that can afflict us all. He does put the dilemma into clear and understandable terms, and it is one that most of us may confront at one time or another. Again, clearly recognizing the problem is mandatory to taking skillful steps to solving it. That underlines the importance of Taking Refuge in Buddhism, where these issues are identified and sorted out. During Pengchan's walking he had plenty of time for directly watching and being aware of his conceptual failures.

Comparing this statement with the task he had set for his students, it is possible to make two very different observations: one, that the task itself was seriously flawed, perhaps impossible at the outset: it was at best based on a confusion

---

[172] ". . .My strength to conduct rational inquiry into these opposites is extremely weakened. I no longer conduct any meaningful rational analysis and it is probably due to this fatigue that I should quit teaching philosophy. [After twenty years.] As far as my awareness is concerned, I have arrived at a junction where truth and falsehood are inseparable, knowledge and ignorance are one; goodness and badness unite and are indivisible; beauty and ugliness are one condition such that no power can possibly separate the two from each other." (Pengchan, pp. 2-3)

of the use of language, and at worst it was wrong minded. And secondly, that the philosophy professor was essentially made grist for the very intellectual mill that he had created and envisioned when he made the claim just prior: "Philosophy is the science of rationality, initiated from the conflict inherent in opposite pairs . . ." (Pengchan, pp. 2-3) and he succumbed to this conflict that is perhaps of his own construction. This duality is a human construct, not an inevitable necessity for life. This is a dramatic misunderstanding of what doing philosophy is about, thinking of it as a science of some sort is often found in academic circles (but that is a very different subject, i.e. refuted by the teachings of Wittgenstein, however a useful one beyond the scope of this discussion). His "rational inquiry" failed because it was destined to fail, being based on a very impossible task. Consider arguing the contrast between Love and Hate, removing the discussion from any specific reality or personal context, and trying to generalize rules about each element of this pair, and what do you get? What kind of scientific rationality is going to help us come up with absolute truths about this pair of opposites? Instead we make progress when we consider each of these abstract concepts separately in the specific context of our own lives during periods of meditation, and by finding the spiritual truths that inspire and derive from each of these human motivations. That is when "arising has been abandoned", when we have achieved unbinding. Are we expected to write our own dictionaries, or does Taking Refuge give us a big head start? This is certainly a rational discussion and food for meditation, but it is not particularly scientific, more an artistic endeavor that can inspire our cultural achievements (e.g. writing poetry, songs and making movies).

What could it mean to say that "truth and falsehood are inseparable?" When would such a statement make sense? The fact that Pengchan recognizes this as a philosophical problem is not unusual, but the fact that he falls victim—to the extent of needing to entirely change his life—is an example of serious suffering. This is perhaps a Realization of a serious existential suffering to which he has become a victim, unknowingly, during the course of his career. And he has only inadvertently described the causes. He is realizing the problem, suffering from it but not initially solving it, although he does offer insight toward the end of the book, gratefully.

Likewise, what could it mean to say ". . . knowledge and ignorance are one..?" How could that be the case? This seems like a gross misuse of language. Is this somehow a paraphrase or Realization of the Emptiness intrinsic to nature described 2,500 years prior by the Buddha? This intellectual paralysis is an example of "binding". Realization of this kind of intellectual suffering is not the solution to the philosophical problem of course, but a target or more or less clear statement of the problem. Realization of the solution will follow in the next two stages of Realization as these are explained in terms of the next two of the Noble Truths.

When would it be the case that " . . . goodness and badness unite . . . ?" That brings to mind the ultimate collapse of Sun some 4 billion years hence. That would seem to be rather destructive to a well-organized and functioning society. And of course, society is not always well organized nor well-functioning, but constantly struggling and flawed as Pengchan describes, especially with his solipsistic complaints against the evils of the power of money and currency. And during the course of Pengchan's trek he seems to discover how much like oil and water goodness and badness are, even though they may be co-resident in any one person at different times, at no time do they unite. This is similar to his assertion that " . . . beauty and ugliness are one condition such that no power can possibly separate the two from each other." This linguistic confusion says less, I believe, about beauty and ugliness, than it does about the failure of this philosophy professor to listen to his own teachings over the years, and his failure to understand the insights of his most perceptive students, perhaps.

He quickly and appropriately recognizes the beauty in the humanity of the generous and hospitable people he encounters, and is surprised by this Realization as if it were an epiphany. He doesn't seem to have been a jaded, cynical man; but to be so surprised by the capacity of people, especially generous Thai people, to be so kind and helpful, a trait they have learned from their Buddhist religious upbringing, strikes me as a serious lack of understanding to begin with. His adventures make good reading, albeit repetitive over the course of 1,000 kilometers as the reader proceeds along the travelogue. This is something like watching a slide show of your well intentioned cousin's recent vacation, and observing similar snapshots which become somewhat boring about half-way through if not sooner.

This is a good example of *Realization;* because it is about changing ones opinion based on a course correction, then incorporating that change into one's life in some significant way. That makes a fairly concise definition of what realization and unbinding are about, although, as we will see in the next chapters, there is more to it than that. If a Realization doesn't change one's life, it is nothing more than a good idea or useful concept that is a non-starter. Something significant and hopefully positive needs to come of it, although I am not advocating that anyone else take such an ascetic trek. Taking Refuge, when properly understood, obviates the necessity for trauma to make such changes in our lives. And of course it is always easier to point to an example from someone else's life rather than from my own, but I have tried in these chapters to make myself likewise vulnerable and describe many of my own experiences.

Step fourteen of Anapanasati deals with the fading away of attachment, which is an essential step in Nirodha. "Watching attachment dissolve is like watching the stains in a cloth slowly fade away . . ."[173] This is where we directly focus on making

---

[173] " . . .is contemplating fading away (viraganupassana) [similar to the dissolving of attachment.] Now we focus upon and study dissolving, or viraga. Vi, in this case, means 'not' or 'not having.' Raga is another name for attachment [also upadana.] Watching attachment dissolve is like watching the stains in a cloth slowly fade away, bleached out by sunlight, until the cloth is white . . . We know that attachment is lessening

Nirodha happen, this is where all the previous preparation has led. When we are "even-minded", we can take social and physical stimulation, or leave it; then we know that we are achieving some significant reduction or cessation of suffering. Start with something simple: I went to a casual dinner and concert recently, knowing before I went that after I ate I would eventually become hungry and need to eat again, but that doesn't cause suffering because I realize the inevitability of this impermanent, albeit temporarily satisfying, event. Likewise, when I left the concert I knew I would be listening to the silence of my own mind, rather than to that pleasant music, but I knew that would happen in advance, so having it come to an end didn't cause suffering. I was not bound by the pleasure of this music. Since I did not have an attachment to the food nor music, their ceasing did not cause suffering as similar endings in other contexts might cause. I was "even-minded" about the stimulation from this social evening by accepting the cultural limitations of such events as a normal happening, no attachment. For what other aspects of our lives do we hold greater attachment? Look at these during meditation with direct awareness, perhaps the attachment can be reduced by knowing about the inevitability of the changes that will occur sooner or later, and because of these new attitudes, these attachments eventually fade away.

In Satipatthana training, it is taught that we can achieve the goal of enlightenment in as little as seven days, and depending on our level of preparation, I believe this attitude change can happen in that short period of time. Furthermore this is another one of those steps to reducing suffering. "We become [as profound as] our deepest knowledge, the wisdom of inner truth."[174] This is not overconfidence, but devotion, a

---

when we are even-minded toward sankhara, [conditioning] namely, toward all things to which we were once attached . . . Contemplate this with every inhalation and exhalation." (Buddhadasa)

[174] "When we reach non-reflective samadhi [concentration] the mind becomes clear and serene, and the clear light of our [virtue] shines out. This is absolute awareness, in which the mind is pervaded by true

sign that our arising has been abandoned. Furthermore there is no confusion about how " . . . knowledge and ignorance are one..?" We have by now Taken Refuge in the Buddha, the Dharma and the Sangha so many times, that this refuge is beginning to turn back onto us as a reward enhancing our stability and peace. We abandon gradually more complex issues, features of our lives that previously bound us to suffering, craving, i.e. a god or being afraid of dead bodies. As we do this and internalize it, we find that we reduce attachment to events, relationships and possessions that previously were thought integral to our lives. This sounds a little preachy, like a good sermon for a Dharma talk or Sunday school lesson, but even so there is an essential message that can be taken and mulled over like a raccoon washing its food.

As we progress, the Dharma begins to make sense in ways that we might not have noticed before. In essence we have constructed a way of explaining nature and society that helps us cope, our assumptions create a formula, like a chemistry solution, that works because of the very nature of our assumptions. "From seeing impermanence, we see unsatisfactoriness . . ."[175] We don't like it when our lives change abruptly especially when we seem to have no control over the changes. Yet these changes have causes that we can often understand, some of which we set in motion perhaps many years prior. By accepting the assumptions of Dharma we have ". . . selected carefully the meanings of truth, knowledge, goodness, and beauty . . ."[176] We see each of these three

---

knowledge and understanding [and merges with our whole Hearts.] We become [as profound as] our deepest knowledge, the wisdom of inner truth." (Forstater, pg. 289)

[175] "Please understand that the realizations of these truths are interrelated. From seeing impermanence, we see unsatisfactoriness . . . and see idappaccayata (conditionality, the law of cause and effect) as well. When impermanence is truly seen, it also has the characteristic of dukkham, namely, it is painful and unbearable." (Buddhadasa)

[176] "It is our duty to individually consider and select carefully the meanings of truth, knowledge, goodness, and beauty for our own use

characteristics of reality (aniccam, dukkham and anatta) in the 10,000 details (Zen) we confront, but in the beginning we settle into the practice based on hope, because we have not yet gained a solid level of confidence or understanding. Each year we learn more about the causes of suffering and how to change our attitudes to eliminate these—that predicts that in subsequent years there are more realizations to come our way, which is a nice hope too.

We have the ability to change our attitudes and change the way we are attached to possessions, and to our own ambitions. ". . . The experience of absorption is a powerful tool to diminish craving and attachment in regard to the five senses . . ." (Analayo, pg. 74) And we have learned that changing these elements of our lives (craving and attachment, etc.) can be the key to reducing a good deal of suffering. " . . . as our erotic love for things to which we were once attached begins to fade."[177] With this process seriously in place, we avoid creating new suffering. We should expect the direction of our lives to change to become more joyful and fulfilling each year.

This understanding of impermanence is an important stage of enlightenment. When we recognize the inevitability of change and movement in our live, and we see the emptiness of the causes of suffering, it only remains that we learn to anticipate this characteristic, and eliminate

---

that is appropriate to us." (Pengchan, pg. 3)

[177] "The result of this fading away of attachment [Nirodha] is the even-minded stillness of non-attachment . . . as our erotic love for things to which we were once attached begins to fade. Anger toward past, or even present, objects of our displeasure dissolves away. We are no longer afraid of the things we once feared . . . hatred, envy, jealousy, worry, anxiety, longing after the past . . . [all defilements] each of these indicators lessens and shrinks until the mind is able to keep still and silent . . . not to grasp, cling, or regard anything as 'I' or 'mine.' Contemplate impermanence until the attachment dissolves, until we can remain still, silent, and even-minded [equanimity.]" (Buddhadasa)

"hatred, envy, jealousy, worry, anxiety, longing after the past . . . in the realization of impermanence there is the simultaneous realization of many other aspects."[178] These results can be felt immediately in our lives, like changing our diets and exercising more, we notice that we begin to lose weight, hopefully. In the beginning of this chapter I asked the question: "Or can we work on the general causes of 'craving, clinging . . . attachments' and make that a significant part of our personal meditation practice?" By understanding impermanence we make some good headway at relieving the underlying causes of a lot of related sufferings. I can recall thinking "Why are all these teachings repeating this simple idea?" "Impermanence, suffering and no-spirit." I accepted this as an obvious truth without realizing or really studying the implications and how unique these teachings are.

And again: If we read this promise at the beginning of chapter 1, it would have seemed confusing, so remote, and an impossible goal. We have moved step by step to achieve this "fruition" and we deserve to have this success by now, to know that because of our effort so much of arising has been abandoned; just as a reward for having read all these chapters, if for no other reason, we can feel special for just a moment—but of course that fades too and we know it's okay. We know how aniccam, dukkham and anatta are interconnected and one flows from the other, but in the experience of jhana (our reward in Chapter 16) we are not thinking, we are not working on eliminating suffering except tangentially, and we are not deliberately progressing substantially toward Nirodha, it just happens, attachment

---

[178] "When this happens we are equipped to accept the lessons of 'piti'. In the second and third Absorptions [jhana, as we learned earlier,] the meditator gradually leaves off thinking entirely, becoming more and more absorbed in the object of meditation alone, and with this increased concentration and simplification he also transcends his feelings of comfort and intellectual pleasure . . . Now, observe that in the realization of impermanence there is the simultaneous realization of many other aspects." (Buddhadasa, 1988, pg. 89)

fades away. However, we may be recharging our Hearts and enhancing our devotional skill, and these are not minor achievements. With unbinding, it's all starting to come together.

Chapter Fifteen

Realization of Nirodha

Key Words:

Thusness (tathata, tathagata), quenching, nirvana, enlightenment, middle-way, penetrative knowledge, un-sated, receptive

Why Should I Meditate?

Meditation leads us into the study of *nirodhanupassana,* the study and contemplation of *quenching* of attachment. *Realization* in meditation is penetrative knowledge that's very subtle and sharp. In meditation if we're distracted by strong emotions, and suffering, focus on the experiences of the emotion (i.e. piti-jhana) as well as causes. In meditation, if we are receptive to melding our minds with Bodhisattvas and inspired teachers of the past, we can be at Nirvana. In the meditation on Right Thought (Intention) we don't invent answers or accept superstitions, then Right View (Understanding) is what guides our lives. In mediation we find a range of choices between debilitating grief, and the stoicism of disregard. When we are absorbed in the object of meditation, with this increased concentration and simplification we can transcend comfort and intellectual pleasure. In meditation we observe quenching of greed, anger, and delusion; and of all experiences of dukkha . . . the arrival of enlightenment. When we eliminate the pride in whom we are during meditation—we sense a satisfaction and wholeness in Buddhism shared with our Sangha.

I find it interesting that such a compassionate and considerate teaching and practice as Buddhism requires so much effort and discipline, although eventually these patterns of behavior become not second nature, but our first nature. Being soft-spoken and polite, as most monks are, disguises the strength and fortitude it takes to follow the Eight-fold Path. "Being resolute is thus different from being severe, because it means being earnest toward everything of every sort in keeping with reason."[179] The best monks, including the Dalai Lama, still have a sense of humor, and no one would question the resoluteness of that great teacher, even a Chinese political leader would give him credit for that. In accepting this admonition there is the implicit agreement that being on the Eight-fold Path and achieving unbinding, is the right thing

---

[179] "A teacher who possesses the Dhamma, who possesses virtue, has to be resolute so as to eliminate evil. . . He can't not be resolute. The stronger the evil, then the more resolute, the stronger his goodness has to be. . . Otherwise it'll get knocked out. Suppose this place were dirty. . . we couldn't clean it just by splashing it with a glass of water, could we? So how would we make it clean? We'd have to use a lot of water. If this place were filled with a pile of excrement, we'd have to splash it with a whole bucket—and not just an ordinary bucket. A great big one. A single splash, and all the excrement would be scattered. The place would become clean because the water was stronger. . . Being resolute is thus different from being severe, because it means being earnest toward everything of every sort in keeping with reason. Take this and think it over. If you act weakly in training yourself, you're not on the path. You have to be strong in fighting with defilement. Don't let the strong defilements step all over you. If we don't have any way of fighting defilement—if we're weak and irresolute—we're good for nothing at all." (Boowa, 1981)

for us to be doing, and the reason for that is to achieve the cessation of suffering; otherwise why go to all the effort and trouble? When we can follow the Buddha's advice: "Vision arose, insight arose, discernment arose, knowledge arose, illumination arose within me with regard to things never heard before: 'This noble truth of the cessation of stress *has been directly* experienced'." (Appendix II) Thus we have come to realize unbinding.

At this point we have gone beyond the need to state this explicitly, although it never hurts. This kind of resolution is what was explained in *Buddhist Sutras: Lesson Book* in Chapter Eleven relating to Right Effort. This is certainly part of being Enlightened, being capable of and disposed to making the appropriate kind of effort to suit the circumstances in pursuing worthwhile and skillful goals. Just as an artist is compelled to paint and create masterpieces, we are all compelled to live for the sake of practicing the Art of Living.

Each time I use these general terms of the Eight-fold Path, I flash examples in my mind to more or less translate the theory to some kind of reality. So what does it mean to be enlightened? And how is that related to being in a state of Nirvana? The last question first, because it is easy to answer: there is no necessary connection. Enlightenment on the other hand is a state of mind that we achieve after study, practice and meditation. It is caused by our Right Thought that also leads to the cessation of suffering. Some authors use "Sound Thought" or "Right Intention" for the title of this step of the Eight-fold Path, If we translate this differently does that change our understanding? Since the success of this step, and each step, requires considerable effort and coaching by skilled teachers, monks and lamas, etc., we can measure our progress toward Enlightenment by how well we utilize and internalize Right (or Sound) View about each of the eight steps. Nirvana is said to be a point of view, a mind-set, an attitude that we achieve as an indirect result. We know that we have and can eliminate suffering, that is like being a confident Sumo wrestler, knowing we can defend ourselves against 99.99 percent of humanity in hand to hand combat.

So perhaps the title or naming Nirvana is not so important, since this emotionless status has no particular causes, which means it is not conditioned, but happens when we are receptive to melding our minds with the Bodhisattvas and inspired teachers of the past. Both states of mind will involve a certain kind of rectitude, i.e. Right Speech, because the words we utter are carried by our sacred breath, and are so central to the development (or not) of future suffering, and are a window to our mental status.

One clue to knowing if we are enlightened or close to "non-returning", is to be comfortable with understanding anatta in its entirety; that our lives are caused by determinants, many of which we can change or control; and that we live an ethical and moral life without knowing all the answers to those four questions which the Buddha refused to discuss or answer. At many preliminary stages we may feel flooded by instructions and good ideas, inundated by advice and "steps to progress" wondering what to do next. Of course that is the conundrum we solve in our meditation (or we don't). We don't invent answers or accept superstitions, we accept that Right View is what guides our lives through discernment and the continued development of wisdom. Here it is appropriate to reference a detailed discussion of unbinding in chapter five of the book *Bodhicitta: Higher Truth.*

Some people notice that this unbinding has been realized with age and the accumulation of experience, but that is not the only possible cause of the growth of wisdom. When we engage in Right Action, for the right reasons that come from inside our own compassionate Hearts, we demonstrate and gain wisdom. This is like a homily that we can repeat and find soothing, and we will discuss this further in chapter 16. Repeating these achievements, perhaps we can write a poem or chant, of course there are many available to choose from, and using these can be a ritual to help us prepare for meditation each day, not unlike fusing incense.

Understanding the details of these "absolutes" is like understanding the significances and differences between lighting a candle or two, heating incense until it smolders,

235

placing flowers in a vase in front of an icon, circumnavigating (barefoot, clockwise) the temple, spinning a chime, or hitting a gong or drum, kneeling, Taking Refuge, bowing three times and reciting a mantra to share merit, etc. Such rituals are as meaningful as we are mindful at the time we conduct them, otherwise they are empty habits like picking our noses.

We do all this ritual because there is no external entity that gives us grace, no substantial spirit in our body that intercedes on our behalf, no saint that will carry our prayer to an ultimate Judge, no law that requires us to act in a certain way, so we have to take it onto ourselves to develop our own purification. Thus our physical actions during these rituals are significant. I see this understanding and acceptance of anatta as a lynch-pin for identifying 'Enlightenment', and knowing why these rituals are useful and important. When we are comfortable in our own skin, independent of the fears and whims of gods or devas, we make our day to day decisions without recourse to such outside influences, we don't concern ourselves about past or future lives to find our motivation, and then we have arrived at the threshold of enlightenment. "The short phrase aniccanupassana (contemplating impermanence) includes the realization of unsatisfactoriness [not-sated,] not-self, voidness, thusness, and conditionality as well."[180] Our very existence is a result of causes, causes that are often momentary, as are our thoughts and ambitions, and our conditioned circumstances that can lead to suffering. There is no destiny or fate; causes, ambitions and conditioning are empty of essence, thus subject

---

[180] "We can also find the characteristic of not-self (anatta) in our mind from the teachings of Dhamma. Each of the three characteristics continues into the next . . . To see aniccam alone, in an incomplete way [it is not enough] that does not include dukkham and anatta, is neither profound nor sufficient to solve our problems. Thus, 'realizing aniccam' [impermanence] in this context must encompass a realization as deep as dukkham, anatta, sunnata, tathata, and idappaccayata . . . The short phrase aniccanupassana (contemplating impermanence) includes the realization of unsatisfactoriness, not-self, voidness, thusness, and conditionality as well." (Mingyur)

to elimination, and we are capable of enlightened choice. From a mathematical perspective, all this understanding is a necessary condition, and being in a state of Nirvana is the ultimate sufficient condition for being at peace. That is perhaps a koan for further contemplation.

Here are some simple instructions that by now should be a matter of course for each person serious about improving their life through meditation. Watch whatever is happening in your mind initially and then direct mindfulness toward a desired agenda that you have accepted as a curriculum. For example, " . . . use your dullness rather than being used by it."[181] This is a back to basics approach from the Tibetan teachings, but is an appropriate instruction even for the most advanced meditator. This kind of problem solving results in the cessation of suffering. The goal has been realized. If you have accepted the list of defilements for a curriculum of objects, that is fine, or earlier begin with "Hindrances". Thus we have some flexibility in how we proceed with our daily religious routines, usually a certain meditation technique will suggest itself, one we haven't engaged for a few weeks perhaps, and we begin our practice with this kind of relaxed receptivity.

The same advice comes from the Theravada teachers, who have emphasized working on the defilements in our meditation. "So why do we fall for the deceits of defilement when it says that death is followed by annihilation, without

---

[181] "If you're distracted by strong emotions, [and suffering from whatever source] you can try focusing, as was taught earlier, on the mind that experiences the emotion. Or you might try switching to tonglen practice, using whatever you're feeling—anger, sadness, jealousy, desire—as the basis for the practice. [Destroying the negative with the in and out breathing. If you get sleepy] There are a couple of ways to deal with this situation. One, which is simply a variation on being mindful of physical sensations, is to rest your attention on the sensation of dullness or sleepiness itself. In other words, use your dullness rather than being used by it. If you can't sit up, just lie down while keeping your spine as straight as possible." (Mingyur, pg. 211)

having the sense to see the harm of its deceits?"[182] I regard this as a serious instruction pointing to current events in my life, so I consider what I did yesterday and see how it fits into some part of this description. Then I lay down a reminder that will have a positive impact on the future (the past is beyond our control). We are being exhorted to "get a hold on the matter" precisely because we can stop the cycles of suffering that are part of our enculturation. It is always difficult to step away from the captivating pleasures of society, but so often these bind us in a cycle of "tricks and deceits". Can we realize the

---

[182] "So. Be earnest, meditators. Don't get discouraged. Give your life to the Buddha. Even though we may have never said that we've given our life to defilement, that's what we've done. . . It's all come from the avijja-paccaya sankhara embedded here in the heart for countless lifetimes. Nothing else in the cosmos has caused us to experience becoming and birth, and to carry the mass of all sufferings, other than this avijja-paccaya sankhara. (The defilement that forms the essence of the cycle (vatta)—'With unawareness as condition, there occur mental formations') For this reason, when they say the mind of a person who dies is annihilated, just where is it annihilated? Use the practice to get a hold on the matter. Don't speak simply in line with the tricks and deceits of defilement that close off our ears and eyes. Defilement says that death is followed by annihilation. See? It's blinded us completely. As for the defilement that causes people to take birth and die, where is it annihilated? If we want to see through its tricks and deceits, why don't we take its arrows to shoot it in return? It causes living beings to lie buried in the cycle, so where is defilement annihilated? [These are the rebirths we experience every day.] And what does it coerce, if it doesn't coerce the mind? If the mind is annihilated, how can defilement coerce it? The mind isn't annihilated, which is why defilement has been able to coerce it into birth, aging, illness, and death all along without ceasing. So why do we fall for the deceits of defilement when it says that death is followed by annihilation, without having the sense to see the harm of its deceits? This sneaky defilement has fooled living beings into falling for it and grabbing at suffering for a long, infinitely long time." (Boowa, 1981)

solution, become saturated with the power that fading away, as described in the last chapter, has in our lives?

Even an enlightened person will have moments of suffering, perhaps upon first hearing about the death of a parent or Sangha member, which are unavoidable, but these feelings are also impermanent. When our Buddhist practice and religious conviction lies firmly in our Hearts, which is when this following teaching begins to make sense. "We see that our body and mind are void of self-hood, which is sunnata . . ."[183] This has been realized when our attachments are quenched and our Hearts come to understand thusness and full-awakening as we read further in this chapter. This may be a kind of cycle of thought that we conceptualize in a few moments, like applying a micro program in a soft-ware application, and the suffering dissipates and we see the details and sad news as facts of nature that we deal with based on our own level of involvement and responsibility. We go on living in a more enlightened way based on the knowledge we have gleaned from our loved ones who have gone and would inspire us if they could to live by the highest moral standards. I have experienced the death of two brothers-in-law and two brothers during the last two years at this writing, which has been a rude awakening as I approach closer to the ages of their deaths. I recall the final years of my mother and father's life separately and how it was comforting to just share the space and air of the room, and when we spoke about trivial details it was like, in retrospect, the song of the angels. Each time I think of them I think of imaginary conversations I might have had with one or the other, and perceive the advice they would give if they could as if we were sitting across from each other relaxing in a living room setting. This visualization is not

---

[183] "As these things are always changing, impermanent, and unsatisfactory [the source of suffering,] and beyond our control, we realize anatta [the causative factors] as well . . . We see that our body and mind are void of self-hood, which is sunnata . . . Impermanence is just thus, just like that, thus-ness [a fact of all nature.] And so, tathata is seen as well." (Buddhadasa)

a moment of grief, but a moment of solace and comfort for me, knowing that in this small way I will never be alone. I am not attached to those memories, they just come around at odd moments, but perhaps I am not "quenched" by these images either.

Of course there are a range of choices like this in between extreme debilitating grief, and the stoicism of disregard. In Buddhism, we let our emotional involvement land somewhere in between. "Realization: This is penetrative knowledge that's very subtle and sharp . . ."[184] and it is bound to have an impact. This is simply a restatement of the possibility and promise of achieving Enlightenment, and then Nirvana blooms. Restating the obvious: This is why Realization comes third in the row of steps to Purification, it is an additive process, dependent first on Recognition (direct knowledge, "what is") and then on Encouragement ("what is to be", full-awakening) that we give ourselves and receive from our Sangha members (including ancients, family members and so many unknown authors). And now we examine how suffering "has been abandoned" by unbinding attachments.

Quenching doesn't happen all at once for most people, in fact it is possible to look back over our personal histories and see where we have given up one or another activity, possession or sensual activity (i.e. we stopped wasting our time playing computer games perhaps). One at a time these propensities and activities connected to defilements have been shed, if we are receptive to change like a snake losing its skin over and over as it grows. That is more accurately labeled fading away in general, but for each detail there is a quenching, so the two go together and the semantic difference is not so important as the progressive, seep-wise reality of it.

---

[184] "The middle way is what can cause all these forms of knowledge to arise. Realization: This is penetrative knowledge that's very subtle and sharp. Even discernment is less penetrating and sharp than it is. Self-awakening. Nibbana: This path leads to nibbana. All of these things without exception come from this middle way. They don't lie beyond range of this middle way at all." (Boowa, 1981)

When we live in and are guided by our own Enlightenment, we realize that our Hearts are not souls in the ordinary sense, just an abstraction of our *compassion, memories, consciousness and mind.* This is the best our nature has to offer, and this is where we make the most important changes in our lives. The knowledge that there is no soul, spirit or Higher Self (in the ordinary religious sense), is a considerable disturbance for most people raised in the Judeo-Islamic-Christian tradition, because as children most Western people are conditioned to accept these teachings, and we have what seems like an instinct. Have you heard that "wee, small voice" that seems to tell us there is a higher power, an inner voice and an inner-Self as taught by Yogi? Buddhism gives us a path to finding a joyful, larger and more pleasurable meaning in life without these challenges and what amounts to mental handicaps—and again: "we are absorbed in the object of meditation alone, and with this increased concentration and simplification we also transcend the feelings of comfort and intellectual pleasure . . ." (Buddhadasa) We get to a neutral point, no attachment to an external deity concept, no silent or psychological craving for a father in heaven, and this is a place of contentment, confidence and tranquility—a kind of enlightened quenching—unbinding.

Considering how this attitude compares to those moments of turmoil and insecurity I suffered in my adolescence, I find this "path to finding joy" a comfortable, relaxed place to be as I proceed with my meditation practice each day. I have heard it said that the preaching we do or the lessons we prepare are often what we need the most ourselves, and this is true with the quenching of attachments, because there are many attachments that are still active in my life, and I still have some hindrances that trouble me from time to time because in my ordinary life I don't follow the Five Precepts strictly. So who am I to talk? Well, I can relay the information for the sake of completion and a little bit of the teaching will rub off on me, more each time I am exposed to it. "A full realization of this step [fifteen] must include all four aspects of dukkha's quenching . . .

[185] but there is a lot to be considered here, so never think that there is no further reason to meditate. Quenching is like drinking water beyond the point of thirst. When we eliminate the pride in whom we are, for example, as part of the growth of our Hearts, we easily show our satisfaction of being involved in Buddhism with our Sangha, and we become generous with our resources, our wisdom, as well as with our time.

When we studied *fading away* (viraganupassana) in the last chapter we noticed that we started the process of overcoming some defilements along with following the Precepts and eliminating Hindrances. But that is just a beginning, quenching in a comprehensive way is the next and detailed phase, as it

---

[185] Step fifteen: " . . .nirodhanupassana is the study and contemplation of quenching of attachment. [In chapter fourteen we learned about fading away.] We observe the cessation of attachment, the nonexistence of attachment, while breathing in and breathing out . . . the quenching of greed, anger, and delusion; and the quenching of all experiences of dukkha . . . When we speak of quenching, remember that the ending of dukkha is what the practice of Dhamma is all about . . .

1) The first aspect is the ending of fearfulness, the horror of birth, aging, illness, and death . . . [These] will never again terrify our mind . . .

2) Next . . . the cessation of the various symptoms or conditions of dukkha, such as sorrow, grief, lamentation, despair, sadness, pain, frustration and depression.

3) . . .our hopes and wants to attractive and unattractive things [is quenched.] Experiencing things we do not like is dukkha. Being separated from the things we like is dukkha. Not getting what we want is dukkha [this is huge.] These aspects of dukkha are quenched as well.

4) Clinging to one of the five khandha (senses, aggregates, clusters), grasping the 'self' (body, feeling, perception, thought, and sense-consciousness) as 'I' or 'mine' is dukkha. These are the summation of all dukkha, the burdens of life. A full realization of this step must include all four aspects of dukkha's quenching . . . We should not underestimate this important realization." (Buddhadasa, 1988, pp. 89-90)

were. And taking the advice of Boowa is like having someone kick you in the butt, but welcome because you respect his knowledge and authority. "That's when we'll attain a great treasure of infinite worth to rule our hearts."[186] When the Dhamma fills the Heart, that is the success of quenching. And just when you think you have accomplished something significant, he comes back and reminds you: there is no room for defilements.

I remember well the steps and evaluation of my thinking when I was in my early 20's and left my religion of birth. There were periods of sadness and regret, in that case for being unable to believe and act as other people expected me to believe. Gradually I became more callous and realized how ridiculous that childhood belief was, now it seems so remote and impossible, simple minded. Yet many bright and substantial people sustain a belief and practice Christianity, Judaism and Islam, etc. I went from fading away of my old beliefs to quenching of any desire or clinging to those old ways of thinking. When we have confidence in our beliefs " . . . the Dhamma has filled the heart and that's plenty enough." And we will have achieved quenching and cessation has been realized as an unbinding of our "contents of consciousness".

This advice was intended for the ears of newly ordained monks, but it carries a lesson for all earnest practitioners: ". . .

---

[186] "So be earnest. Shilly-shallying around, thinking of sleep, thinking of our stomachs: These are habits long embedded in our hearts. They're all an affair of defilement. So flip over a new leaf, making the heart an affair of the Dhamma, in keeping with the fact that we're disciples of the Tathagata who have given ourselves to be [active] in his religion and to follow the principles of his Dhamma. That's when we'll attain a great treasure of infinite worth to rule our hearts. When the Dhamma rules the heart, how is it different from defilement ruling the heart? As I've said before, the Dhamma ruling the heart is something supreme and magnificent: We're fully free with our full heart—not grasping, not hungry, not searching, not hoping to depend on anything—for the Dhamma has filled the heart and that's plenty enough." (Boowa, 1981)

not grasping, not hungry, not searching, not hoping to depend on anything . . ." When we achieve this, the simple details of our lives take on new significance and become sources of satisfaction and joy, such as keeping our toilets clean and orderly, feeding birds, planting and tending flowers (even in window pots), and reading interesting books. Our lives can be enjoyable and satisfying without all the exciting new styles of pleasures, such as sky-diving, hang-gliding or other risk taking adventures. There is joy to be found in pursuing a peaceful, quiet life.

Chapter Sixteen

Realization—Precepts and Path

Key Words:

Equanimity, vipassana, upadana, Lokuttara, persistence auras, supernatural, bodichitta, (absolute and relative) aspiration, application, compassion, conviction, lokya

Why Should I Meditate?

We become the object of meditation as we experience jhana, and this represents a useful skill in the manipulation of one's own experience. It is not intuitively obvious, but the recognition of aniccam (impermanence) during meditation dissolves the sources of suffering. In meditation our "absolute" bodichitta grows along with our Buddha-nature. Meditation takes the place of any supernatural disposition, since the arising of these phenomena is liable to bar the way to the Path and Fruit. In Buddhist meditation we are concerned with improving the ethical and moral aspects of our lives, because there are practical advantages. When we seek Right Livelihood—we will realize the benefits that come from treating our customers not only with charm and grace, but with honesty. We expand the factors of compassion as "relative" bodichitta guides our minds during meditation. In meditation we realize and acknowledge the true power of our minds, and the usefulness of our Hearts and we gain control over our experiences. We develop goals and "aspirations" to improve our lives. In meditation experiences that seemed as obstacles become opportunities, deepening understanding of the mind's unimpeded nature. We implement a *purified* life plan and monitor progress. In meditation we achieve Lokuttara for our Hearts. After you *realize* the stages of Bodhicitta, you will feel useful inspiration surging into your discipline.

If you were to design a system of self-improvement you would have in it one or maybe two rewarding experiences, immediate payoffs, that made people feel like they had accomplished something when they achieved their objective. The student might get a massage upon graduation or a coupon for a discount at a popular book store. What do those who read this book completely get? The experience of the great masters tells us that there are four levels of jhana, each somewhat more in depth, less mentally active, and more peaceful and these can be thought of as rewarding experiences. This practice of jhana (Zen) is ". . . representing specific useful skills in the manipulation of one's own experience."[187] Thus if there are specific signs or images beyond "an abiding sense of firm equanimity . . ." these relate to the emotional consequences of previous experiences.

Can this be our reward—as with the experience of Buddha's enlightenment? "Vision arose, insight arose, discernment arose, knowledge arose, illumination arose within me with regard to things never heard before: 'This noble truth of the *way of practice* leading to the cessation of stress *has been developed*'." (Appendix II) This fourth jhana or absorption, is

---

[187] "And finally, in the fourth Absorption, the meditator is aware only of the object, and of an abiding sense of firm equanimity, beyond feelings of pain or pleasure. . . Indeed from this point of view he might be said to have increasingly become the object of meditation . . . [this jhana is] representing specific useful skills in the manipulation of one's own experience." (Carrithers, 1983, pp. 32-33)

the epitome of calm, a realization of unbinding and peace of mind. This is like being out of the mind and looking back onto ourselves with objectivity, using our well-developed mind's eye to see ourselves sitting in meditation, pliant, humble, rewarded (in 3D?), receptive and yet resourceful.

Coincidentally, I just read an article in *"Discover:* science, technology, and the future" magazine, a digest of several scientific papers, that described the kind of experiences that are taught as being potential aspects of jhana, and have been reported and described for thousands of years by Buddhist monks and disciples. It can no longer be thought of as a religious superstition to suggest such unusual or special images and perceptions during meditation. Experiments created sensations "Producing out-of-body experiences in volunteers . . ."[188] and these were measured as a scientific reality. So now when someone recounts such experiences, we should at least take them seriously, even though it may not teach us anything in particular. Since each of us has a different combination of intelligences and aptitudes, we also

---

[188] "What if your perception could be altered so that you could be anyone and anyplace at all—leaving without traveling?" is the question under investigation. They studied the centers in the brain that control self-perception. 1) They showed that the brain ". . .could feel ownership of a body part that was not truly its own. . . The illusion involves interconnected areas of the brain, including the premotor cortex in the frontal lobe, and the intraparietal cortex in the parietal lobe." 2) "The physical sensation of floating outside the body. . . the treatment he briefly zapped the temporoparietal junction, a brain region that integrates sound, touch, vision, balance perception, and the sense of location in space." 3) "Subjects feel immersed in a representation of another person" involving video cameras and illusions. 4) Others ". . .reproduced a semblance of their plots by giving test subjects the sensation of swapping bodies with an 11 -1/2in. Barbie doll or a 13 foot tall mannequin." 5) "Producing out-of-body experiences in volunteers who face their own bodies and shake their own hands, seeming to encounter themselves from the outside." (July-August, 2012, pp. 50-56) (italics mine)

have different activity in these various sections of our brains, for so many reasons: nutrition, drug heritage, and our intrinsic DNA. If we are tired and sleepy our minds operate differently; If I am reading something when I am too tired, I can create a narrative for a story when I am half asleep and my mind just flows to deceive me as in a dream so it can sleep on another level. Very clever that. I perceive that I am reading, but I'm actually asleep. I have no comprehension of the actual material and I have to stand up and reread a page or two.

Resting your mind between objectless meditation and object-based meditation gives you a chance to assimilate whatever you have experienced.

We have discussed the experience of jhana and the ramifications of that kind of peaceful, to the extreme, experience. This level of meditation has very little direct relationship to the Precepts that are the broad ethical guidelines of Buddhism, or to the Eight-fold Path which has been described as the operating system of our lives from Buddhist Dharma. To expect to experience jhana we have to be well ensconced into the devotion and ritual of Buddhist practice, however, and these teachings are the essential precursors to that. Here is another warning relating to jhana. ". . . the arising of these phenomena is liable to bar the way to the true Path and Fruit."[189] In other

---

[189] "There exist several obstacles to this further progress [through the fourth jhana,] which usually arise in the course of Vipassana practice. While the mind is in a concentrated state, there are likely to arise various strange phenomena with which the meditator may become overawed, such as wonderful impressive auras seen in the mind's eye (the physical eyes being shut.) If these effects are purposely encouraged, they can become highly developed; and if the meditator jumps to the conclusion that 'this is the Fruit of Vipassana practice,' or congratulates himself saying, 'This is something supernatural; this will do me' and the like, the arising of these phenomena is liable to bar

teachings these visions are referred to as delusions, on the same level as falling asleep during meditation. Interpretation of these phenomena is so subjective, how could we hope to understand it, let alone gain from it, in any rational way? Is this just a trick of our brain? The best advice is to take these experiences with a grain of salt, don't seek them or get bogged down with searching for these. If we learn something that changes our lives, like an inspiration that we can conceptualize into words, so much the better.

On a related topic, what kind of effort will we need to make before we see the kind of gains we expect from our meditation practice (a kind of religious self-improvement project)? Do we have to make ourselves suffer (as an ascetic) in order to accomplish Nirodha, the cessation of suffering? "Upadana [sources of suffering] dissolves until less and less remains." And one benefit of *Realization* is that it resolves attachments.[190] That is the promise and general reward. Do we have to give up our possessions and return to a stone-age existence? Elsewhere I have read that this is the wrong kind of compassion. What we need is to realize that the Eight-fold Path has been cultivated to the point of unbinding.

There is a certain irony here that we need to attend to—if we need to suffer to eliminate suffering, what would be the point? No one said it would be easy; however, just understanding all the Pali words is an accomplishment. But the result of realizing impermanence, which I have always been willing to concede, is the key to making progress, so how hard can that be? And when we do this in advance of an activity or decision, then we prepare ourselves to enjoy our lives without the risk of creating

---

the way to the true Path and Fruit. Consequently, teachers consider it a side track, a blind alley." (Buddhadasa, 2005, pg. 118)

[190] "Now, observe—study closely until you see it—that the realization of aniccam dissolves upadana, and dissolves attachment. This is crucial. Realizing aniccanupassana dissolves attachment because we realize the pain and suffering of the attachment. Upadana [sources of suffering] dissolves until less and less remains. Such is the [end] result of realizing impermanence." (Buddhadasa, 1988, pp. 83-88)

more causes of conditioned (dependent co-origination) suffering. Most of our possessions, like our clothing, will wear out or become obsolete, and gradually we will lose interest in most of the adult toys we acquire. When this happens, and we donate these otherwise useful items to a not-for-profit charity, is this in part satisfying the directive to eliminate clinging and attachments? We can learn to apply a new kind of scrutiny when we are considering what to buy or how much to eat, for example keeping our choices wholesome and minimal. If we purchase a work of art made by a "starving artist" or member of our Sangha, is that a worthy action? Open questions.

From the methodological point of view, this following teaching is the secret of meditation, as opposed to expecting visions: ". . . to develop a degree of mental stability . . ."[191] as we have discussed in previous chapters. We have discussed this in different ways, but receiving confirmation from this Tibetan tradition is encouraging. Most people are familiar with Attention Deficit Disorder, where the mind is skittish and unable to sustain concentration for a useful period of time. Symptoms and causes can vary substantially; even young students take serious medication, so there is no simple cure or explanation. Some people who might wish to meditate could be victims of this organic disorder, as well as affected family members, and

---

[191] ". . .It's very important during each session to alternate between focusing on an object [sati] and simply resting your mind in objectless meditation [samadhi—that leads to jhana.] The point of working with supports for meditation is to develop a degree of mental stability that allows you to be aware of your own mind as it perceives things. Resting your mind between objectless meditation and object-based meditation gives you a chance to assimilate whatever you have experienced. By alternating between these two states, no matter what situation you find yourself in—whether you're dealing with your own thoughts and emotions or with a person or a situation that appears 'out there'—you'll gradually learn to recognize that whatever is going on is intimately connected with your own awareness." (Mingyur, pg. 195)

will need to develop strategies to overcome the debilitating consequences of this challenge.

It is easy to say, but at times difficult to have the required patience (if we can), and add to that the realization—the necessity to gain skillful knowledge of the possibilities of our practice through preparation and study.[192] Imbedded in these simple directives is the key word "purity"—which we know to mean purification: "recognition, encouragement and realization." We are at the last step of Realization (unbinding has been cultivated) at this point, so we have almost all the information, preparation and experience we need to achieve our final success. Even when we do, it will be useful to repeat this sixteen step training of Anapanasati many times. Buddhism is concerned with improving the ethical and moral aspects of our lives, in part because there are practical advantages in doing so, such as Right Livelihood—and we will realize the benefits that come from treating our clients, family members and/or customers not only with charm and grace, but with honesty. In that way we will not only reduce our own suffering but theirs as well.

Look around at others you know to see if they share the changes and success you feel (or at least, do they appreciate the changes you have made?) Does this following statement feel valid? "Pain, sadness, fear, anxiety, and all other forms of suffering no longer disrupt your life as forcefully as they used to."[193] What will it take to get to that point? Don't be

---

[192] "With repeated practice we will produce a result eventually . . . We will be able to attain the path of purity. The most important point for the practice which is a must, is knowledge and understanding on the practice so that we can succeed eventually." (Wee, pp. 118-119)

[193] "To the extent that you can acknowledge the true power of your mind, [and you acknowledge the development and usefulness of your Heart,] you can begin to exercise more control over your experience. Pain, sadness, fear, anxiety, and all other forms of suffering no longer disrupt your life as forcefully as they used to. Experiences that once seemed to be obstacles become opportunities for deepening your understanding of the mind's unimpeded nature." (Mingyur, pg. 102)

disappointed if the changes in your life are slow and subtle like a melting glacier. Since the emphasis in Anapanasati steps thirteen through sixteen is on mental formations and contents of consciousness, seeing these negative aspects of our "mental continuum" disappear or dissipate when they do, ought to be very encouraging; a reason to recommend the entire process of meditation up to this point. If we redouble our effort, will this move this cleansing along at a more rapid pace? Perhaps—but be specific; consider one or more serious issues or difficulty experienced ten years ago; fear of public speaking, for example. In the meantime how many occasions have there been when such a requirement was eminent and the fear returned? Did it lessen? Or was the stage fright less consequential to the positive outcome of the speaking engagement? Have strategies presented themselves, i.e. more preparation, coaching and practice, to reduce the impact of fear and enhance the quality of the resulting appearances? Apply this same kind of analysis to any of the mental contents that have a negative impact on work or family experiences. Develop a strategy based on successful patterns, share it, ask for advice, problem solve, and then take it to the cushion for Insight. But like any good patient, try every known effective medical cure; don't rely strictly on meditation to fix all those problems, use reason and discernment (wisdom).

Here is a story that tells a useful point about the kind and intensity of effort we should employ. Boowa was a relatively new monk talking to Ajan Man (Mun) his teacher and he was diligent and even overwrought about achieving success from meditation. He relates how his teacher gave him some valuable directions which described an essential aspect of the middle way. "When its rebelliousness weakens, the harsh treatment can be relaxed . . ."[194] So when we do make progress and

---

[194] "I continued sitting all night in meditation and kept telling him the Dhamma I had gained. Sitting in meditation all night—I did it more than nine or ten times that Rains Retreat, and I wasn't just sitting as normal, because I was wrestling with my full strength, both because of the marvels I was seeing and because of my frustration over the

accomplish some positive changes, accept them and move on to new challenges. Perhaps if we torture our body it will rebel and this will end up being a counterproductive process. Some authors suggest that self-torture is little more than a lingering psychological problem of self-loathing, thus it is not a skillful strategy.

In the sixteenth step we learn to focus on compassion for others and what that means (and we practice that by feeling compassion for ourselves as well). "Absolute bodhicitta is the direct insight into the nature of mind . . ."[195] We have discussed the various constituents of the brain in some specific applications, such as that relating to jhana above. We have discussed the purpose and usefulness of walking meditation

---

way my mind had regressed earlier. These two got added together, so that the mind had the full strength of frustration and daring. As time passed though, Ven. Acariya Mun finally gave me a warning—a single flash: 'The defilements don't lie in the body,' he said. 'They lie in the heart'."

"He then gave a comparison with a horse. 'When a horse is unruly and won't listen to its master, the master has to give it really harsh treatment. If he has to make it starve, he should make it starve—really treat it harshly until it can't make a move. Once it finally stops being rebellious, though, he can let up on the harsh treatment. When its rebelliousness weakens, the harsh treatment can be relaxed.' That's all he said—and I understood immediately." (Boowa, 1981)

[195] "There are two aspects of bodichitta, absolute and relative. Absolute bodhicitta is the direct insight into the nature of mind . . . there is no distinction between subject and object, self and other; all sentient beings are spontaneously recognized as perfect manifestations of Buddha nature [as are you.] . . .relative bodhicitta shares the same goal: the direct experience of Buddha nature, or awakened mind, [seeing and using the connections we make with our Hearts] . . . In the practice of relative bodhicitta, however, we're still working within the framework of a relationship between subject and object or self and other. Finally, according to many great teachers . . . development of absolute bodhicitta depends on developing relative bodhicitta." (Buddhadasa)

and the development of mindfulness, for example. When we write in our journals we not only use our talent but we get to review our progress over the years and see how much better our minds work after years of practice. This explanation of our mental capacities is a little difficult to follow, so here is an easy reference:

Absolute bodichitta—we recognize the innate Buddha nature in every person.

Relative bodichitta—we make comparisons between subject and object, between ourselves and others within the framework of a content area i.e. compassion.

Then we break down the relative comparison even further: ". . . relative bodhicitta always involves two aspects: *aspiration and application.*"[196] This is a kind of theoretical framework that operates on specific details of our lives, but the ramifications are not obvious, so that is where meditation can be helpful.

Aspiration bodichitta—emphasizes results of our practice, goals, liberation from attachments . . . etc. comparing these to the intention of our original goals. This might be as specific as a list of, or the next defilements we intend to work on and overcome.

Application bodichitta—here we figure out how to do this, taking the steps (as with the Eight-fold Path.) This is

---

[196] "Developing *relative* bodhicitta always involves two aspects: aspiration and application. Aspiration bodhicitta involves cultivating the Heartfelt desire to raise all sentient beings to the level at which they recognize their Buddha nature . . . Aspiration bodhicitta focuses on the fruit, or the result, of practice . . . Application bodhicitta—often compared in classic texts to actually taking the steps to arrive at an intended destination—focuses on the path of attaining the goal of aspiration bodhicitta: the liberation of all sentient beings from all forms and causes of suffering through recognition of their Buddha nature . . . When we generate the motivation to lift not only ourselves but all sentient beings to the level of complete recognition of Buddha nature, an odd thing happens: The dualistic perspective of 'self' and 'other' begins very gradually to dissolve, and we grow in wisdom and power to help others as well as ourselves." (Buddhadasa)

the nuts and bolts: step by step we breathe in and out, we chant bud—dho, and we walk in meditation and improve mindfulness. (For me writing this book, as with the previous three, is both a passion and a compulsion and an example of Application Bodhicitta.) We develop a strategy as above and apply known and effective cures, i.e. diet and exercise to reduce high levels of harmful cholesterol. This returns us to the absolute recognition of the growth of wisdom and power to help others and ourselves (our Buddha nature). This is a cycle that repeats in a positive way. When it does we know that we have successfully cultivated the elements of the Eight-fold Path and we have realized unbinding. This is where we begin to experiment with different techniques and strategies to accomplish our intentions because we have the bigger picture and confidence in what we are doing.

After you have realized the importance of these distinctions and bodichitta in general, you will feel the inspiration surging into your discipline. In the book *Bodhicitta: Higher Truth*, I developed the discussion about ways to gain wisdom with the purpose of helping others as well as ourselves, I discussed ways to escape from under the "burdens of life". "This is called 'living beneath the world' [lokiya] or 'drowning in the world'." This is true for drug addicts, often for incarcerated criminals, gang members and so many people who suffer from their own under-achievement. "Once we can toss away the burdens that hold us down . . . we ascend . . . We are 'lords of the world.' [Lokuttara]."[197] This could be a song or anthem for our practice. Certainly if not that, then it is as easy to understand—just like living in the poem of Buddhism. Obviously this is a rhetorical

---

[197] "Throw away the burdens of life. Throw them away until no burdens remain. Before, we lived under their weight; their heaviness oppressed us. This is called 'living beneath the world' [lokiya] or 'drowning in the world.' Once we can toss away the burdens that hold us down, that trap us beneath the world, we ascend . . . We are 'lords of the world.' [Lokuttara] This is the true meaning of freedom and well-being." (Buddhadasa, 1988, pg. 92)

flourish intended to be inspiring, and perhaps we should have stated it in the beginning instead of here at the ending.

As for the Dhamma, we realize that this is the path to follow as taught by the Buddha, it has *conviction* as its basis—in other words, conviction in the path to be followed for good results—and *persistence* in making the effort to follow the path unflaggingly. By now our conviction should be something we take for granted, no more asking "What do I do next?" nor "Is this sitting on my cushion, lighting incense etc., worthwhile?" We realize the path and we are on it. As to persistence, that is something we need to recharge from time to time, this should be expected and anticipated. That is what a Sangha is for too. We can expect our development (progress toward purification and elimination of suffering) to proceed at a pace in direct proportion to how well we follow the Precepts and other ethical teachings.

Mindfulness is what guides our efforts as we follow the path, realizing each moment to take that moment in whole. While we measure our passion with Buddhism based on how well we accept and follow the Five Precepts, realize that this is a minimum standard of morality. Recall the practice of stepping in segments during walking meditation, and consider the object lessons learned from that training. This is a prerequisite to developing *Concentration* which comes from firmness of the heart in following the Eight-fold Path; we realize the benefit of being one pointed in achieving each of our objectives, as if our mind was a stage with a spotlight on the particular object (subject of Application Bodhicitta) and we are the audience watching it with direct awareness and our best contemplation. Our immediate reward is peace and tranquility, we have cultivated unbinding, and we accept this at the same time we move to share this with others. And we realize *discernment* as a kind of circumspection and the growth of wisdom in following the path step by step. "When we have these five qualities—conviction, persistence, mindfulness, concentration, and discernment constantly with us, there's no need to doubt that the results will appear as a well-deserved reward."[198] As we develop our Heart in line with our strength and abilities, we share our merit completely. The words and teachings of Boowa are dripping with compassion, inspiration and empathy. If we develop these five qualities so that they are powerful within our Hearts, the promise of our natural Buddha-hood will be achieved. When we turn around, it will be there as proclaimed—*nibbana* the unconditioned reward, the same for every true seeker.

These are the characteristics of Enlightenment, and create the potential in those who achieve them to accomplish the goals they seek. "Make your persistence adequate to the task." (Boowa)

---

[198] "When we have these five qualities—conviction, persistence, mindfulness, concentration, and discernment constantly with us, there's no need to doubt that the results will appear as a well-deserved reward. So I ask that you as meditators nourish your conviction in the Dhamma and in your own capabilities. Make your persistence adequate to the task. Concentration will then appear as a result, so try to make it adequate, and take mindfulness and discernment as your guardians. The results will then appear to your full satisfaction. You don't have to worry about where the paths, fruitions, and nibbana lie. Try to nourish the causes I have explained here and make them adequate. Nothing will then be able to prevent the results that will arise from those causes." (Boowa, 1996) "

Bibliography

This bibliography is an accumulation of the references that I have used, studied and from which I have quoted in four books, *Buddhist Sutras: Lesson Book; Bodhicitta: Higher Truth; The Path to Nirodha; and Canto Kusala (Dharma Chantings)*.

Aitken, Robert, 1982. Taking the Path of Zen. New York: North Point Press.

Analayo, PhD. (ne Steffens), 2003. Satipatthana, The Direct Path to Realization. Cambridge: Windhorse Publications Ltd.

Armstrong, Karen, 2006. The Great Transformation, The beginning of our Religious Traditions. Alfred A. Knopf: New York.

Baba, Meher, 1967. Discourses. Sheriar Press, Inc. USA.

Bloom, Alfred, 2007. Translated by Ruben Habito. The Essential Shinran, A Buddhist path of true entrusting. Bloomington, IN: World Wisdom, Inc.

Brown, Daniel P., PhD., 2006. Pointing Out The Great Way, The stages of meditation in the Mahamudra tradition. Boston: Wisdom Publications.

Boowa, Venerable Acayiya Maha Boowa Nanasampanno, 1998. Free Book, A Life of Inner Quality, A comprehensive guide to Buddhist practice. Udorn Thani: Wat Pa Baan Taad, c/o Songserm Service. 41000 Thailand. Boowa, http://www.what-buddha-taught.net/Books4/Maha_Boowa_Amata_Dhamma.pdf

Irv Jacob

Boowa, 1996. Things as they are. A collection of talks on the Training of the Mind. Translated by Thanissaro Bhikku. http://www.accesstoinsight.org/lib/thai/boowa/thingsas.html#frames

Buddhadasa Bhikkhu, May18-20, 2548/2005. Handbook for Mankind, International Buddhist Conference on the United Nations Day of Vesak, UNESCO, Bangkok: Thammasapa Press.

- 2006. The Truth of Nature. The Master Buddhadasa Explains the Buddha's Teachings. Bangkok: Amarin Publishing.
- 2003. A Handbook for a perfect form of Anapanasati-Bhavana. Condensed by: Chien Nurn Eng. Translated by James RtanaNantho Bhikku. Bangkok: Mental Health Publishing House.
- 2001. Happiness and Hunger, brochure by Atammayata for Wisdom and Perfection Project.
- 1999. Keys to Natural Truth, translated by Santikaro Bhikkhu, Rod Bucknell and others. Bangkok: The Dhamma Study & Practice Group. Third printing: Mental Health Publishing.
- 1993. No Religion, brochure by buddhadharma Meditaton Center, Hinsdale, Il. The Dhammadana Foundation.
- 1988. Mindfulness with Breathing, A manual for Serious Beginners. Translated by Santikaro Bhikkhu, Chaing Mai: Silkworm Books.
- 1988b, The A, B, C of Buddhism, the meditative development of mindfulness of breathing. Translated by Santikaro, Chaiya: Thailand.

Buddhaghosa, Bhadantacariya, 400 CE abt. The path of purification, **Visuddhimagga.** Translated from the Pali by Bhikkhu Nanamoli. Singapore: Singapore Buddhist Meditation Centre.

Bullitt, John, 2005. What is Theravada Buddhism? http://www.accesstoinsight.org/lib/authors/bullitt/ theravada.html

Carrithers, Michael, 1983. The Buddha. Oxford: Oxford University Press (Past Masters).

Chah, Venerable Ajahn, 2007. In the shape of a circle. Four Dharma Talks. Translated by Thanissaro Bhikkhu. Printed for free distribution by The Shangha, Ubon Ratchathani, Thailand.

*2007b, Living Dharma. Ubon Rachathani, Thailand: The Sangha, Wat Nong Pah Pong.

Chan, Victor; and His Holiness the Dalai Lama, 2004. The Wisdom of Forgiveness. Intimate Conversations and Journeys. New York: Riverhead Books—Penguin Group (USA) Inc.

Chapman, Gary, 1992. The Five Love Languages, How to Express Heartfelt Commitment to Your Mate. Chicago: Northfield Publishing.

Chittaviveka, 2001. Buddhist Rituals & Observances, by Ajahns Sucitto and Candasiri, Amaravati Publications, from the internet.

Dalai Lama, 2005. The Essential Dalai Lama, His important teachings. Edited by Rajiv Mehrotra, New York: Viking.

Dattajeevo, Phra Phadet, 2007. Dhamma Talk by Phrabhavanaviriyakhun, Bangkok: Rung Silp Printing Co. Ltd.

de Bary, Theodore, et. al. 1969. The Buddhist Tradition, in India, China, and Japan. New York: Random House, Inc. de Bary, Wm. Theodore, (ed) 1960. Sources of Chinese Tradition. New York: Columbia University Press.

Dhammapada, The. Translated by Valerie j. Roebuck. London: Penguin Classics, 2010.

Edwards, Paul. Editor in Chief, 1967. The Encyclopedia of Philosophy. New York: Macmillan Publishing Co., Inc. & The Free Press.

Erricker, Clive, 1995. Buddhism, world faiths. London: Hodder Headline Plc.

Forstater, Mark, and Jo Manuel, 2002. Yoga Masters, How Yoga theory can deepen your practice and meditation. Cambridge University Press.

Frost, Gavin and Yvonne Frost, 1989. Tantric Yoga, The Royal Path to Raising Kundalini Power. York Beach, Maine: Samuel Weiser, Inc.

Forman, Judith, 1987. Bhagwan: The Buddha for the Future. Poona, India: The Rebel Publishing House.

Gardner, Howard. (1999) "Intelligence Reframed: Multiple Intelligences for the 21st Century." New York: Basic Books.

Garfield, Jay L., 1995. The Fundamental Wisdom of the Middle Way; Nagarjuna's Mulamadhyamakakarika. Oxford: Oxford University Press.

Getty, Alice, 1988. The gods of northern Buddhism. New York, Dover Publications, Inc.

Goddard, Dwight, 1938. A Buddhist Bible. Boston: Beacon Press.

Inthisan, Phramaha Thanat, 2007. Walking on the Path of The Buddha, edited by Duwayne Engelhart. Samutprakarn, Thailand: Pimpinit Printing Ltd., Part.

Hall, Stephen S., 2010. Wisdom from Philosophy to Neuroscience. Borsoi/ Alfred A. Knopf: New York.

Hanh, Thich Nhat, 2004. Taming the Tiger Within, Meditations on Transforming Difficult Emotions. Eddited by Pritam Singh. New York, Riverhead Books (Peguin Group).
1998. The Heart of the Buddha's Teaching, Transforming Suffering into Peace, Joy, and Liberation. New York: Broadway Books.

Holymtn: http://www.holymtn.com/teapots/sutra.htm

Jacob, Irvin H. 1967-91. Jack and Lucky. Internet Book

Kagyu Thubten Choling, 1999. Karmapa: The Sacred Prophecy. Eds. Willa Baker et al. Wappinger Falls, NY: Kagyu Thubten Choling Publications Committee.

Khippapanno, Phra Acariya Thoon. Methods of concentration development, Walking meditation (Cankama). Preparation for Cankama Walk. Internet

Kornfield, Jack and Paul Breiter, eds. 1985. A still forest Pool: The Insight Meditation of Achaan Chah. Weaton, IL: Theosophical Publishing House.

Kornfield, Jack, 1993. A Path with Heart, The classical guide through the perils and promises of spiritual life. London: Rider.

Loori, John Daido, 1992. The Eight Gates of Zen, a program of Zen training. Boston: Shambhala. By the Mountains and Rivers Order.

McLeod, Melvin, 2009. The best Buddhist writing. Edited. Boston: Shambhala Publications, Inc.

Mehrotra, Rajiv editor,—and Dalai Lama. 2005. The Essential Dalai Lama, His Important Teachings. New Delhi: The Foundation for Universal Responsibility of His Holiness the Dalai Lama.

Mingyur, Yongey Rinpoche, 2007. The Joy of Living. Unlocking the secret and science of happiness. New York, Harmony Books. (written with Eric Swanson.)

Mizuno, Kogen, 1980. The beginnings of Buddhism. (Bukkyo no Genten) Translated by Richard L. Gage. Tokyo: Kosei Publishihng Co.

Mondo: http://goliath.ecnext.com/coms2/gi_0199-1543776/The-Zen-Mondo-an-analytical.html

Nyanatiloka, Mahathera, 2004. Buddhist Dictionary, A Manual of Buddhist terms and Doctrines. Chaing Mai: Silkworm Books.

Pannapadipo, Pra Peter, 1998. One Step at a Time, Buddhist meditation for absolute beginners. Bangkok: The Post Publishing Plc.

Payutto, P.A., 1994. Dependent Origination, The Buddhist law of conditionality, translated from the Thai by Burce Evans. Bangkok: Buddhadhamma Foundation.

Pengchan, Pramuan, 2007. Walk to Freedom, William B. Shaw: Editor. Bangkok: Sukhapabjai Publishing House.

Plamintr, Sunthorn, Ph. D. 2007. The discovery of Buddhism. splamintr01@yahoo.com. Nueng, Nonthaburi: Write & Read Publishing Co., Ltd.

Radhakrishnan, Sarvepalli; and Charles A. Moore, 1957. A Source Book In Indian Philosophy. Princeton, NJ: Princeton University Press.

Saddhatissa, Ven. Dr. H., 2007. An Introduction to Buddhism. The Council of Thai Bhikkhus in U.S.A. Wat Mongkolratanaram of Florida.

Salzberg, Sharon, 2002. Lovingkindness, The Revolutionary Art of Happiness. Boston & London: Shambhala.

Sangharakshita, 1997. The rainbow road. Melksham, Wiltshire: The Cromwell Press.
~ 1957 and seventh edition 1993. A Survey of Buddhism, its doctrines and methods through the Ages. Glasgow: Windhorse Publication.

Sayaedaw, Veneragle, 1974. A Discourse on Viipassana, Spiritual Insight. Delivered at the Yangon University Dhammæyon, Burma.

Schettini, Stephen, 2009. The Novice, why I became a Buddhist monk, why I quit and what I learned. Austin TX: Greenleaf Book Group Press

Shoshanna, Brenda, Ph.D., 2002. Zen Miracles, Finding Peace in an Insane World. New York: John Wiley & Sons, Inc.

Smith, Huston; and Philip Novak, 2003. Buddhism: A Concise Introduction. San Francisco: Harper Collins. http://www.harpercollins.com

Snelling, John, 1991. The Buddhist Handbook, A complete guide to Buddhist schools, teaching, practice, and History. Rochester, VT: Inner Traditions International.

Stanford Encyclopedia of Philosophy (Schopenhauer) 2003. http://plato.stanford.edu/entries/schopenhauer/

Sunnahonline:http://www.sunnahonline.com/ilm/dawah/0020.html

Surya Das, Lama, 2007. Buddha is as Buddha does. San Francisco: HarperCollins

Suvanno, Loo-Ang Por Kamkee-an, 2006. Watching: Not 'Being', following the Satipatthana Sutta. Translanted by Venerable Tone Jinavamao (A.G.J. van der Bom). Bangkok: Kled Thai, Ltd.

Suzuki, D. T., 1956. Zen Buddhism, selected writings of d.t.suzuki. William Barrett, Ed. New York, Doubleday, Image Books, 1996.

Thanissaro Bhikkhu, 2011. Selves & Not-self, The Buddhist Teaching on Anatta, internet text.

Thera, Venerable K. Sri Dhammananda Maha. http://www. budsas.org/ebud/whatbudbeliev/217.htm

Ussivakul, Archan Vinai, 2003 (2546). An introduction to Buddhist Meditation for results. Bangkok: Tipitaka Study Center, Tippayawisuit Ltd., Partnership. (Courtesy of Sally and Ian Timm.)

Vishvapani, 2001. Introducing the Friends of the Western Buddhist Order. Birmingham: Windhorse Publications.

Watson, Burton, 1993. The Lotus Sutra. New York: Columbia University Press.

Watts, Alan W., 1957. The Way of Zen. New York: Vintage Books, Alfred A. Knopf, Inc., Random House, Inc., Pantheon books Inc.

Wee, Handyman, 2007. Techniques and Tips on Concentration Meditation and Insight Meditation in Buddhism. Translated from Thai by Saichol Chuncharoephol. Bangkok: National Office of Buddhist Printing.

Wellpage.com; Oregon Health Foundation, Seaside, OR. (expired page)

Wittgenstein, Ludwig,1953. Philosophical Investigations, translated by G.E.M. Anscombe. New York: The Macmillan Company.

Zimmer, Heinrich, 1951. Philosophies of India. Edited by Joseph Campbell. Bollingen Foundation Inc., New York: Meridian Books, Inc.

Appendix I

Satipatthana Sutta

I have heard that on one occasion the Blessed One was staying in the Kuru country. Now there is a town of the Kurus called Kammasadhamma. There the Blessed One addressed the monks, "Monks."

"Lord," the monks replied.

The Blessed One said this: "This is the direct path for the purification of beings, for the overcoming of sorrow & lamentation, for the disappearance of pain & distress, for the attainment of the right method, & for the realization of Unbinding—in other words, the four frames of reference. Which four? [body, feelings, mind, mental qualities]

"There is the case where a monk remains focused on the body in & of itself—ardent, alert, & mindful—putting aside greed & distress with reference to the world. He remains focused on feelings . . . mind . . . mental qualities in & of themselves—ardent, alert, & mindful—putting aside greed & distress with reference to the world.

A. Body

"And how does a monk remain focused on the body in & of itself?

267

[1] "There is the case where a monk—having gone to the wilderness, to the shade of a tree, or to an empty building—sits down folding his legs crosswise, holding his body erect and setting mindfulness to the fore [lit: the front of the chest]. Always mindful, he breathes in; mindful he breathes out.

"Breathing in long, he discerns that he is breathing in long; or breathing out long, he discerns that he is breathing out long. Or breathing in short, he discerns that he is breathing in short; or breathing out short, he discerns that he is breathing out short. He trains himself to breathe in sensitive to the entire body and to breathe out sensitive to the entire body. He trains himself to breathe in calming bodily fabrication and to breathe out calming bodily fabrication. Just as a skilled turner or his apprentice, when making a long turn, discerns that he is making a long turn, or when making a short turn discerns that he is making a short turn; in the same way the monk, when breathing in long, discerns that he is breathing in long; or breathing out short, he discerns that he is breathing out short . . . He trains himself to breathe in calming bodily fabrication, and to breathe out calming bodily fabrication.

"In this way he remains focused internally on the body in & of itself, or externally on the body in & of itself, or both internally & externally on the body in & of itself. Or he remains focused on the phenomenon of origination with regard to the body, on the phenomenon of passing away with regard to the body, or on the phenomenon of origination & passing away with regard to the body. Or his mindfulness that 'There is a body' is maintained to the extent of knowledge & remembrance. And he remains independent, unsustained by (not clinging to) anything in the world. This is how a monk remains focused on the body in & of itself.

[2] "Furthermore, when walking, the monk discerns that he is walking. When standing, he discerns that he is standing. When sitting, he discerns that he is sitting. When lying down, he discerns that he is lying down. Or however his body is disposed, that is how he discerns it.

"In this way he remains focused internally on the body in & of itself, or focused externally . . . unsustained by anything in the world. This is how a monk remains focused on the body in & of itself.

[3] "Furthermore, when going forward & returning, he makes himself fully alert; when looking toward & looking away . . . when bending & extending his limbs . . . when carrying his outer cloak, his upper robe & his bowl . . . when eating, drinking, chewing, & savoring . . . when urinating & defecating . . . when walking, standing, sitting, falling asleep, waking up, talking, & remaining silent, he makes himself fully alert.

"In this way he remains focused internally on the body in & of itself, or focused externally . . . unsustained by anything in the world. This is how a monk remains focused on the body in & of itself.

[4] "Furthermore . . . just as if a sack with openings at both ends were full of various kinds of grain—wheat, rice, mung beans, kidney beans, sesame seeds, husked rice—and a man with good eyesight, pouring it out, were to reflect, 'This is wheat. This is rice. These are mung beans. These are kidney beans. These are sesame seeds. This is husked rice,' in the same way, monks, a monk reflects on this very body from the soles of the feet on up, from the crown of the head on down, surrounded by skin and full of various kinds of unclean things: 'In this body there are head hairs, body hairs, nails, teeth, skin, flesh, tendons, bones, bone marrow, kidneys, heart, liver, pleura, spleen, lungs, large intestines, small intestines, gorge, feces, bile, phlegm, pus, blood, sweat, fat, tears, skin-oil, saliva, mucus, fluid in the joints, urine.'

"In this way he remains focused internally on the body in & of itself, or focused externally . . . unsustained by anything in the world. This is how a monk remains focused on the body in & of itself.

[5] "Furthermore . . . just as a skilled butcher or his apprentice, having killed a cow, would sit at a crossroads cutting it up into pieces, the monk contemplates this very body—however it stands, however it is disposed—in terms of properties: 'In this body there is the earth property, the liquid property, the fire property, & the wind property.'

"In this way he remains focused internally on the body in & of itself, or focused externally . . . unsustained by anything in the world. This is how a monk remains focused on the body in & of itself.

[6] "Furthermore, as if he were to see a corpse cast away in a charnel ground—one day, two days, three days dead—bloated, livid, & festering, he applies it to this very body, 'This body, too: Such is its nature, such is its future, such its unavoidable fate' . . .

"Or again, as if he were to see a corpse cast away in a charnel ground, picked at by crows, vultures, & hawks, by dogs, hyenas, & various other creatures . . . a skeleton smeared with flesh & blood, connected with tendons . . . a fleshless skeleton smeared with blood, connected with tendons . . . a skeleton without flesh or blood, connected with tendons . . . bones detached from their tendons, scattered in all directions—here a hand bone, there a foot bone, here a shin bone, there a thigh bone, here a hip bone, there a back bone, here a rib, there a breast bone, here a shoulder bone, there a neck bone, here a jaw bone, there a tooth, here a skull . . . the bones whitened, somewhat like the color of shells . . . piled up, more than a year old . . . decomposed into a powder: He applies it to this very body, 'This body, too: Such is its nature, such is its future, such its unavoidable fate.'

"In this way he remains focused internally on the body in & of itself, or externally on the body in & of itself, or both internally & externally on the body in & of itself. Or he remains focused on the phenomenon of origination with regard to the body, on the phenomenon of passing away with regard to the body, or on the phenomenon of origination & passing away with regard to the body. Or his mindfulness that 'There is a body' is maintained to the extent of knowledge & remembrance. And he remains independent, unsustained by (not clinging to) anything in the world. This is how a monk remains focused on the body in & of itself.

B. Feelings

"And how does a monk remain focused on feelings in & of themselves? There is the case where a monk, when feeling a painful feeling, discerns that he is feeling a painful feeling. When feeling a pleasant feeling, he discerns that he is feeling a pleasant feeling. When feeling a neither-painful-nor-pleasant feeling, he discerns that he is feeling a neither-painful-nor-pleasant feeling.

"When feeling a painful feeling of the flesh, he discerns that he is feeling a painful feeling of the flesh. When feeling a painful feeling not of the flesh, he discerns that he is feeling a painful feeling not of the flesh. When feeling a pleasant feeling of the flesh, he discerns that he is feeling a pleasant feeling of the flesh. When feeling a pleasant feeling not of the flesh, he discerns that he is feeling a pleasant feeling not of the flesh. When feeling a neither-painful-nor-pleasant feeling of the flesh, he discerns that he is feeling a neither-painful-nor-pleasant feeling of the flesh. When feeling a neither-painful-nor-pleasant feeling not of the flesh, he discerns that he is feeling a neither-painful-nor-pleasant feeling not of the flesh.

"In this way he remains focused internally on feelings in & of themselves, or externally on feelings in & of themselves, or both internally & externally on feelings in & of themselves. Or he remains focused on the phenomenon of origination with regard to feelings, on the phenomenon of passing away with regard to feelings, or on the phenomenon of origination & passing away with regard to feelings. Or his mindfulness that 'There are feelings' is maintained to the extent of knowledge & remembrance. And he remains independent, unsustained by (not clinging to) anything in the world. This is how a monk remains focused on feelings in & of themselves.

C. Mind

"And how does a monk remain focused on the mind in & of itself? There is the case where a monk, when the mind has passion, discerns that the mind has passion. When the mind is without passion, he discerns that the mind is without passion. When the mind has aversion, he discerns that the mind has aversion. When the mind is without aversion, he discerns that the mind is without aversion. When the mind has delusion, he discerns that the mind has delusion. When the mind is without delusion, he discerns that the mind is without delusion.

"When the mind is constricted, he discerns that the mind is constricted. When the mind is scattered, he discerns that the mind is scattered. When the mind is enlarged, he discerns that the mind is enlarged. When the mind is not enlarged, he discerns that the mind is not enlarged. When the mind is surpassed, he discerns that the mind is surpassed. When the mind is unsurpassed, he discerns that the mind is unsurpassed. When the mind is concentrated, he discerns that the mind is concentrated. When the mind is not concentrated, he discerns that the mind is not concentrated. When the mind is released, he discerns that the mind is released. When the mind is not released, he discerns that the mind is not released.

"In this way he remains focused internally on the mind in & of itself, or externally on the mind in & of itself, or both internally & externally on the mind in & of itself. Or he remains focused on the phenomenon of origination with regard to the mind, on the phenomenon of passing away with regard to the mind, or on the phenomenon of origination & passing away with regard to the mind. Or his mindfulness that 'There is a mind' is maintained to the extent of knowledge & remembrance. And he remains independent, unsustained by (not clinging to) anything in the world. This is how a monk remains focused on the mind in & of itself.

D. Mental Qualities

"And how does a monk remain focused on mental qualities in & of themselves?

[1] "There is the case where a monk remains focused on mental qualities in & of themselves with reference to the *five hindrances.* And how does a monk remain focused on mental qualities in & of themselves with reference to the five hindrances? There is the case where, there being sensual desire present within, a monk discerns that 'There is sensual desire present within me.' Or, there being no sensual desire present within, he discerns that 'There is no sensual desire present within me.' He discerns how there is the arising of unarisen sensual desire. And he discerns how there is the abandoning of sensual desire once it has arisen. And he discerns how there is no future arising of sensual desire that has been abandoned. (The same formula is repeated for the remaining hindrances: ill will, sloth & drowsiness, restlessness & anxiety, and uncertainty.)

"In this way he remains focused internally on mental qualities in & of themselves, or externally on mental qualities in & of themselves, or both internally & externally on mental qualities in & of themselves. Or he remains focused on the phenomenon of origination with regard to mental qualities, on the phenomenon of passing away with regard to mental qualities, or on the phenomenon of origination & passing away with regard to mental qualities. Or his mindfulness that 'There are mental qualities' is maintained to the extent of knowledge & remembrance. And he remains independent, unsustained by (not clinging to) anything in the world. This is how a monk remains focused on mental qualities in & of themselves with reference to the five hindrances.

[2] "Furthermore, the monk remains focused on mental qualities in & of themselves with reference to the *five*

clinging-aggregates. And how does he remain focused on mental qualities in & of themselves with reference to the five clinging-aggregates? There is the case where a monk [discerns]: 'Such is form, such its origination, such its disappearance. Such is feeling . . . Such is perception . . . Such are fabrications . . . Such is consciousness, such its origination, such its disappearance.'

"In this way he remains focused internally on the mental qualities in & of themselves, or focused externally . . . unsustained by anything in the world. This is how a monk remains focused on mental qualities in & of themselves with reference to the five clinging-aggregates.

[3] "Furthermore, the monk remains focused on mental qualities in & of themselves with reference to the *sixfold internal & external sense media.* And how does he remain focused on mental qualities in & of themselves with reference to the sixfold internal & external sense media? There is the case where he discerns the eye, he discerns forms, he discerns the fetter that arises dependent on both. He discerns how there is the arising of an unarisen fetter. And he discerns how there is the abandoning of a fetter once it has arisen. And he discerns how there is no future arising of a fetter that has been abandoned. (The same formula is repeated for the remaining sense media: ear, nose, tongue, body, & intellect.)

"In this way he remains focused internally on the mental qualities in & of themselves, or focused externally . . . unsustained by anything in the world. This is how a monk remains focused on mental qualities in & of themselves with reference to the sixfold internal & external sense media.

[4] "Furthermore, the monk remains focused on mental qualities in & of themselves with reference to the *seven factors for Awakening.* And how does he remain focused on mental qualities in & of themselves with reference to the seven factors for Awakening? There is the case where, there being mindfulness as a factor for Awakening present within, he discerns that 'Mindfulness as a factor

for Awakening is present within me.' Or, there being no mindfulness as a factor for Awakening present within, he discerns that 'Mindfulness as a factor for Awakening is not present within me.' He discerns how there is the arising of unarisen mindfulness as a factor for Awakening. And he discerns how there is the culmination of the development of mindfulness as a factor for Awakening once it has arisen. (The same formula is repeated for the remaining factors for Awakening: analysis of qualities, persistence, rapture, serenity, concentration, & equanimity.)

"In this way he remains focused internally on mental qualities in & of themselves, or externally . . . unsustained by (not clinging to) anything in the world. This is how a monk remains focused on mental qualities in & of themselves with reference to the seven factors for Awakening.

[5] "Furthermore, the monk remains focused on mental qualities in & of themselves with reference to the *four noble truths.* And how does he remain focused on mental qualities in & of themselves with reference to the four noble truths? There is the case where he discerns, as it has come to be, that 'This is stress.' He discerns, as it has come to be, that 'This is the origination of stress.' He discerns, as it has come to be, that 'This is the cessation of stress.' He discerns, as it has come to be, that 'This is the way leading to the cessation of stress.' 1

"In this way he remains focused internally on mental qualities in & of themselves, or externally on mental qualities in & of themselves, or both internally & externally on mental qualities in & of themselves. Or he remains focused on the phenomenon of origination with regard to mental qualities, on the phenomenon of passing away with regard to mental qualities, or on the phenomenon of origination & passing away with regard to mental qualities. Or his mindfulness that 'There are mental qualities' is maintained to the extent of knowledge & remembrance. And he remains independent, unsustained by (not clinging to) anything in the world. This is how a monk remains focused on mental qualities in & of themselves with reference to the four noble truths . . .

E. Conclusion

"Now, if anyone would develop these four frames of reference in this way for seven years, one of two fruits can be expected for him: either gnosis right here & now, or—if there be any remnant of clinging/sustenance—non-return.

"Let alone seven years. If anyone would develop these four frames of reference in this way for six years . . . five . . . four . . . three . . . two years . . . one year . . . seven months . . . six months . . . five . . . four . . . three . . . two months . . . one month . . . half a month, one of two fruits can be expected for him: either gnosis right here & now, or—if there be any remnant of clinging/sustenance—non-return.

"Let alone half a month. If anyone would develop these four frames of reference in this way for seven days, one of two fruits can be expected for him: either gnosis right here & now, or—if there be any remnant of clinging/sustenance—non-return.

"'This is the direct path for the purification of beings, for the overcoming of sorrow & lamentation, for the disappearance of pain & distress, for the attainment of the right method, & for the realization of Unbinding—in other words, the four frames of reference.' Thus was it said, and in reference to this was it said."

That is what the Blessed One said. Gratified, the monks delighted in the Blessed One's words.

Appendix II

Dhammacakkappavattana Sutta:

Setting the Wheel of Dhamma in Motion

translated from the Pali
byThanissaro Bhikkhu
© 1993-2012

I have heard that on one occasion the Blessed One was staying at Varanasi in the Game Refuge at Isipatana. There he addressed the group of five monks:

"There are these two extremes that are not to be indulged in by one who has gone forth. Which two? That which is devoted to sensual pleasure with reference to sensual objects: base, vulgar, common, ignoble, unprofitable; and that which is devoted to self-affliction: painful, ignoble, unprofitable. Avoiding both of these extremes, the middle way realized by the Tathagata—producing vision, producing knowledge—leads to calm, to direct knowledge, to self-awakening, to Unbinding.

"And what is the middle way realized by the Tathagata that—producing vision, producing knowledge—leads to calm, to direct knowledge, to self-awakening, to Unbinding? Precisely this Noble Eightfold Path: right view, right resolve, right speech, right action, right livelihood, right effort, right mindfulness, right concentration. This is the middle way realized by the Tathagata that—producing vision, producing knowledge—leads to calm, to direct knowledge, to self-awakening, to Unbinding.

"Now this, monks, is the noble truth of stress:[1] Birth is stressful, aging is stressful, death is stressful; sorrow, lamentation, pain, distress, & despair are stressful; association with the unbeloved is stressful, separation from the loved is stressful, not getting what is wanted is stressful. In short, the five clinging-aggregates are stressful.

"And this, monks, is the noble truth of the origination of stress: the craving that makes for further becoming—accompanied by passion & delight, relishing now here & now there—i.e., craving for sensual pleasure, craving for becoming, craving for non-becoming.

"And this, monks, is the noble truth of the cessation of stress: the remainderless fading & cessation, renunciation, relinquishment, release, & letting go of that very craving.

"And this, monks, is the noble truth of the way of practice leading to the cessation of stress: precisely this Noble Eightfold Path—right view, right resolve, right speech, right action, right livelihood, right effort, right mindfulness, right concentration.

"Vision arose, insight arose, discernment arose, knowledge arose, illumination arose within me with regard to things never heard before: 'This is the noble truth of stress.' Vision arose, insight arose, discernment arose, knowledge arose, illumination arose within me with regard to things never heard before: 'This noble truth of stress is to be comprehended.' Vision arose, insight arose, discernment arose, knowledge arose, illumination arose within me with regard to things never heard before:' This noble truth of stress has been comprehended.'

"Vision arose, insight arose, discernment arose, knowledge arose, illumination arose within me with regard to things never heard before: 'This is the noble truth of the origination of stress' . . . 'This noble truth of the origination of stress is to be abandoned' [2] . . . 'This noble truth of the origination of stress has been abandoned.'

"Vision arose, insight arose, discernment arose, knowledge arose, illumination arose within me with regard to things never heard before: 'This is the noble truth of the cessation of stress' . . . 'This noble truth of the cessation of stress is to be directly experienced' . . . 'This noble truth of the cessation of stress has been directly experienced.'

"Vision arose, insight arose, discernment arose, knowledge arose, illumination arose within me with regard to things never heard before: 'This is the noble truth of the way of practice leading to the cessation of stress' . . . 'This noble truth of the way of practice leading to the cessation of stress is to be developed' . . . 'This noble truth of the way of practice leading to the cessation of stress has been developed.' [3]

"And, monks, as long as this—my three-round, twelve-permutation knowledge & vision concerning these four noble truths as they have come to be—was not pure, I did not claim to have directly awakened to the right self-awakening unexcelled in the cosmos with its deities, Maras, & Brahmas, with its contemplatives & brahmans, its royalty & commonfolk. But as soon as this—my three-round, twelve-permutation knowledge & vision concerning these four noble truths as they have come to be—was truly pure, then I did claim to have directly awakened to the right self-awakening unexcelled in the cosmos with its deities, Maras & Brahmas, with its contemplatives & brahmans, its royalty & commonfolk. Knowledge & vision arose in me: 'Unprovoked is my release. This is the last birth. There is now no further becoming.'"

That is what the Blessed One said. Gratified, the group of five monks delighted at his words. And while this explanation was being given, there arose to Ven. Kondañña the dustless, stainless Dhamma eye: Whatever is subject to origination is all subject to cessation.

And when the Blessed One had set the Wheel of Dhamma in motion, the earth devas cried out: "At Varanasi, in the Game Refuge at Isipatana, the Blessed One has set in motion the unexcelled Wheel of Dhamma that cannot be stopped by brahman or contemplative, deva, Mara or God or anyone in the cosmos." On hearing the earth devas' cry, the devas of the Four Kings' Heaven took up the cry . . . the devas of the Thirty-three . . . the Yama devas . . . the Tusita devas . . . the Nimmanarati devas . . . the Paranimmita-vasavatti devas . . .

the devas of Brahma's retinue took up the cry: "At Varanasi, in the Game Refuge at Isipatana, the Blessed One has set in motion the unexcelled Wheel of Dhamma that cannot be stopped by brahman or contemplative, deva, Mara, or God or anyone at all in the cosmos."

So in that moment, that instant, the cry shot right up to the Brahma worlds. And this ten-thousand fold cosmos shivered & quivered & quaked, while a great, measureless radiance appeared in the cosmos, surpassing the effulgence of the devas.

Then the Blessed One exclaimed: "So you really know, Kondañña? So you really know?" And that is how Ven. Kondañña acquired the name Añña-Kondañña—Kondañña who knows. http://www.what-buddha-taught.net/Articles/turning_of_the_wheel.htm#Thanissaro